Microsoft

W9-ARU-918

Step by Step

Microsoft® Office
Access 2003

Online Training Solutions, Inc.

PUBLISHED BY
Microsoft Press
A Division of Microsoft Corporation
One Microsoft Way
Redmond, Washington 98052-6399

Library of Congress Cataloging-in-Publication Data
Microsoft Office Access 2003 Step by Step / Online Training Solutions, Inc.
       p. cm.
     Includes index.
     ISBN 0-7356-1517-9
     1. Microsoft Access. 2. Database management. I. Online Training Solutions (Firm)

   QA76.9.D3M5733   2003
   005.75'65--dc21   2003052694

Printed and bound in the United States of America.

12 13 14 15 QWE 8 7 6

Distributed in Canada by H.B. Fenn and Company Ltd.

A CIP catalogue record for this book is available from the British Library.

Microsoft Press books are available through booksellers and distributors worldwide. For further information about international editions, contact your local Microsoft Corporation office or contact Microsoft Press International directly at fax (425) 936-7329. Visit our Web site at www.microsoft.com/mspress. Send comments to *mspinput@microsoft.com*.

Acquisitions Editor: Alex Blanton
Project Editor: Aileen Wrothwell

Body Part No. X09-71428

Contents

Contents

5   Locating Specific Information   117

6   Keeping Your Information Accurate   145

7   Working with Reports   175

8   Making It Easy for Others to Use Your Database   201

What's New in Microsoft Office Access 2003

You'll notice some changes as soon as you start Microsoft Office Access 2003. The new Getting Started task pane links you to common start-up options, and the user interface has a new, softer look.

New in Office 2003

Most of the features that are new or improved in this version of Access won't be apparent to you until you start using the program. To help you quickly identify features that are new or improved with this version, this book uses the icon in the margin whenever those features are discussed or shown.

The following table lists the new features that you might be interested in, as well as the chapters in which those features are discussed.

To learn how to	Using this feature	See
Track types of data, such as dates, names, and addresses, that can be used in multiple ways	Smart Tags	Chapter 2
Transform script to data when you import or export it	Transform	Chapter 3
Change your display theme	Support for Windows XP Theming	Chapter 4
Quickly update input mask options	Property Update Options	Chapter 6
Identify and correct errors in forms and reports	Automatic Error Checking	Chapter 7
Quickly back up your database with the click of a button	Back Up Database	Chapter 8
Summarize data in tabular or graphical format	Pivot Tables and Pivot Charts	Chapter 10

Getting Help

Every effort has been made to ensure the accuracy of this book and the contents of its CD-ROM. If you do run into problems, please contact the appropriate source for help and assistance.

Getting Help with This Book and Its CD-ROM

If your question or issue concerns the content of this book or its companion CD-ROM, please first search the online Microsoft Press Knowledge Base, which provides support information for known errors in or corrections to this book, at the following Web site:

www.microsoft.com/mspress/support/search.asp

If you do not find your answer at the online Knowledge Base, send your comments or questions to Microsoft Press Technical Support at:

mspinput@microsoft.com

Getting Help with Microsoft Office Access 2003

If your question is about Microsoft Office Access 2003, and not about the content of this Microsoft Press book, your first recourse is Access's Help system. This system is a combination of help tools and files stored on your computer when you installed The Microsoft Office System 2003 and, if your computer is connected to the Internet, help files available from Microsoft Office Online.

To find out about different items on the screen, you can display a *ScreenTip*. To display a ScreenTip for a toolbar button, for example, point to the button without clicking it. Its ScreenTip appears, telling you its name. In some dialog boxes, you can click a question mark icon to the left of the Close button in the title bar to display the Microsoft Office Access Help window with information related to the dialog box.

When you have a question about using Access, you can type it in the "Type a question for help" box at the right end of the program window's menu bar. Then press Enter to display a list of Help topics from which you can select the one that most closely relates to your question.

Another way to get help is to display the Office Assistant, which provides help as you work in the form of helpful information or a tip. If the Office Assistant is hidden when a tip is available, a light bulb appears. Clicking the light bulb displays the tip, and provides other options.

If you want to practice getting help, you can work through this exercise, which demonstrates two ways to get help.

BE SURE TO start Access before beginning this exercise.

1 At the right end of the menu bar, click the **Type a question for help** box.

2 Type How do I get help?, and press `Enter`.

A list of topics that relate to your question appears in the Search Results task pane.

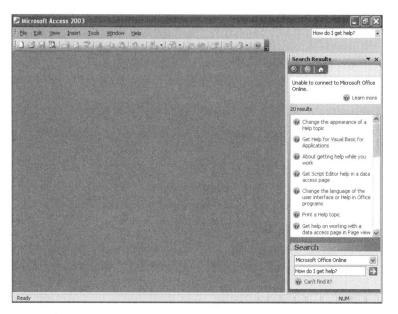

You can click any of the help topics to get more information or instructions.

3 In the **Search Results** task pane, scroll down the results list, and click **About getting help while you work**.

The Microsoft Office Access Help window opens displaying information about that topic.

Maximize

4 At the right end of the Microsoft Office Access Help window's title bar, click the **Maximize** button and then click **Show All**.

The topic content expands to provide in-depth information about getting help while you work.

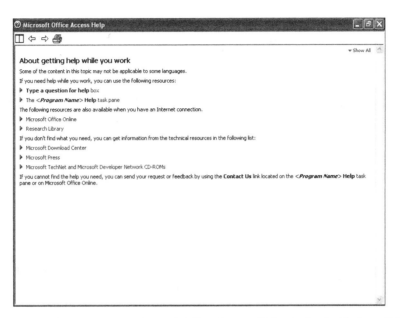

Close

5 At the right end of the Microsoft Office Access Help window's title bar, click the **Close** button, to close the window.

6 On the **Help** menu, click **Microsoft Office Access Help**.

The Access Help task pane opens.

7 In the task pane, click **Table of Contents**.

The task pane now displays a list of help topics organized by category, like the table of contents in a book.

Back

8 On the toolbar at the top of the task pane, click the **Back** button.

Notice the categories of information that are available from the Microsoft Office Online Web site. You can also reach this Web site by clicking Microsoft Office Online on the Help menu.

More Information

If your question is about a Microsoft software product, including Access 2003, and not about the content of this Microsoft Press book, please search the appropriate product support center or the Microsoft Knowledge Base at:

support.microsoft.com

In the United States, Microsoft software product support issues not covered by the Microsoft Knowledge Base are addressed by Microsoft Product Support Services. The Microsoft software support options available from Microsoft Product Support Services are listed at:

support.microsoft.com

Outside the United States, for support information specific to your location, please refer to the Worldwide Support menu on the Microsoft Product Support Services Web site for the site specific to your country:

support.microsoft.com

Using the Book's CD-ROM

The CD-ROM included with this book contains all the practice files you'll use as you work through the exercises in this book. By using practice files, you won't waste time creating sample content with which to experiment—instead, you can jump right in and concentrate on learning how to use Microsoft Office Access 2003.

What's On the CD-ROM?

In addition to the practice files, the CD-ROM contains some exciting resources that will really enhance your ability to get the most out of using this book and Access 2003, including the following:

■ *Microsoft Office Access 2003 Step by Step* in e-book format.

■ *Insider's Guide to Microsoft Office OneNote 2003* in e-book format.

■ *Microsoft Office System Quick Reference* in e-book format.

■ *Introducing the Tablet PC* in e-book format.

■ *Microsoft Computer Dictionary, Fifth Edition* in e-book format.

■ 25 business-oriented templates for use with programs in The Microsoft Office System.

■ 100 pieces of clip art.

Important   The CD-ROM for this book does not contain the Access 2003 software. You should purchase and install that program before using this book.

Minimum System Requirements

To use this book, you will need:

■ **Computer/Processor**

Computer with a Pentium 133-megahertz (MHz) or higher processor; Pentium III recommended

■ **Memory**

64 MB of RAM (128 MB recommended) plus an additional 8 MB of RAM for each program in The Microsoft Office System (such as Access) running simultaneously

- **Hard Disk**

  - 245 MB of available hard disk space with 115 MB on the hard disk where the operating system is installed

  - An additional 20 MB of hard disk space is required for installing the practice files.

  Hard disk requirements will vary depending on configuration; custom installation choices may require more or less hard disk space

- **Operating System**

  Microsoft Windows 2000 with Service Pack 3 (SP3) or Microsoft Windows XP or later

- **Drive**

  CD-ROM drive

- **Display**

  Super VGA (800 × 600) or higher-resolution monitor with 256 colors

- **Peripherals**

  Microsoft Mouse, Microsoft IntelliMouse, or compatible pointing device

- **Software**

  Microsoft Office Access 2003 and Microsoft Internet Explorer 5 or later

Important In order to complete some of the exercises in this book, you will need to install the Jet 4.0 Service Pack 7, which you can obtain from the Windows Update Web site at *windowsupdate.microsoft.com*.

Installing the Practice Files

You need to install the practice files on your hard disk before you use them in the chapters' exercises. Follow these steps to prepare the CD's files for your use:

1 Insert the CD-ROM into the CD-ROM drive of your computer.

The Step by Step Companion CD End User License Agreement appears. Follow the on-screen directions. It is necessary to accept the terms of the license agreement in order to use the practice files. After you accept the license agreement, a menu screen appears.

Important   If the menu screen does not appear, start Windows Explorer. In the left pane, locate the icon for your CD-ROM drive and click this icon. In the right pane, double-click the StartCD executable file.

2   Click **Install Practice Files.**

3   Click **Next** on the first screen, and then click **Yes** to accept the license agreement on the next screen.

4   If you want to install the practice files to a location other than the default folder (*My Documents\Microsoft Press\Access 2003 SBS*), click the **Browse** button, select the new drive and path, and then click **OK.**

5   Click **Next** on the **Choose Destination Location** screen, click **Next** on the **Select Features** screen, and then click **Next** on the **Start Copying Files** screen to install the selected practice files.

6   After the practice files have been installed, click **Finish.**

Within the installation folder are subfolders for each chapter in the book.

7   Close the Step by Step Companion CD window, remove the CD-ROM from the CD-ROM drive, and return it to the envelope at the back of the book.

Using the Practice Files

Each exercise is preceded by a paragraph or paragraphs that list the files needed for that exercise and explains any file preparation you need to take care of before you start working through the exercise, as shown here:

BE SURE TO start Word before beginning this exercise.
USE the TrackChange document in the practice file folder for this topic. This practice file is located in the My Documents\Microsoft Press\Office 2003 SBS\Collaborating\Tracking folder and can also be accessed by clicking Start/All Programs/Microsoft Press/Office 2003 Step by Step.
OPEN the TrackChange document.

Usually you will be instructed to open the practice files from within the application in which you are working. However, you can also access the files directly from Windows by clicking the Start menu items indicated. Locate the file in the chapter sub-folder and then double-click the file to open it.

The following table lists each chapter's practice files.

Chapter	Folder	Subfolder	Files
Chapter 1: Getting to Know Microsoft Access 2003	KnowAccess	Open	GardenCo
		Tables	GardenCo
		Queries	GardenCo
		Forms	GardenCo
		Reports	GardenCo
		Print	GardenCo
Chapter 2: Creating a New Database	CreateNew	CheckDB	Contacts
		Refine	GardenCo
		Manipulate	GardenCo
Chapter 3: Getting Information Into and Out of a Database	Importing	ImportExcel	GardenCo Customers
		ImportDText	GardenCo Employees
		ImportFText	GardenCo Suppliers
		ImportAccess	GardenCo Products
		ImportDbase	GardenCo Shippers
		ImportHTML	GardenCo NewCust
		ImportXML	GardenCo Orders OrderDetails
		Export	GardenCo
		Link	GardenCo LinkDatabase LinkWorksheet
		OfficeLink	GardenCo
Chapter 4: Simplifying Data Entry with Forms	Forms	FormByWiz	GardenCo
		Properties	GardenCo tgc_bkgrnd
		Layout	GardenCo
		Controls	GardenCo tgc_logo2
		Events	GardenCo AftUpdate
		AutoForm	GardenCo
		Subform	GardenCo

Chapter	Folder	Subfolder	Files
Chapter 5: Locating Specific Information	Queries	Sort	GardenCo
		FilterDS	GardenCo
		FilterForm	GardenCo
		AdvFilter	GardenCo
		QueryDes	GardenCo
		QueryWiz	GardenCo
		Aggregate	GardenCo
Chapter 6: Keeping Your Information Accurate	Accurate	FieldSize	Field Test
		InputMask	Field Test
		ValRules	Field Test
		Lookup	Field Test
		QueryUp	GardenCo
		QueryDel	GardenCo
Chapter 7: Working with Reports	Reports	RepByWiz	GardenCo
		Modify	GardenCo
		ByDesign	GardenCo
		Subreport	GardenCo
		Print	GardenCo
Chapter 8: Making It Easy for Others to Use Your Database	Switchbrd	SBManager	GardenCo
		Splash	GardenCo
			tgc_logo1
			Paragraphs
		Startup	GardenCo
		Health	GardenCo
Chapter 9: Keeping Your Information Secure	Secure	Encrypt	GardenCo
		Password	GardenCo
		Share	GardenCo
		Replicate	GardenCo
		Split	GardenCo
		Multi	GardenCo
		VBA	GardenCo
		MDE	GardenCo
Chapter 10: Working with Pages and Modules	PgsMods	Static	GardenCo
		VBA	GardenCo
		AutoPage	GardenCo
		Wizard	GardenCo
		Analyze	GardenCo

Uninstalling the Practice Files

After you finish working through this book, you should uninstall the practice files to free up hard disk space.

1   On the Windows taskbar, click the **Start** button, and then click **Control Panel**.

2   In Control Panel, click **Add or Remove Programs**.

3   In the list of installed programs, click **Microsoft Office Access 2003 Step By Step**, and then click the **Remove** or **Change/Remove** button.

4   In the **Uninstall** dialog box, click **OK**.

5   After the files are uninstalled, click **Finish**, and then close the Add or Remove Programs window and Control Panel.

Important   If you need additional help installing or uninstalling the practice files, please see "Getting Help" earlier in this book. Microsoft Product Support Services does not provide support for this book or its CD-ROM.

Conventions and Features

You can save time when you use this book by understanding how the *Step by Step* series shows special instructions, keys to press, buttons to click, and so on.

Convention	Meaning
Microsoft Office Specialist	This icon indicates a topic that covers a Microsoft Office Specialist exam objective.
New in Office 2003	This icon indicates a new or greatly improved feature in Microsoft Office Access 2003.
	This icon indicates a reference to the book's companion CD.
BE SURE TO	These words are found at the beginning of paragraphs preceding or following step-by-step exercises. They point out items you should check or actions you should carry out either before beginning an exercise or after completing an exercise.
USE OPEN	These words are found at the beginning of paragraphs preceding step-by-step exercises. They draw your attention to practice files that you'll need to use in the exercise.
CLOSE	This word is found at the beginning of paragraphs following step-by-step exercises. They give instructions for closing open files or programs before moving on to another topic.
1 2	Numbered steps guide you through hands-on exercises in each topic.
●	A round bullet indicates an exercise that has only one step.
Troubleshooting	These paragraphs show you how to fix a common problem that might prevent you from continuing with the exercise.
Tip	These paragraphs provide a helpful hint or shortcut that makes working through a task easier.
Important	These paragraphs point out information that you need to know to complete a procedure.

Convention	Meaning
[Save icon] Save	The first time you are told to click a button in an exercise, a picture of the button appears in the left margin. If the name of the button does not appear on the button itself, the name appears under the picture.
Ctrl + Home	A plus sign (+) between two key names means that you must hold down the first key while you press the second key. For example, "press Ctrl + Home " means "hold down the Ctrl key while you press the Home key."
Black bold characters	In steps, the names of program elements, such as buttons, commands, and dialog boxes, are shown in black bold characters.
Blue bold characters	Anything you are supposed to type appears in blue bold characters.
Blue italic characters	Terms that are explained in the glossary at the end of the book are shown in blue italic characters.

Taking a Microsoft Office Specialist Certification Exam

As desktop computing technology advances, more employers rely on the objectivity and consistency of technology certification when screening, hiring, and training employees to ensure the competence of these professionals. As a job seeker or employee, you can use technology certification to prove that you have the skills businesses need, and can save them the trouble and expense of training. Microsoft Office Specialist is the only Microsoft certification program designed to assist employees in validating their Microsoft Office System skills.

About the Microsoft Office Specialist Program

A Microsoft Office Specialist is an individual who has demonstrated worldwide standards of Microsoft Office skill through a certification exam in one or more of the Microsoft Office System desktop programs including Microsoft Word, Excel, PowerPoint®, Outlook®, Access and Project. Office Specialist certifications are available at the "Specialist" and "Expert" skill levels. Visit *www.microsoft.com/officespecialist/* to locate skill standards for each certification and an Authorized Testing Center in your area.

What Does This Logo Mean?

This Microsoft Office Specialist logo means this courseware has been approved by the Microsoft Office Specialist Program to be among the finest available for learning Access 2003. It also means that upon completion of this courseware, you might be prepared to become a Microsoft Office Specialist.

Selecting a Microsoft Office Specialist Certification Level

When selecting the Microsoft Office Specialist certification(s) level that you would like to pursue, you should assess the following:

- The Office program ("program") and version(s) of that program with which you are familiar
- The length of time you have used the program
- Whether you have had formal or informal training in the use of that program

Candidates for Specialist-level certification are expected to successfully complete a wide range of standard business tasks, such as formatting a document or spreadsheet. Successful candidates generally have six or more months of experience with the program, including either formal, instructor-led training or self-study using Microsoft Office Specialist-approved books, guides, or interactive computer-based materials.

Candidates for Expert-level certification are expected to complete more complex, business-oriented tasks utilizing the program's advanced functionality, such as importing data and recording macros. Successful candidates generally have one or more years of experience with the program, including formal, instructor-led training or self-study using Microsoft Office Specialist-approved materials.

Microsoft Office Specialist Skill Standards

Every Microsoft Office Specialist certification exam is developed from a set of exam skill standards that are derived from studies of how the Office program is used in the workplace. Because these skill standards dictate the scope of each exam, they provide you with critical information on how to prepare for certification.

Microsoft Office Specialist Approved Courseware, including the Microsoft Press Step by Step series, are reviewed and approved on the basis of their coverage of the Microsoft Office Specialist skill standards.

The Exam Experience

Microsoft Office Specialist certification exams for Office 2003 programs are performance-based exams that require you to complete 15 to 20 standard business tasks using an interactive simulation (a digital model) of a Microsoft Office System program. Exam questions can have one, two, or three task components that, for example, require you to create or modify a document or spreadsheet:

Modify the existing brochure by completing the following three tasks:

1 Left-align the heading *Premium Real Estate*.

2 Insert a footer with right-aligned page numbering. (Note: accept all other default settings.)

3 Save the document with the file name Broker Brochure in the My Documents folder.

Candidates should also be aware that each exam must be completed within an allotted time of 45 minutes and that in the interest of test security and fairness, the Office Help system (including the Office Assistant) cannot be accessed during the exam.

Passing standards (the minimum required score) for Microsoft Office Specialist certification exams range from 60 to 85 percent correct, depending on the exam.

The Exam Interface and Controls

The exam interface and controls, including the test question, appear across the bottom of the screen.

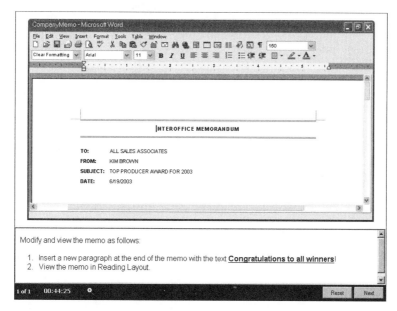

■ The **Counter** is located in the left corner of the exam interface and tracks the number of questions completed and how many questions remain.

■ The **Timer** is located to the right of the Counter and starts when the first question appears on the screen. The Timer displays the remaining exam time. If the Timer is distracting, click the Timer to remove the display.

Important Transition time between questions is not counted against total allotted exam time.

■ The **Reset** button is located to the left of the **Next** button and will restart a question if you believe you have made an error. The **Reset** button will not restart the entire exam nor extend the total allotted exam time.

■ The **Next** button is located in the right corner. When you complete a question, click the **Next** button to move to the next question. It is not possible to move back to a previous question on the exam.

Test-Taking Tips

■ Follow all instructions provided in each question completely and accurately.

■ Enter requested information as it appears in the instructions, but without duplicating the format. For example, all text and values that you will be asked to enter will appear in the instructions with bold and underlined text formats (for example, text), however, you should enter the information without applying these formats unless you are specifically instructed to do otherwise.

- Close all dialog boxes before proceeding to the next exam question unless you are specifically instructed otherwise.

- There is no need to close task panes before proceeding to the next exam question unless you are specifically instructed otherwise.

- There is no need to save your work before moving on to the next question unless you are specifically instructed to do otherwise.

- For questions that ask you to print a document, spreadsheet, chart, report, slide, and so on, please be aware that nothing will actually be printed.

- Responses are scored based on the result of your work, not the method you use to achieve that result (unless a specific method is indicated in the instructions), and not the time you take to complete the question. Extra keystrokes or mouse clicks do not count against your score.

- If your computer becomes unstable during the exam (for example, if the exam does not respond or the mouse no longer functions) or if a power outage occurs, contact a testing center administrator immediately. The administrator will restart the computer and return the exam to the point where the interruption occurred with your score intact.

Certification

At the conclusion of the exam, you will receive a score report, which you can print with the assistance of the testing center administrator. If your score meets or exceeds the passing standard (the minimum required score), you will be mailed a printed certificate within approximately 14 days.

College Credit Recommendation

The American Council on Education (ACE) has issued a one-semester hour college credit recommendation for each Microsoft Office Specialist certification. To learn more, visit *www.microsoft.com/traincert/mcp/officespecialist/credit.asp*.

For More Information

To learn more about Microsoft Office Specialist certification, visit *www.microsoft.com /officespecialist/*.

To learn about other Microsoft Office Specialist approved courseware from Microsoft Press, visit *www.microsoft.com/mspress/certification/officespecialist/*.

Microsoft Office Specialist Skill Standards

Each Microsoft Office Specialist certification has a set of corresponding skill standards that describe areas of individual, Microsoft Office program use. You should master each skill standard to prepare for the corresponding Microsoft Office Specialist certification exam.

Microsoft Office Specialist

This book will fully prepare you for the Microsoft Office Specialist certification at the Specialist level. Throughout this book, content that pertains to a Microsoft Office Specialist skill standard is identified with the logo shown in the margin.

Standard	Skill	Page
AC03S-1	**Structuring Databases**	
AC03S-1-1	Create Access databases	32, 41
AC03S-1-2	Create and modify tables	41, 44, 51
AC03S-1-3	Define and create field types	44, 146, 160
AC03S-1-4	Modify field properties	150, 152
AC03S-1-5	Create and modify one-to-many relationships	106
AC03S-1-6	Enforce referential integrity	106
AC03S-1-7	Create and modify queries	129, 138, 166
AC03S-1-8	Create forms	84, 104
AC03S-1-9	Add and modify form controls and properties	86, 95
AC03S-1-10	Create reports	176, 186
AC03S-1-11	Add and modify report control properties	180
AC03S-1-12	Create a data access page	283
AC03S-2	**Entering Data**	
AC03S-2-1	Enter, edit and delete records	36, 170
AC03S-2-2	Find and move among records	6
AC03S-2-3	Import data to Access	58, 61, 63, 66, 68, 69, 71

Standard	Skill	Page
AC03S-3	**Organizing Data**	
AC03S-3-1	Create and modify calculated fields and aggregate functions	129, 140
AC03S-3-2	Modify form layout	92, 95, 186
AC03S-3-3	Modify report layout and page setup	191
AC03S-3-4	Format datasheets	51
AC03S-3-5	Sort records	118, 126
AC03S-3-6	Filter records	121, 123
AC03S04	**Managing Databases**	
AC03S-4-1	Identify and modify object dependencies	217
AC03S-4-2	View objects and object data in other views	197
AC03S-4-3	Print database objects and data	22, 197
AC03S-4-4	Export data from Access	73
AC03S-4-5	Back up a database	238
AC03S-4-6	Compact and repair databases	217

About the Authors

Online Training Solutions, Inc. (OTSI)

OTSI is a traditional and electronic publishing company specializing in the creation, production, and delivery of computer software training. OTSI publishes the Quick Course® series of computer and business training products. The principals of OTSI are:

Joyce Cox has over 20 years' experience in writing about and editing technical subjects for non-technical audiences. For 12 of those years she was the principal author for Online Press. She was also the first managing editor of Microsoft Press, an editor for Sybex, and an editor for the University of California.

Steve Lambert started playing with computers in the mid-seventies. As computers evolved from wire-wrap and solder to consumer products, he evolved from hardware geek to programmer and writer. He has written over 14 books and a wide variety of technical documentation and has produced training tools and help systems.

Gale Nelson honed her communication skills as a technical writer for a SQL Server training company. Her attention to detail soon led her into software testing and quality assurance management. She now divides her work time between writing and data conversion projects.

Joan Preppernau has been contributing to the creation of excellent technical training materials for computer professionals for as long as she cares to remember. Joan's wide-ranging experiences in various facets of the industry have contributed to her passion for producing interesting, useful, and understandable training materials.

The OTSI publishing team includes the following outstanding professionals:

Susie Bayers
Jan Bednarczuk
Keith Bednarczuk
RJ Cadranell
Liz Clark
Nancy Depper
Leslie Eliel
Joseph Ford
Jon Kenoyer
Marlene Lambert
Aaron L'Heureux
Lisa Van Every
Michelle Ziegwied

For more information about Online Training Solutions, Inc., visit *www.otsi.com*.

Quick Reference

3   Navigate to the folder that contains the database, click the file, and then click **Import**.

4   Click the **Options** button to select any import options you want.

5   Select the objects you want to import, or click **Select All** to import all objects, and then click **OK**.

68 To import information from another database

1   On the **File** menu, point to **Get External Data**, and then click **Import** to open the **Import** dialog box.

2   In the **Files of type** list, click the database type you want to import.

3   Navigate to the folder that contains the database, click the file, and then click **Import**.

4   Follow the wizard's instructions, and click **Finish** to complete the process, and then click **OK**.

69 To import information from an HTML file into an existing table

1   On the **File** menu, point to **Get External Data**, and then click **Import**.

2   In the **Files of type** list, click **HTML Documents**.

3   Navigate to the folder that contains the HTML file, click the file, and then click **Import**.

4   Follow the instructions on the **Import HTML File Wizard**, click **Finish** to complete the process, and then click **OK**.

71 To import information from an XML file into an existing table

1   On the **File** menu, point to **Get External Data**, and then click **Import**.

2   In the **Files of type** list, click **XML**.

3   Navigate to the folder that contains the XML file, click the file, click **Import**, and then click the **Options** button to display the import options.

4   Click the **Options** button to select any import options you want, and then click **OK** twice.

73 To export information to another program

1   In the database window, click the table you want to export.

2   On the **File** menu, click **Export** to display the **Export Table To** dialog box.

3   Navigate to the folder where you want to store the exported file, select the appropriate **Save as type** option, type a name for the file, and then click **Export**.

76 To link a table in one database to another

1   On the **File** menu, point to **Get External Data**, and then click **Link Tables**.

2 In the **Link** dialog box, navigate to the folder that contains the database to which you want to link, select the appropriate **Files of type** setting, select the file, and then click **Link**.

3 In the **Link Tables** dialog box, click the name of the table that you want to link to, and then click **OK**.

76 **To link a database to an Excel worksheet**

1 On the **File** menu, point to **Get External Data**, and then click **Link Tables**.

2 Navigate to the folder that contains the worksheet to which you want to link. In the **Files of type** list, click **Microsoft Excel**, select the worksheet, and then click **Link**.

3 Follow the instructions of the **Link Spreadsheet Wizard**, click **Finish**, and then click **OK**.

78 **To copy and paste Access data into an Excel worksheet**

1 Open the table in Datasheet view.

2 Select the records you want to copy by pointing to the row selector of the first record you want to select (the pointer changes to a right arrow), holding down the left mouse button and dragging to the last record you want to select. Then on the toolbar, click the **Copy** button.

3 Start Excel, and with cell A1 of a new blank worksheet selected, click the **Paste** button on Excel's toolbar.

Chapter 4 **Simplifying Data Entry with Forms**

Page 84 **To create a form by using a wizard**

1 On the **Objects** bar, click **Forms**.

2 Double-click **Create form by using wizard** to display the first page of the **Form Wizard**.

3 Follow the instructions of the **Form Wizard**, and then click **Finish**.

86 **To change the properties in a form**

1 Display the form in Design view.

2 Use the buttons and boxes on the Formatting toolbar to change the formatting of labels and controls.

3 To change the properties of a control, in the form, right-click the control you want to change, and click **Properties** from the shortcut menu.

4 Click the appropriate tab, click the property you want to change, and then change the property setting.

86   **To change the background color of a label**

1   Open the form in Design view.

2   Right-click the label you want to change, and then click **Properties** from the shortcut menu.

3   Click the **Format** tab, click the **Back Color ...** button, select the color you want, and then click **OK**.

92   **To rearrange or move the controls in a form**

1   Display the form in Design view.

2   To resize a control, select it, and drag the left, right, top or bottom edge of the control.

3   To move a control, select it, and when the pointer changes to a hand, drag it to its new location.

95   **To add a graphic and a caption to a form**

1   Display the form in Design view.

2   Click the **Image** control in the Toolbox, and then drag a rectangle in the location where you will add the graphic.

3   Navigate to the folder that contains the graphic, and double-click the graphic file.

4   To add a caption, click the **Label** control in the Toolbox, and then drag another rectangle in the location where you will add the caption.

5   Type the caption, and press Enter.

104   **To create a form by using AutoForm**

1   On the **Objects** bar, click **Forms**.

2   On the database window's toolbar, click the **New** button.

3   Click the AutoForm format that you want from the list, click the **Table/Query** down arrow, select the table or query on which you want to base the form, and then click **OK**.

4   Click the **Save** button, enter a name for the form in the **Save As** dialog box, and then click **OK**.

106   **To add a subform to a form**

1   Make sure the tables on which you want to base your main form and the subform have a relationship.

2   Open the main form in Design view and if necessary, open the Toolbox and make sure the **Control Wizards** button is active (is orange).

3 On the Toolbox, click the **Subform/Subreport** button, and drag a rectangle to the location on your main form where you want to insert a subform.

4 Follow the instructions on the **Subform Wizard**, and click **Finish** on the wizard's last page to complete the process.

5 Adjust the size and location of the objects on your form as necessary.

114 **To create a form and subform by using a wizard**

1 To create the form in your database, on the **Objects** bar, click **Forms**, and then click the **New** button on the database window's toolbar.

2 Click **Form Wizard**, select the form's base table from the list at the bottom of the page, and then click **OK**.

3 Verify that the table you selected is shown in the **Table/Queries** list and then double-click each field that you want to include in the new form to move it to the **Fields in my new table** list.

4 To create the subform, display the **Tables/Queries** list, and select the table on which you want to base the subform.

5 Double-click each field you want to add to the subform, and then click **Next**.

6 Follow the instructions on the wizard, and then click **Finish** to create the form and subform.

Chapter 5 **Locating Specific Information**

Page 118 **To sort a field in ascending or descending order**

1 Open the table in Datasheet view.

2 Click anywhere in the column you want to sort, and then click the **Sort Ascending** or **Sort Descending** button.

3 To reverse the sort order, click the opposite **Sort** button.

4 To sort on more than one column of information, arrange the columns so that they are side-by-side in the order you want to sort them, select the columns, and then use the **Sort** buttons.

121 **To filter a table by selection**

1 Open the table in Datasheet view.

2 Click any instance of the selection by which you want to filter, and then click the **Filter By Selection** button.

121 **To remove a filter**

● Click the **Remove Filter** button.

121   **To exclude a field from a filter process**

    ●   Right-click the field you want to exclude, and click **Filter Excluding Selection** on the shortcut menu

123   **To filter by form in a form**

    1   Open the table or form you want to work with in either Datasheet or Form view.

    2   Click the **Filter By Form** button on the toolbar.

    3   Click the field or fields in which you want to create the filter, type the filter criteria you want, and press `Enter`; or select the criteria from the list of options. (Repeat this step for any other fields you want to filter.)

    4   To add additional filter criteria for a particular field, click the **Or** tab and enter the criteria as necessary.

    5   Click the **Apply Filter** button.

126   **To filter by multiple criteria**

    1   Open the table in Datasheet view.

    2   On the **Records** menu, point to **Filter**, and then click **Advanced Filter/Sort**.

    3   If the design grid is not blank, on the **Edit** menu, click **Clear Grid**.

    4   Select the criteria by which to filter.

    5   On the **Filter** menu, click **Apply Filter/Sort** to view the records that match the criteria.

129   **To create a select query in Design view**

    1   On the **Objects** bar, click **Queries**.

    2   Double-click **Create query in Design view**.

    3   In the **Show Tables** dialog box, double-click each table that you want to include in the query, and then close the dialog box.

    4   To include a field in the query, drag it from the field list at the top of the window to consecutive columns in the design grid. To copy all fields to the grid, double-click the title bar above the field list to select the entire list, and then drag the selection over the grid.

    5   Click the **Run** button to run the query and display the results in Datasheet view.

129   **To add an expression to a query**

    1   Open the query in Design view.

    2   Right-click the appropriate cell in the design grid, and then click **Build** on the shortcut menu.

3   In the **Expression Builder** dialog box, double-click the **Functions** folder in the first column of the elements area, and then click **Built-in Functions**.

4   Build your expression, and then click **OK**.

5   Press [Enter] to move the insertion point out of the field, which completes the entry of the expression.

6   To rename the expression, double-click **Expr1**, and then type the name you want.

7   Click the **Run** button to run the query and see the results in Datasheet view.

138 **To create a query by using a wizard**

1   On the **Objects** bar, click **Queries**, and then double-click **Create query by using wizard**.

2   In the **Tables/Queries** list, click the table on which you want to base the query.

3   Double-click each field that you want to include in the query to move it to the **Selected Fields** list.

4   If you want to include more than one table in your query, repeat steps 2 and 3.

5   Follow the instructions of the **Simple Query Wizard**, and then click **Finish** to complete the process and see the results.

6   If you want to use a field in a query but don't want to see the field in the results datasheet, click the **View** button to switch to Design view, and then clear the **Show** check box for fields you don't want to display.

7   Switch to Datasheet view to see the results.

140 **To perform a calculation in a query**

1   Open the query in which you want to perform a calculation.

2   Click in the field in which you want to perform the calculation, and then click the **Totals** button on the toolbar.

3   In the new **Totals** cell for the field, click the down arrow, and then click the calculation you want to perform from the drop-down list.

Chapter 6 Keeping Your Information Accurate

Page 146 **To specify data type settings**

1   Display the table in Design view.

2   Click in the **Data Type** cell of the field you want to change, click the down arrow, and then click the data type you want.

150 **To set a field's size property**

1 Display the table in Design view.

2 Click in the field you want to change, and then in the **Field Properties** area, click in the **Field Size** box, click the down arrow, and change the setting to what you want.

152 **To create a custom input mask**

1 Display the table in Design view.

2 Select the field for which you want to set an input mask, and in the **Field Properties** area, click **Input Mask**.

3 Click the ... button to start the **Input Mask Wizard**. (Click **Yes** if you are prompted to first save the table or install this feature.)

4 Select an input mask from the options, or enter your own input mask in the **Try It** box, and then click **Next**.

5 Specify whether you want to store the symbols with the data, and then click **Finish**.

6 Press ⌷Enter⌷ to accept the mask.

157 **To set a field validation rule**

1 Display the table in Design view.

2 Select the field you want to add a rule to, and in the **Field Properties** area, click the **Validation Rule** box,

3 Click the ... button at the right end of the **Validation Rule** box to open the Expression Builder, or type an expression and press ⌷Enter⌷.

4 In the **Validation Text** box, type a description of the rule.

5 Click in the **Caption** box, and indicate the type of entry that can be made in the field,, by typing, for example, Phone Number.

6 Save and close the table.

160 **To use a Lookup List to restrict data**

1 Display the table in Design view.

2 Click the **Data Type** cell for the field in which you want to use a Lookup List, click the down arrow, and then click **Lookup Wizard**.

3 Select the option to either look up the values in a table or query, or to type in the values that you want, and click **Next**.

4 Follow the wizard's instructions, (which will be determined by your choice in step 3), and then click **Finish**.

166 **To create and run an update query**

1 Create a query that displays the information you want and then open the query in Design view.

2 On the **Query** menu, click **Update Query**.

3 In the **Update To** row of the field you want to update, type the text you want, or create an expression.

4 Click the **Run** button, click **Yes** when Access warns you that you are about to update records, and save and close the query.

170 **To create and run a delete query**

1 Create a query that displays the information you want and then open the query in Design view.

2 On the **Query** menu, click **Delete Query**.

3 Type the text you want in the **Criteria** row under the appropriate field.

4 Click the **Run** button to run the delete query and click **Yes** when Access warns you that you are about to delete records.

5 Save and close the query.

Chapter 7 **Working with Reports**

Page 176 **To create a report by using a wizard**

1 On the **Objects** bar, click the table on which you want to base your report.

2 On the **Insert** menu, click **Report** to display the **New Report** dialog box.

3 Double-click **Report Wizard**.

4 Follow the instructions of the **Report Wizard**, and then click **Finish** to preview the report.

180 **To change the height of a report section**

1 Open the report in Design view.

2 Point to the top of the selector of the section you want to resize, and when the pointer changes to a two-headed vertical arrow, drag the selector up or down to expand or collapse the section.

180 **To create a custom date format in a Report Header**

1 Open the report in Design view.

2 Click the **Toolbox** button to open it, if necessary.

3   In the Toolbox, click the **Text Box** control, and then click where you want to insert the date in the **Report Header** section.

4   Click the label that was created with the new text box, and press ⌷Del⌷ to delete it.

5   Click the text box, and then press the ⌷F4⌷ key to display the **Properties** dialog box.

6   On the **Data** tab, click **Control Source**, enter your custom date format, for example: =Format(Date(), "dd,mm,yyyy"), and then press ⌷Enter⌷.

180   **To add a group header or footer**

1   Open the report in Design view, and then click the **Sorting and Grouping** button on the toolbar.

2   In the **Group Properties** area, double-click **Group Header** or **Group Footer** to change it to **Yes**.

180   **To report properties**

1   Open the report in Design view.

2   Select the control you want to modify, press ⌷F4⌷ to display the **Properties** dialog box, if necessary, and then click the appropriate tab.

3   Click the property you want to change, and then enter new values, or select a new setting from the drop-down list.

186   **To use a query as the basis for a report**

1   On the **Objects** bar, click **Queries**.

2   Click the query on which you want to base the report.

3   On the **Insert** menu, click **Report**.

4   Click **Report Wizard**, and then click **OK**.

5   Follow the wizard's instructions, and then click **Finish**.

186   **To insert a title in a report**

1   Open the report in Design view.

2   If the Toolbox isn't displayed, click the **Toolbox** button on the toolbar.

3   To give the report a title, click the **Label** control in the Toolbox, and then click the top of the **Report Header** section.

4   Name the report, and press ⌷Enter⌷.

5   Scroll down, and set the label's font properties.

6   If necessary, on the **Format** menu, point to **Size**, and then click **To Fit**.

7   Move the label to the location you want it.

To insert the date and time into a report

> **1** On the **Insert** menu, click **Date and Time** to display the **Date and Time** dialog box.
>
> **2** Make sure that **Include Date** is selected, and choose the date format you want. If you want to include the time, make sure that **Include Time** is selected, choose the time format, and then click **OK**.
>
> **3** Drag the new text box containing *=Date()* to where you want it, and adjust its width and position as needed using the buttons and boxes on the Formatting toolbar.

To give a report a label

> **1** Click the **Label** button in the Toolbox, click in the location on the report where you want the label, type the label name, and then press ⌷Enter⌷.
>
> **2** Set the font properties for the label, and then fine-tune the position of the label, in necessary.

To insert a page number in a report

> **1** In the **Page Footer** section, click **Page Numbers** on the **Insert** menu to display the **Page Numbers** dialog box.
>
> **2** Select the options you want, and then click **OK**.

To add a subreport to a report

> **1** Open the main report in Design view.
>
> **2** Open the Toolbox, if necessary, click **Subform/Subreport** on the Toolbox, and then click on the report where you want to insert the subreport.
>
> **3** Follow the instructions of the **SubReport Wizard**, and then click **Finish**.

To format a subreport

> **1** Open the main report with the subreport in Design view.
>
> **2** Click the subreport control, and press ⌷F4⌷.
>
> **3** Use the options in the **Properties** dialog box to make the necessary changes.
>
> **4** Save your changes, and switch to Print Preview to view the results.

To use the Expression Builder in a text box in a report

> **1** Open the report in Design view.
>
> **2** Click an unbound text box control and press ⌷F4⌷ to open the **Properties** dialog box.
>
> **3** Click the **Data** tab, click **Control Source**, and click the ... button to open the **Expression Builder**.
>
> **4** Build your expression, and then click **OK** to close the **Expression Builder**.
>
> **5** Press ⌷Enter⌷ to enter the calculation in the unbound text box.

4 Scroll through the list, click each entry in turn, and read through all the analysis notes, and click the **Optimize** button.

5 Close the **Performance Analyzer** dialog box.

To run the Documenter

1 On the **Tools** menu, point to **Analyze**, and then click **Documenter**.

2 Click the **All Object Types** tab.

3 Click **Select All**, and then click **OK** to start the documentation process.

Keeping Your Information Secure

To encrypt a database

1 Open the database, and on the **Tools** menu, point to **Security**, and then click **Encrypt/Decrypt Database**.

2 Navigate to the folder in which you want to store the encrypted file, name the encrypted file you are creating, and click **Save**.

To decrypt a database

1 With the database closed, on the **Tools** menu, point to **Security**, and click **Encrypt/Decrypt Database**.

2 In the **Encrypt/Decrypt Database** dialog box, navigate to the folder that contains the encrypted database, click the encrypted database file, and then click **OK**.

3 In the **File name** box, type a name for the decrypted database, and click **Save**.

To assign a password to a database

1 On the Database toolbar, click the **Open** button.

2 In the **Open** dialog box, navigate to the folder that contains the database you want to assign a password to, and click the file name.

3 Click the **Open** button's down arrow, and then click **Open Exclusive**.

4 On the **Tools** menu, point to **Security**, and click **Set Database Password**.

5 In the **Password** box, type a password, and press `Tab`.

6 In the **Verify** box, type the password again, and then click **OK**.

7 Close and reopen the database (you will have to type the password).

To share a database

1 Open the database you want to share, and on the **Tools** menu, click **Options** to display the **Options** dialog box.

2 Click the **Advanced** tab.

3   In the **Default open mode** area, make sure that the **Shared** option is selected.

4   Select the options you want, and then click **OK** to close the dialog box.

233   **To replicate a database**

1   Right-click the desktop, point to **New**, and then click **Briefcase** on the shortcut menu.

2   Rename the briefcase, and press ⟨Enter⟩.

3   Click the Windows **Start** button, and navigate to the folder that contains the database you want to replicate.

4   Reduce the size of the window, and position it so that you can see both the database file and briefcase on your desktop.

5   Drag the database to the briefcase.

6   Click **Yes** to continue.

7   Click **Yes** to have Briefcase make a backup copy of your database.

8   Click **OK** to accept the option to allow design changes only in the original copy of the database and to finish the replication process.

238   **To split a database**

1   Open the database you want to split, and on the **Tools** menu, point to **Database Utilities**, and click **Database Splitter**.

2   Click **Split Database**.

3   In the **Create Back-end Database** dialog box, navigate to the folder where you want to store the database components. In the **File name** box, type the name you want, and then click **Split**.

240   **To create a workgroup**

1   Open the database, and on the **Tools** menu, point to **Security**, and then click **User-Level Security Wizard**.

2   On the first page of the **Security Wizard**, click **Next** to create a new workgroup information file (WIF).

3   Replace the text in the **WID** box by selecting it and typing a new workgroup ID.

4   Accept the default selection to create a shortcut to open the security-enhanced database, and click **Next**.

5   Click **Next** to accept the default selections and secure all objects.

6   Select the check boxes for **Full Data Users** and **New Data Users**, and then click **Next**.

7   Click **Next**.

8   To add users to the list, in the **User name** box, type a name of a user, in the **Password** box, type a password, and then click **Add This User to the List**.

9 Click **Next**.

10 Click **Finish** in the wizard's final page to accept the default name for the backup copy of your unsecured database.

253 **To secure the VBA code in a database**

1 With the database open, press [Alt]+[F11] to open the VBA Editor.

2 On the VBA Editor's **Tools** menu, click the **Properties** command for the database you have open.

3 In the **Project Properties** dialog box, click the **Protection** tab, and click the **Lock project for viewing** check box.

4 In the **Password** box, type a password, and press [Tab].

5 In the **Confirm Password box**, type the password again, and then click **OK**.

6 Press [Alt]+[F11] to return to Access, and then close the database.

254 **To convert a database to Access 2002-2003 format**

1 With the database you want to convert closed, on the **Tools** menu, point to **Database Utilities**, point to **Convert Database**, and click **To Access 2002 – 2003 File Format**.

2 In the **Database to Convert From** dialog box, navigate to the folder that contains the database you want to convert, and double-click the file name.

3 In the **File name** box, type a name for the converted database, and click **Save**.

4 Click **OK**.

254 **To secure a database by saving it as an MDE file**

1 Make sure the database you want to secure as an MDE file is first converted to Access 2002-2003 format.

2 With the database closed, on the **Tools** menu, point to **Database Utilities**, and click **Make MDE File**.

3 In the **Database To Save As MDE** dialog box, navigate to the folder that contains the file you want to save as an MDE file, click the file, and then click **Make MDE**.

4 In the **File name** box, type a name for the file, and then click **Save**.

Chapter 10 Working with Pages and Modules

Page 261 **To convert a report to a set of static Web pages**

1 On the **Objects** bar, click **Reports**, and double-click the report you want to convert.

2 On the **File** menu, click **Export** to display the **Export** dialog box.

3 Navigate to the folder where you want to save the Web pages, in the **File name** box, type a name for the pages, in the **Save as type** box, click **HTML Documents**, select the **Autostart** check box, and then click **Export**.

4 In the **HTML Output Options** dialog box, make sure the **Select a HTML Template** check box is cleared, and then click **OK**.

5 If you don't see the HTML page, click the file name on the taskbar to display it. Click the **Next** hyperlink to scroll through the pages of the file.

276 **To create a data access page with AutoPage**

1 With the database open, on the **Objects** bar, click **Pages**.

2 On the database window's toolbar, click the **New** button to display the **New Data Access Page** dialog box.

3 Click the **AutoPage** option you want, display the list of tables and queries, click the table or query you want, and then click **OK**.

4 Click the **Save** button on the toolbar to save your new page.

5 In the **Save As Data Access Page** dialog box, navigate to the folder where you want to store the file, give the file a name, and click **Save**.

6 If Access warns you that the connection string for this page uses an absolute page, click **OK** to dismiss the message. (A UNC path is appropriate if you are using a file on a network computer.)

283 **To create a data access page with the Page Wizard**

1 With the database open, on the **Objects** bar, click **Pages**.

2 At the top of the database window, click the **New** button.

3 In the **New Data Access Page** dialog box, click **Page Wizard**. In the list of tables and queries, click the table on which you want to base the data access page, and then click **OK**.

4 Click the **>>** button to move fields from the **Available Fields** list to the **Selected Fields** list, and then click **Next**.

5 Double-click **CategoryName**, and then click **Next**.

6 In the first sort box, click **ProductName**, and click **Next**.

7 Select the **Do you want to apply a theme to your page** check box, and click **Finish**.

287 **To create a data access page by hand**

1 With the database open, on the **Objects** bar, click **Pages**.

2 Double-click **Create data access page in Design view** to open a blank data access page.

287 **To add a PivotTable to a data access page**

1 Open the data access page that you want to add a PivotTable to in Design view.

2 If the Field List is not displayed, click the **Field List** button on the toolbar.

3 Make sure the Toolbox is open, click the **Office PivotTable** tool, and then click a blank section of the upper-left corner on the page.

4 Click in the PivotTable, and then double-click its frame to open the **Properties** dialog box.

5 Click the **Other** tab, click the **DataMember** property, select the table or query on which the PivotTable will be based from the list, and close the **Properties** dialog box.

6 In the **Field List**, select the same table or query.

7 Drag a field from the Field List to the horizontal box labeled **Drop Filter Fields Here**.

8 Drag a field to the vertical box labeled **Drop Row Fields Here**.

9 Drag a field to the horizontal box labeled **Drop Column Fields Here**.

10 Drag a field to the box labeled **Drop Totals** or **Detail Fields Here**.

11 Click the **View** button to switch to Page view, and experiment with the PivotTable to make sure it works.

12 Save the page.

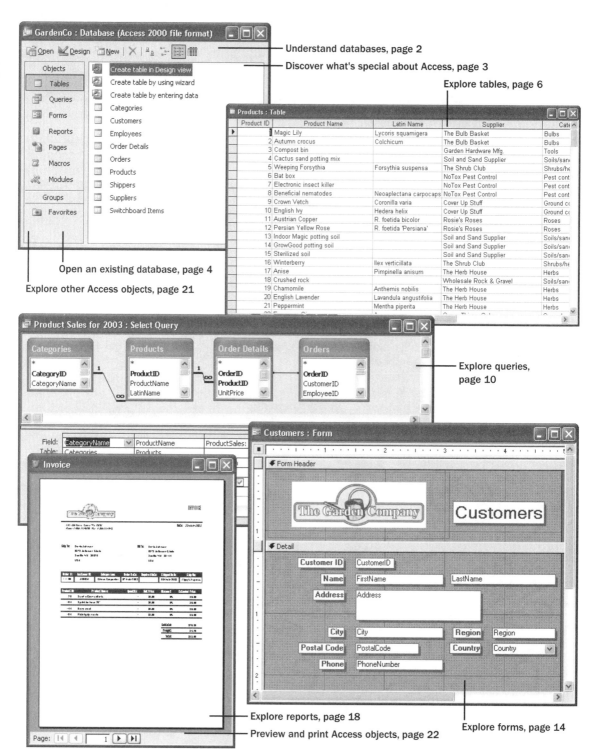

Understand databases, page 2

Discover what's special about Access, page 3

Explore tables, page 6

Open an existing database, page 4

Explore other Access objects, page 21

Explore queries, page 10

Explore reports, page 18

Preview and print Access objects, page 22

Explore forms, page 14

Chapter 1 at a Glance

1 Getting to Know Microsoft Access 2003

In this chapter you will learn to:

✔ Understand databases.

✔ Discover what's special about Access.

✔ Open an existing database.

✔ Explore tables.

✔ Explore queries.

✔ Explore forms.

✔ Explore reports.

✔ Explore other Access objects.

✔ Preview and print Access objects.

Microsoft Office Access 2003 is part of The Microsoft Office System, so the basic interface objects—menus, toolbars, dialog boxes—will be familiar if you have used other Office products or other Microsoft Windows applications. However, Access has more dimensions than most of those programs, so it might seem more complex until you become familiar with it.

This book gives you straightforward instructions for using Access to create databases. It takes you from knowing little or nothing about Access—or, for that matter, about databases—to a level of expertise that will enable you to develop database programs for use by one person or by many.

This chapter introduces you to the concept of a database, explains a little about Access, and takes you on a tour of the program. The database you will use for the tour belongs to The Garden Company, a fictional garden supply and plant store. (You will be working with this database throughout this book.) This tour will give you a firm foundation from which to begin working with Access to create your own databases. After exploring the structure of the GardenCo database, you will look at some of the objects used to store and manipulate the data it contains. Finally, you will preview and print the various Access objects.

See Also   Do you need only a quick refresher on the topics in this chapter? See the Quick Reference entries on pages xxix–xxx.

Important Before you can use the practice files in this chapter, you need to install them from the book's companion CD to their default location. See "Using the Book's CD-ROM" on page xiii for more information.

Understanding Databases

In its most basic form, a database is the computer equivalent of an organized list of information. Typically, this information has a common subject or purpose, such as the list of employees shown here:

ID	Last name	First name	Title	Hire date
1	Dale	Martha	Sales Rep	May 1, 1992
2	Fuller	Joanna	V.P, Sales	Aug 14, 1992
3	Lee	Mark	Sales Rep	Apr 1, 1992
4	Penn	Daniel	Sales Rep	May 3, 1993

This list is arranged in a *table* of columns and rows. Each column (*field*) stores a particular type of information about an employee: first name, last name, date of hire, and so on. Each row (*record*) contains information about a different employee.

If a database did nothing more than store information in a table, it would be as useful as a paper list. But because the database stores information in an electronic format, you can manipulate the information in powerful ways to extend its utility.

For example, a phone book for your city is probably sitting on a shelf within a few feet of you. If you want to locate a person or a business in your city, you can do so, because the information in the telephone book is organized in an understandable manner. If you want to get in touch with someone a little further away, you can go to the public library and use its collection of phone books, which probably includes one for each major city in the country. However, if you want to find the phone numbers of all the people in the country with your last name, or if you want the phone number of your grandmother's neighbor, these phone books won't do you much good because they aren't organized in a way that makes that information easy to find.

When the information published in a phone book is stored in a database, it takes up far less space, it costs less to reproduce and distribute, and, if the database is designed correctly, the information can be retrieved in many ways. The real power of a database isn't in its ability to store information; it is in your ability to quickly retrieve exactly the information you want from the database.

Discovering What's Special About Access

Simple *database programs*, such as the Database component of Microsoft Works, can store information in only one table, which is often referred to as a flat file. These simple databases are often called *flat databases*. More complex database programs, such as Microsoft Access, can store information in multiple related tables, thereby creating what are often referred to as *relational databases*. If the information in a relational database is organized correctly, you can treat these multiple tables as a single storage area and pull information electronically from different tables in whatever order meets your needs.

A table is just one of the types of *objects* that you can work with in Access. The following graphic shows all the Access object types:

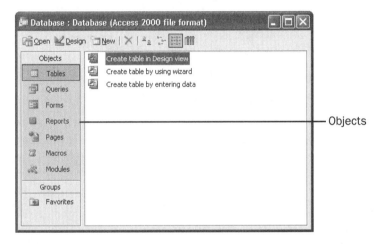

Objects

Tip   For maximum compatibility with existing databases, the default format for new databases created with Access 2003 is Access 2000.

Of all these object types, only one—the table—is used to store information. The rest are used to manage, manipulate, analyze, retrieve, display, or publish the table information—in other words, to make the information as accessible and therefore as useful as possible.

Over the years, Microsoft has put a lot of effort into making Access not only one of the most powerful consumer database programs available, but also one of the easiest to learn and use. Because Access is part of The Microsoft Office System, you can use many of the techniques you know from using other Office programs, such as Microsoft Office Word and Microsoft Office Excel, when using Access. For example, you can use familiar commands, buttons, and keyboard shortcuts to open and edit the information in Access tables. And because Access is integrated with other members of the suite, you can easily share information between Access and Word, Excel, or other programs.

Opening an Existing Database

The Garden Company's database, which is called *GardenCo*, contains information about its employees, products, suppliers, and customers that is stored in a series of tables. As you complete the exercises in this book, you will work with these tables to develop an assortment of queries, forms, reports, data access pages, macros, and modules that can be used to enter, edit, and manipulate the information in the tables in many ways.

In this exercise, you will open the GardenCo database, explore some of its objects, and then close the database. You won't find a lot of detailed explanation here, because this is just an overview.

BE SURE TO start your computer, but don't start Access yet.
USE the *GardenCo* database in the practice file folder for this topic. This practice file is located in the *My Documents\Microsoft Press\Access 2003 SBS\KnowAccess\Open* folder and can also be accessed by clicking *Start/All Programs/Microsoft Press/Access 2003 Step by Step*.

1 On the taskbar, click the **Start** button, point to **All Programs** and then **Microsoft Office**, and click **Microsoft Office Access 2003**.

As with other Office programs, Access has a menu bar and one or more toolbars across the top of the window. When you click either New or File Search on the File menu, or click Office Clipboard on the Edit menu, the New File task pane is displayed at the right side of this window.

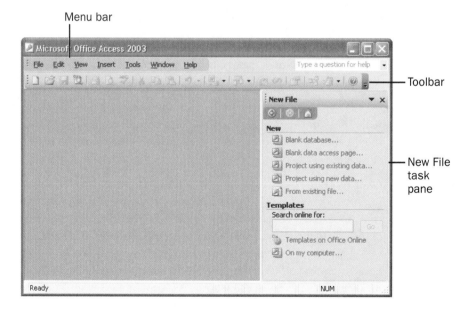

Open

2 On the toolbar, click the **Open** button, navigate to the *My Documents\Microsoft Press \Access 2003 SBS\KnowAccess\Open* folder, and then double-click **GardenCo**. If Access warns you that unsafe expressions are not blocked, click **Yes**. Then click **Open**.

The Garden Company introductory screen, called a *splash screen*, appears.

Tip There are a couple of other ways you can open a database. On the File menu, you can click New to display the New File task pane, which offers a variety of options for opening new or existing databases. You can also double-click a database in Windows Explorer, or My Documents, My Computer or My Network Places. (Access databases have a file name extension *.mdb*.)

3 Select the **Don't show this screen again** check box, and then click **OK**.

The database's switchboard appears. A *switchboard* is used to easily access the database objects needed to perform common tasks.

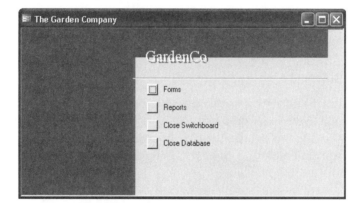

4 Click **Close Switchboard** to close the switchboard.

The GardenCo *database window* appears.

See Also For more information about switchboards, see "Creating a Switchboard by Using Switchboard Manager" in Chapter 8.

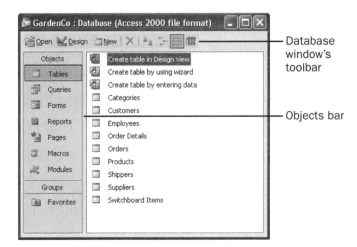

Across the top of the window is a toolbar and along the left edge is the Objects bar, which lists the Access database objects. Because Tables is selected, the right pane of the window lists the tables contained in the database.

5   On the **File** menu, click **Close** to close the GardenCo database.

Exploring Tables

*Microsoft
Office
Specialist*

Tables are the core database objects. Their purpose is to store information. The purpose of every other database object is to interact in some manner with one or more tables. An Access database can contain thousands of tables, and the number of records each table can contain is limited more by the space available on your hard disk than anything else.

Tip   For detailed information about Access specifications, such as the maximum size of a database or the maximum number of records in a table, click the Ask A Question box at the right end of the menu bar, type **Access specifications**, and press the Enter key.

Every Access object has two or more *views*. For tables, the two most common views are *Datasheet view*, in which you can see and modify the table's data, and *Design view*, in which you can see and modify the table's structure. Clicking the View button toggles the view of the open table between Datasheet and Design views. You can also click the down arrow to the right of the View button and select a view from the drop-down list.

When you view a table in Datasheet view, you see the table's data in columns (fields) and rows (records).

Row selector
Row (record)   Column (field)   Column header

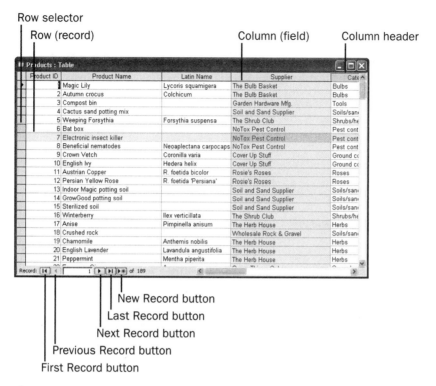

New Record button
Last Record button
Next Record button
Previous Record button
First Record button

If two tables have one or more fields in common, you can embed the datasheet for one table in another. With the embedded datasheet, which is called a *subdatasheet*, you can see the information in more than one table at the same time. For example, you might want to embed an Orders datasheet in a Customers table so that you can see the orders each customer has placed.

In this exercise, you will open existing tables in the GardenCo database and explore their structure in different views.

USE the *GardenCo* database in the practice file folder for this topic. This practice file is located in the *My Documents\Microsoft Press\Access 2003 SBS\KnowAccess\Tables* folder and can also be accessed by clicking *Start/All Programs/Microsoft Press/Access 2003 Step by Step*.
OPEN the *GardenCo* database and acknowledge the safety warning, if necessary.

1   On the **Objects** bar, click **Tables**.

2   On the toolbar at the top of the database window, click the **Details** button.

Details

A description of each of the objects listed in the window is displayed to the right of its name.

Tip　You can resize the columns in the database window by dragging the vertical bar that separates columns in the header. You can set the width of a column to the width of its widest entry by double-clicking the vertical bar.

Maximize

3　Click the **Maximize** button in the upper-right corner of the database window.

The database window expands to fill the Access window. Note that the first three items in the Name column are not tables; they are shortcuts to three commands you can use to create a new table.

Tip　If you don't want these shortcuts at the top of each list of objects, on the Tools menu, click Options, click the View tab in the Options dialog box, clear the New object shortcuts check box, and then click OK.

4　Click the **Restore Down** button.

Restore Down

The database window shrinks.

Open

5　Click the **Categories** table, and then click the **Open** button at the top of the database window to open the table in Datasheet view.

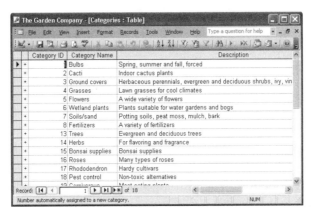

This datasheet contains a list of the categories of products sold by The Garden Company. As you can see, there are fields for Category ID, Category Name, and Description.

6　Click the plus sign to the left of the record for the Bulbs category.

Clicking the plus sign expands an embedded subdatasheet. The category records from the Categories table and product records from the Products table are displayed simultaneously.

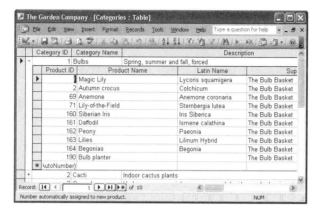

Notice that the plus sign has changed to a minus sign.

7　Click the minus sign to the left of the Bulbs record to collapse the subdatasheet.

8　On the **File** menu, click **Close** to close the Categories table. If you are prompted to save changes to the table layout, click **Yes**.

Tip　You can also close a window by clicking the Close button in the window's upper-right corner. When an object window is maximized, this button is called the Close Window button to avoid confusion with the Close button at the right end of the Access window's title bar. Be careful to click the correct button, or else you will quit Access.

9　Double-click **Orders** to open the table in Datasheet view.

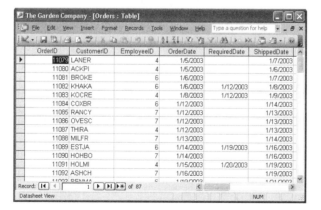

The navigation area at the bottom of the window indicates that this table contains 87 records and that the active record is number 1.

Next Record

10 Move the selection one record at a time by clicking the **Next Record** button several times.

The selection moves down the OrderID field, because that field contains the insertion point.

Tip You can move the selection one record at a time by pressing the ↑ or ↓ key, one screen at a time by pressing the [Page Up] or [Page Down] key, or to the first or last field in the table by pressing [Ctrl]+[Home] or [Ctrl]+[End].

11 Move directly to record 40 by selecting the current record number, typing 40, and pressing [Enter].

12 Close the Orders table, clicking **No** if you are prompted to save changes to the table's layout.

13 Double-click **Products** in the list of tables to open it in Datasheet view.

Notice that this table contains 189 records.

View

14 On the toolbar, click the **View** button to switch the view of the Products table to Design view.

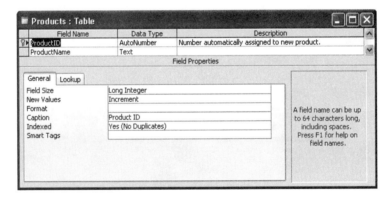

In Datasheet view, you see the data stored in the table, whereas in Design view, you see the underlying table structure.

Close

15 Close the Products table by clicking its **Close** button. If prompted to save changes to the table layout, click **No**.

CLOSE the *GardenCo* database.

Exploring Queries

One way you can locate information in an Access database is to create queries. You use queries to locate information so that you can view, change, or analyze it in various ways. You can also use the results of queries as the basis for other Access objects.

A *query* is essentially a question. For example, you might ask, "Which records in the Customer table have the value 98052 in the Postal Code field?" When you *run a query* (the equivalent of asking a question), Access looks at all the records in the table or tables you have specified, finds those that match the criteria you have defined, and displays them in a datasheet.

For Access to be able to answer your questions, you have to structure queries in a specific way. Each type of question has a corresponding type of query. The primary query types are *select, crosstab*, and *parameter*. Less common types are *action, AutoLookup*, and *SQL (Structured Query Language)*. Access includes wizards that guide you through the creation of the common queries; less common ones have to be created by hand in a *design grid* in Design view. Here's what a typical query looks like:

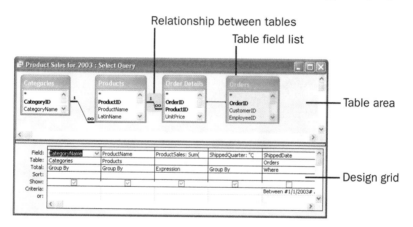

At the top of this query window are four small windows listing the fields in the four tables that will be included in this query. The lines connecting the tables indicate that they are related by virtue of common fields. The first row of the grid contains the names of the fields to be included in the query, and the second row shows which table each field belongs to. The third row (labeled *Total*) performs calculations on the field values, and the fourth row indicates whether the query results will be sorted on this field. A check mark in the check box in the fifth row (labeled *Show*) means that the field will be displayed in the results datasheet. (If the check box isn't selected, the field can be used in determining the query results, but it won't be displayed.) The sixth row (labeled *Criteria*) contains criteria that determine which records will be displayed, and the seventh row (labeled *or*) sets up alternate criteria.

Don't worry if this all sounds a bit complicated at the moment. When you approach queries logically, they soon begin to make perfect sense. And don't worry if they sound like a lot of work. The Query Wizard is available to help you structure the query, and if you create a query that you are likely to run more than once, you can save it. It then becomes part of the database and is displayed in the database window when you click Queries on the Objects bar.

In this exercise, you will explore a few of the queries that have already been defined and saved in the GardenCo database.

USE the *GardenCo* database in the practice file folder for this topic. This practice file is located in the *My Documents\Microsoft Press\Access 2003 SBS\KnowAccess\Queries* folder and can also be accessed by clicking *Start/All Programs/Microsoft Press/Access 2003 Step by Step*.
OPEN the *GardenCo* database and acknowledge the safety warning, if necessary.

1 On the **Objects** bar, click **Queries**.

The database window displays all the queries that have been saved as part of the GardenCo database.

2 Double-click the title bar of the database window to maximize the window.

The top two entries in this window are commands for creating queries. The remaining entries are queries that have already been created.

Details

3 Click the **Details** button.

12

The description of each query explains its purpose. The icon in the Name column is an indication of the query's type, as is the information in the Type column, which you can see by scrolling the window to the right.

Restore
Window

4 Click the **Restore Window** button on the menu bar (not the title bar).

The database window is restored to its original size.

Open

5 Open the **Products by Category** query in Datasheet view by selecting it and clicking the **Open** button at the top of the database window.

When you open the query, Access processes it (described as *running a query*) and produces a datasheet that displays the results.

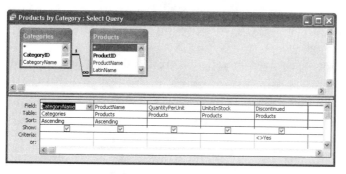

The Navigation bar tells you that 171 records are displayed. The Products table contains 189 records. To find out why 18 of the records are missing, you need to look at this query in Design view.

View

6 On the toolbar, click the **View** button to view the query in Design view.

In the top part of the query window, two boxes list the fields of the tables this query is designed to work with. The bottom part is the design grid, where the query is formed. Each column of the grid can refer to one field from one of the tables above. Notice that <> *Yes (not equal to Yes)* has been entered in the Criteria row for the Discontinued field. This query therefore finds all the records that don't have a value of *Yes* in that field (in other words, that have not been discontinued).

Run

7   As an experiment, in the **Criteria** row of the **Discontinued** field, select the text **<>Yes**, type **=Yes**, and then click the **Run** button on the toolbar.

Tip   You can also run a query by switching to Datasheet view.

The query is changed so that it now finds all the records that have a value of *Yes* in the Discontinued field (in other words, that have been discontinued).

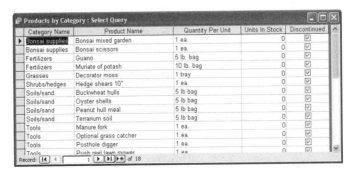

The 18 discontinued products account for the difference in the number of records in the Products table and the number of records displayed by the original query.

8   Close the query window, clicking **No** when prompted to save the design changes.

CLOSE the *GardenCo* database.

Exploring Forms

Access tables are dense lists of raw information. If you create a database that only you will use, you will probably be very comfortable working directly with tables. But if you create a database that will be viewed and edited by people who don't know much about it—and don't necessarily want to know about it—working with your tables might be overwhelming. To solve this problem, you can design forms to guide users through your database, making it easier for them to enter, retrieve, display, and print information.

A *form* is essentially a window in which you can place *controls* that either give users information or accept information that they enter. Access provides a toolbox that includes many standard Windows controls, such as labels, text boxes, option buttons, and check boxes. With a little ingenuity, you can use these controls to create forms that look and work much like the dialog boxes in all Microsoft Windows applications.

You use forms to edit the records of the underlying tables or enter new records. As with tables and queries, you can display forms in several views. The three most common views are *Form view*, in which you enter data; *Datasheet view*, which looks essentially like a table; and *Design view*, in which you work with the elements of the form to refine the way it looks and works. This graphic shows what a form looks like in Design view:

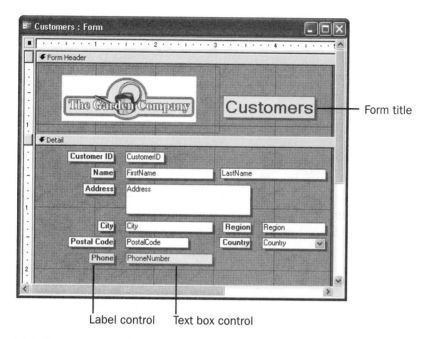

Form title

Label control　Text box control

This form consists of a *main form* that is linked to just one table. But a form can also include *subforms* that are linked to other tables. Arranged in the form are *label controls* containing text that appears in the form in Form view, and *text box controls* that will contain data from the table. Although you can create a form from scratch in Design view, you will probably use this view most often to refine the forms you create with a wizard.

In this exercise, you will take a look at a few of the forms in the GardenCo database that have been designed to make viewing tables, editing existing information, and adding new information easier and less error-prone.

USE the *GardenCo* database in the practice file folder for this topic. This practice file is located in the *My Documents\Microsoft Press\Access 2003 SBS\KnowAccess\Forms* folder and can also be accessed by clicking *Start/All Programs/Microsoft Press/Access 2003 Step by Step*.
OPEN the *GardenCo* database and acknowledge the safety warning, if necessary.

1　On the **Objects** bar, click **Forms**, and then double-click **Switchboard** to open the main switchboard.

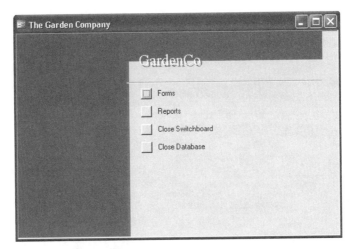

The Switchboard form has a customized title bar at the top, a title for the GardenCo database, and four command buttons. The first two buttons open switchboards—other forms—that have the same name as the button.

2 On the switchboard, click the **Forms** button to display the Forms switchboard.

3 Click **Edit/Enter Orders** to display the **Orders** form.

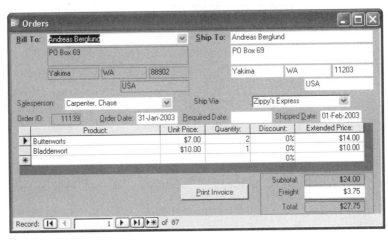

This form consists of a main form and a subform.

4 On the Navigation bar, click the **Next Record** button to display that record's information.

5 Click the **New Record** button (the one with asterisk) to display a blank form where you could enter a new order.

Next Record

New Record

6 Close the **Orders** form, and in the Forms switchboard, click **Return** to redisplay the main switchboard.

7 Click the **Close Switchboard** button.

8 In the database window, double-click **Products** in the **Forms** list to open the form.

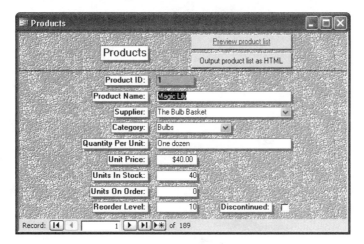

You use this form to edit the records of current products or enter new ones.

View

9 You are currently looking at the form in Form view. On the toolbar, click the down arrow to the right of the **View** button, and click **Datasheet View**.

Now the form looks essentially like the Products table in Datasheet view but without gridlines.

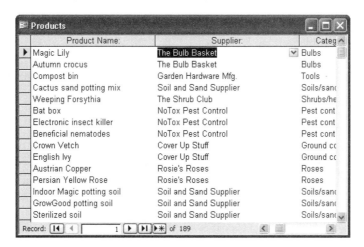

10 Click the **View** button again to switch to Design view, and then maximize the form window.

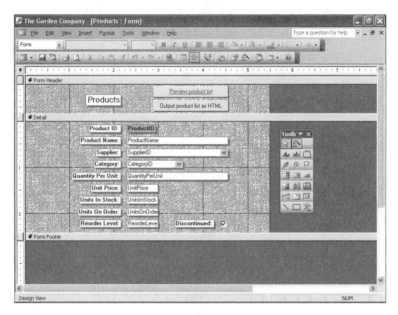

Toolbox

11 If the Toolbox is not displayed, on the toolbar, click the **Toolbox** button.

> **Tip** If the Toolbox is in the way, drag it by its title bar to a location where it's not obscuring anything.

12 Point to each of the icons in the Toolbox until the name of the tool is displayed.

These are the tools you use to build custom forms for your database.

13 Close the Toolbox.

14 Close the **Products** form.

CLOSE the *GardenCo* database.

Exploring Reports

Microsoft Office Specialist

You use *reports* to display the information from your tables in nicely formatted, easily accessible ways, either on your computer screen or on paper. A report can include items of information selected from multiple tables and queries, values calculated from information in the database, and formatting elements such as headers, footers, titles, and headings.

You can look at reports in three views: *Design view*, in which you can manipulate the design of a report in the same way that you manipulate a form; *Print Preview*, in which you see your report exactly as it will look when printed; and *Layout Preview*, which shows you how each element will look but without all the detail of Print Preview. A report in Design view looks like this:

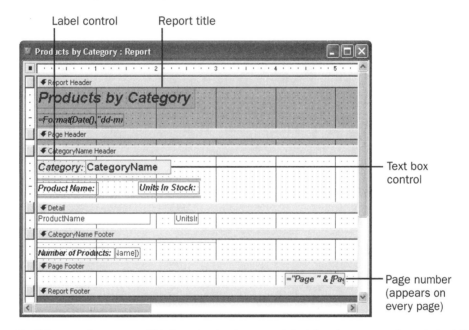

In this exercise, you will take a look at a report that has been saved as part of the GardenCo database, just to get an idea of what is possible.

USE the *GardenCo* database in the practice file folder for this topic. This practice file is located in the *My Documents\Microsoft Press\Access 2003 SBS\KnowAccess\Reports* folder and can also be accessed by clicking *Start/All Programs/Microsoft Press/Access 2003 Step by Step*.
OPEN the *GardenCo* database and acknowledge the safety warning, if necessary.

1 On the **Objects** bar, click **Reports**.

The top two entries in this window are commands you can use to create reports. The remaining entries are reports that have already been created.

2 Click **Customer Labels**, and then click the **Preview** button at the top of the database window to display the report.

This report prints customer names and addresses in a mailing label format. You are looking at it in a view that is much like Print Preview in other Microsoft Office programs.

Tip Access provides a wizard that can help you create a mailing label report. You can also use the Customer table in this database with Word's mail merge feature to create these labels.

3 Click in the form to change the zoom level.

Tip If the report is too small to read in Print Preview, you can also select a zoom level in the Zoom box on the toolbar.

4 Close the **Customer Labels** report.

5 In the database window, select the **Invoice** report, and click the **Preview** button to see the invoice.

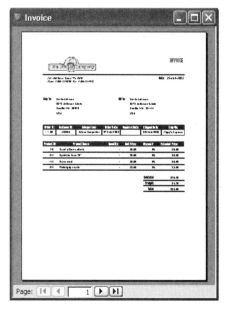

6 Check out each page by clicking the navigation buttons at the bottom of the window.

View

7 On the Database toolbar, click the **View** button to display the report in Design view, and then maximize the report window.

20

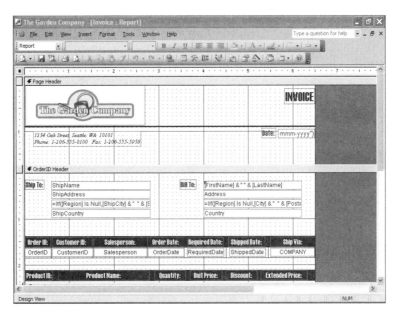

In this view, the report looks similar to a form, and the techniques you use to create forms can also be used to create reports.

8   Close the report.

CLOSE the *GardenCo* database.

Exploring Other Access Objects

Tables, queries, forms, and reports are the objects you will use most frequently in Access. You can use them to create powerful and useful databases. However, if you need to create a sophisticated database, you can use data access pages, macros, and modules to substantially extend the capabilities of Access. To round out this introduction to Access databases, this section provides a brief overview of these objects.

Pages

To enable people to view and manipulate your database information over an intranet or the Internet, you can create *pages*, also known as *data access pages*. Working with a data access page on the World Wide Web is very much like working directly with a table or form in Access—users can work with the data in tables, run queries, and enter information in forms.

Although publishing database information on the Web seems like a fairly difficult task, Access provides a wizard that does most of the tedious work of creating data access pages for you. You can use a wizard-generated page as-is, or you can add your own personal touch in Design view.

Macros

You use *macros* to have Access respond to an event, such as the click of a button, the opening of a form, or the updating of a record. Macros can be particularly handy when you expect that other people who are less experienced with Access than you will work in your database. For example, you can make routine database actions, such as opening and closing forms or printing reports, available as command buttons on switchboards. And by grouping together an assortment of menu commands and having users carry them out by using a macro with the click of a button, you can ensure that everyone does things the same way.

Modules

More powerful than macros, *modules* are Microsoft Visual Basic for Applications (VBA) programs. VBA is a high-level programming language developed by Microsoft for the purpose of creating Windows programs. A common set of VBA instructions can be used with all programs in The Microsoft Office System, and each program has its own set as well. Whereas macros can automate four to five dozen actions, VBA includes hundreds of commands and can be extended indefinitely with third-party add-ins. You could use VBA to carry out tasks that are too complex to be handled with macros, such as opening an Excel spreadsheet and retrieving specific information.

Tip The Microsoft Office XP installation CD-ROM includes several sample databases that illustrate many of the principles of creating and using a database. One of these, the Northwind Traders database, is used as an example in many topics in Access online Help, so it is a particularly good database for you to explore. You'll find a link to this database on the Access Help menu, under *Sample Databases*.

Previewing and Printing Access Objects

Microsoft Office Specialist

Because Access is a Windows application, it interacts with your printer through standard Windows dialog boxes and drivers. This means that any printer that you can use from other programs can be used from Access, and any special features of that printer, such as color printing or duplex printing, are available in Access.

As you have seen in this chapter, you can use different Access objects—tables, forms, reports, and so on—to display the information stored in your database. Within each object there are several views available: Design view, Datasheet view, and so on. You can choose the view you want by selecting it from the View menu (the views available will depend on the object that is active).

Like most Windows applications, Access includes the Page Setup, Print Preview, and Print commands on the File menu. These commands are available when their use would be appropriate, which is determined by the object displayed and the current view of that object.

This table shows the relationships for the primary objects:

View\Object	Table	Query	Form	Report
Design			PP, P	PP, P
Datasheet	PP, P	PP, P	PP, P	
PivotTable	PP, P	PP, P	PP, P	
PivotChart	PP, P	PP, P	PP, P	
SQL				
Form			PP, P	
Layout Preview				

If a cell is shaded, that object supports that view. PP in a cell indicates Print Preview is supported for that object in that view. P indicates that Print and Page Setup are supported for that object in that view.

The less common objects—Pages, Macros, and Modules—offer more limited views and print commands, as shown here:

View\Object	Page	Macro	Module
Design		PP, P	
Page	P		
Web Page Preview			
Code			P
Object			P

These tables make the process of previewing and printing your data seem a little complex, but the point is that the appropriate print commands are generally available when you need them.

Tip   When printing tables in Datasheet view, you will often find that printing in Landscape orientation will provide the best image.

In this exercise, you will preview and print employee information that is in a table and a form in the GardenCo database.

USE the *GardenCo* database in the practice file folder for this topic. This practice file is located in the *My Documents\Microsoft Press\Access 2003 SBS\KnowAccess\Print* folder and can also be accessed by clicking *Start/All Programs/Microsoft Press/Access 2003 Step by Step*.
OPEN the *GardenCo* database and acknowledge the safety warning, if necessary.

1   On the **Objects** bar, click **Tables**.

2   Double-click the **Employees** table to open it in Datasheet view.

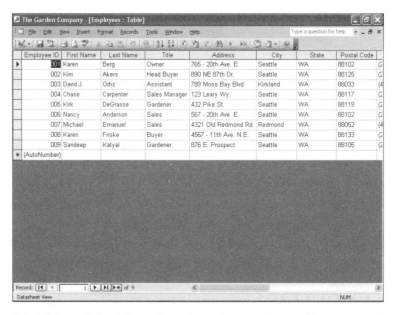

This table contains information about nine employees. You can see that there are more fields than will fit on the screen.

3   On the **File** menu, click **Print Preview** to display the first page of the datasheet printout.

4 Move the pointer over the table—the pointer will become a magnifying glass—and then click to zoom in. Click again to return to a reduced view.

Next Record

5 Click the **Next Record** button at the bottom of the screen to preview the next page. Click it again.

You can see that there will be three short pages if you print this datasheet.

6 On the toolbar, click the **Setup** button to display the **Page Setup** dialog box.

This is the same dialog box you would see if you clicked Page Setup on the File menu. You can use this dialog box to control margin and page layout settings.

7 On the **Page** tab, click **Landscape** and then **OK**.

The preview page is displayed lengthwise across the screen, and displays more fields. There are now only two pages.

Print

8 Click the **Print** button to send this datasheet to your default printer.

Tip If your computer is connected to more than one printer and you would like to send a job to a printer other than the default one, on the File menu, click Print, and then select the desired printer from the list near the top of the dialog box.

Close

9 Click the **Close** button to close Print Preview.

10 On the **File** menu, click **Close** to close the datasheet.

11 On the **Objects** bar, click **Forms**.

12 Double-click the **Employees** form to open it in Form view.

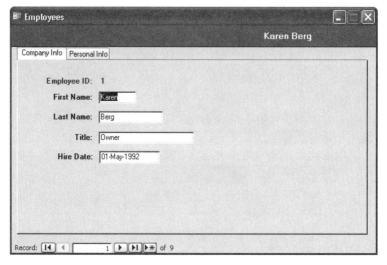

The information for each employee appears on its own page. Notice that there are two tabs at the top of the page, one for company information and one for personal information.

13 Click the **Personal Info** tab to see the information that is listed there, and then return to the **Company Info** tab.

Print Preview

14 On the toolbar, click the **Print Preview** button to preview the printout.

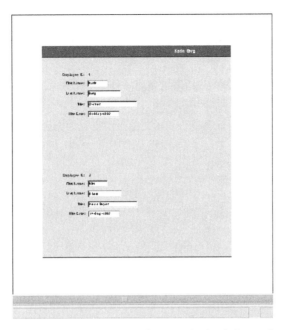

Notice that the preview shows only the information that was on the active tab. If you want to print the information on a different tab you need to make that tab active first.

15   Click the **Close** button to close the Print Preview window.

16   On the **File** menu, click **Print** to display the **Print** dialog box.

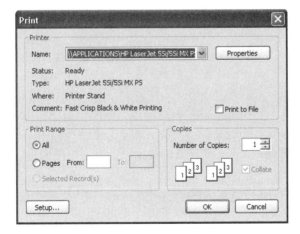

The dialog box you see will depend on the printer you have installed. Use this dialog box to select a printer, set the range of pages to be printed, and do other things.

See Also You use essentially the same methods to print information displayed in different Access objects. For an example of printing a report, see "Previewing and Printing a Report" in Chapter 7.

---

17 Click **Close** to close the dialog box.

CLOSE the *GardenCo* database and quit Access.

Key Points

- Microsoft Access is part of The Microsoft Office System, so the basic interface objects—menus, toolbars, dialog boxes—work basically the same as other Office products or other Microsoft Windows applications.

- A database is the computer equivalent of an organized list of information. The power of a database is in your ability to quickly retrieve precise information from it. In Access, data is organized in tables comprised of columns and rows, called fields and records. Access is a relational database, so you can treat the multiple tables in one database as a single storage area and easily pull information from different tables in whatever order and format suits you.

- A table is just one of the types of objects that you can work with in Access. The other object types are: queries, forms, reports, data access pages, macros and modules. Tables are the core database objects and the purpose of every other database object is to interact with one or more tables.

- Every Access object has two or more views. For example, you view data in a table in Datasheet view and define how the data is displayed in Design view.

- One way you can locate information in an Access database is to create and run a query. You use queries to locate information so that you can view, change, or analyze it in various ways. Queries can be viewed in Datasheet view or Design view, but you can also use the results of a query as the basis for other Access objects, such as a form or report.

- Forms make it easy for users to enter, retrieve, display and print information stored in tables. A form is essentially a window in which you can place controls that either give users information or accept information they enter. Forms can be viewed in Form view, Datasheet view, or Design view.

■ Reports display information from your tables in a nicely formatted, easily accessible way, either on your computer screen or on paper. A report can include items of information selected from multiple tables and queries, values calculated from information in the database, and formatting elements such as headers, footers, titles, and headings. Reports can be viewed in Design view, Print Preview, and Layout Preview.

■ Data access pages, macros, and modules substantially extend the capabilities of Access. Data access pages enable people to view and manipulate your database information over an intranet or the Internet. Macros can be used to make routine database actions available as command buttons in forms, which help less experienced users work in your database. Modules are Microsoft Visual Basic for Applications (VBA) programs. Whereas macros can automate many actions, VBA can be used to carry out tasks that are too complex to be handled with macros.

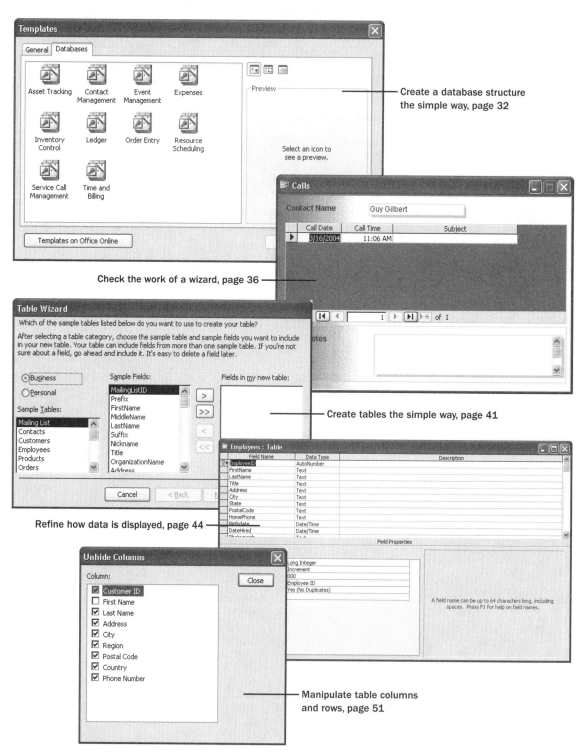

Create a database structure the simple way, page 32

Check the work of a wizard, page 36

Create tables the simple way, page 41

Refine how data is displayed, page 44

Manipulate table columns and rows, page 51

Chapter 2 at a Glance

2 Creating a New Database

In this chapter you will learn to:

✔ Create a database structure the simple way.

✔ Check the work of a wizard.

✔ Create tables the simple way.

✔ Refine how data is displayed.

✔ Manipulate table columns and rows.

Creating the structure for a database is easy. But an empty database is no more useful than an empty Microsoft Office Word document or an empty Microsoft Office Excel worksheet. It is only when you fill, or *populate*, a database with data in tables that it starts to serve a purpose. As you add queries, forms, and reports, it becomes easier to use. If you customize it with a switchboard and your tools, it moves into the realm of being a *database application*.

Not every database has to be refined to the point that it can be classified as an application. Databases that only you or a few experienced database users will work with can remain fairly rough-hewn. But if you expect an administrative assistant to enter data or your company's executives to generate their own reports, spending a little extra time in the beginning to create a solid database application will save a lot of work later. Otherwise, you'll find yourself continually repairing damaged files or walking people through seemingly easy tasks.

Microsoft Office Access 2003 takes a lot of the difficult and mundane work out of creating and customizing a database by providing *wizards* that you can use to create entire databases or individual tables, forms, queries, and other objects. It is generally easier to use a wizard to create something that is similar to what you need and then modify it than it is to create the same thing by hand.

In this chapter, you'll create a couple of databases from scratch, first by using a wizard to rapidly create the structure for a sophisticated contact management database, complete with tables, queries, forms, and reports. After exploring this database and entering a few records to get an idea of what a wizard can provide in the way of a starting point, you will discard this database and start working on a simpler contacts database for The Garden Company. By the end of this chapter, you will have a GardenCo database containing three tables that will serve as the foundation for many of the exercises in this book.

See Also   Do you need only a quick refresher on the topics in this chapter? See the Quick Reference entries on pages xxx–xxxi.

Important   Before you can use the practice files in this chapter, you need to install them from the book's companion CD to their default location. See "Using the Book's CD-ROM" on page xiii for more information.

Creating a Database Structure the Simple Way

A few years ago (the distant past in computer time), creating a database structure from scratch involved first analyzing your needs and then laying out the database design on paper. You would decide what information you needed to track and how to store it in the database. Creating the database structure could be a lot of work, and after you had created it and entered data, making changes could be difficult. Wizards have changed this process. Committing yourself to a particular database structure is no longer the big decision it once was. By using the Database Wizard, you can create a dozen database applications in less time than it used to take to sketch the design of one on paper. Access wizards might not create exactly the database application you want, but they can quickly create something very close.

In this exercise, you will use the Database Wizard to create a new database structure. The new database, in this case, will contain the structure for a contact management database.

BE SURE TO start Access before beginning this exercise.

New

1   If the **New File** task pane is not displayed, open it by clicking the **New** button on the Database toolbar.

2   In the **Templates** area of the task pane, click **On my computer,** and then click the **Databases** tab to display the available templates.

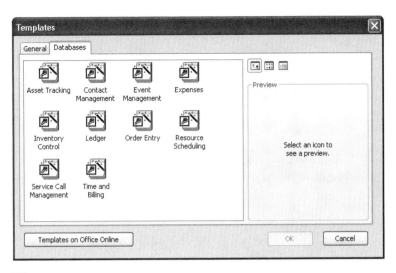

Tip   The Database Wizard uses predefined *templates* to create fairly sophisticated database applications. In addition to the templates provided with Access, if you are connected to the Internet, you will find additional templates and other resources by following the link to "Templates on Microsoft.com" that is on the New File task pane.

3   Double-click **Contact Management**.

The File New Database dialog box appears so that you can provide a name for your new database and specify where to store it.

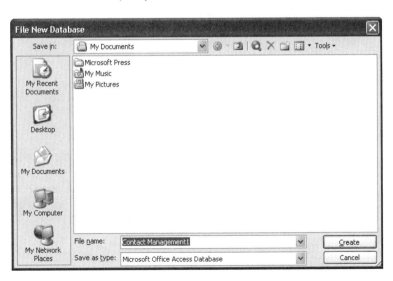

Tip The default folder for storing Access database files is My Documents. You can change this default to any other folder by clicking Options on the Tools menu when a database file is open, entering a new path in the Default database folder box on the General tab, and clicking OK.

4 Navigate to the *My Documents\Microsoft Press\Access 2003 SBS\CreateNew* folder, in the **File name** box, replace *Contact Management1* with Contacts, and then click **Create**.

Tip Naming conventions for Access database files follow those for Microsoft Windows files. A file name can contain up to 215 characters including spaces, but creating a file name that long is not recommended. File names cannot contain the following characters: \ / : * ? " < > |. The extension for an Access database file is *.mdb*.

The database window is displayed, and then you see the first page of the Database Wizard, which tells you the type of information that will be stored in this database.

5 This page requires no input from you, so click **Next** to move to the second page of the **Database Wizard**.

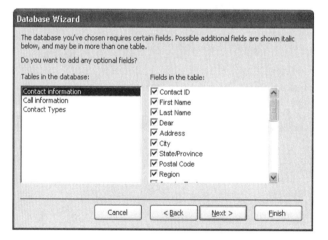

This page lists the three tables that will be included in the Contacts database. The box on the right lists the fields you might want to include in the table selected in the box on the left. Required fields have a check mark in their check boxes. Optional fields are italic. You can select the check box of an optional field to include it in the selected table.

6   Click each table name, and browse through its list of fields, just to see what is available.

7   Indicate that you want to include all the selected fields in the three tables by clicking **Next** to move to the next page of the wizard.

The next page of the wizard appears, displaying a list of predefined styles that determine what the elements of the database will look like.

Tip   Whenever the Back button is active (not gray) at the bottom of a wizard's page, you can click it to move back through previous pages and change your selections. If the Finish button is active, you can click it at any time to tell a wizard to do its job with no further input from you. Most of the options set by a wizard can be modified later, so clicking Finish does not mean that whatever the wizard creates is cast in stone.

8   Click each of the styles to see what they look like.

9   Click **Blends**, and click **Next**.

10   Click each of the report styles to see what they look like.

11   Click **Bold**, and click **Next**.

12   Change the proposed database name to Contacts, leave the **Yes, I'd like to include a picture** check box cleared, and click **Next**.

The Next button is unavailable on this page, indicating that this is the wizard's last page. By default, the "Yes, start the database" check box is selected, and the "Display Help on using a database" check box is cleared.

13   Leave the default settings as they are, and click **Finish**.

The process of creating a database can take from several seconds to several minutes. While the wizard creates the database, an alert box tells you what is happening and how much of the process is complete. When the wizard finishes its work, it opens the newly created Contacts database with the switchboard displayed.

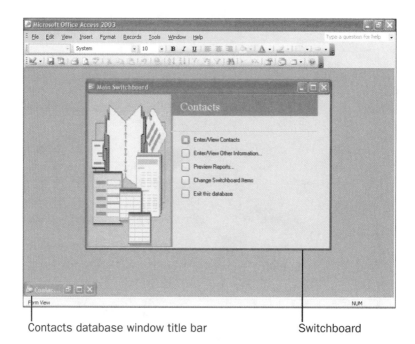

Contacts database window title bar   Switchboard

The switchboard opens, and the Contacts database window is minimized. (You can see its title bar in the lower left corner of the Access window.)

Close

14 At the right end of the Main Switchboard window's title bar, click the **Close** button.

15 At the right end of the Contacts database window title bar, click the **Close** button to close the database.

Checking the Work of a Wizard

Microsoft Office Specialist

Using a wizard to create a database is quick and painless, but just what do you end up with? The Database Wizard creates a database application, complete with a switchboard, several tables, and some other objects. In many cases, all you have to do to have a working database application is add the data. If the wizard's work doesn't quite suit your needs, you can modify any of the database objects or use another type of wizard to add more objects.

For example, if you tell the Database Wizard to create a contact management database, it creates three tables. It doesn't create any queries for this type of database, but it does for some of the other types. It creates forms that you can use to enter or view data, and two reports that you can use to list contacts or summarize the calls made or received during the week. Finally, it creates a switchboard so that users can quickly access the parts of the database needed to perform specific tasks.

In this exercise, you'll use the switchboard to take a quick tour of the Contacts database that the Database Wizard has created. You can't check out some of the objects unless the database contains data, so along the way, you will enter information in several of the tables.

USE the *Contacts* database in the practice file folder for this topic. This practice file is located in the *My Documents\Microsoft Press\Access 2003 SBS\CreateNew\CheckDB* folder and can also be accessed by clicking *Start/All Programs/Microsoft Press/Access 2003 Step by Step.*
OPEN the *Contacts* database and acknowledge the safety warning, if necessary.

1 In the switchboard, click the **Enter/View Other Information** button to display the Forms Switchboard window.

This switchboard has two buttons: the first opens a form you can use to enter or view contact types, and the second returns you to the Main Switchboard window.

2 Click **Enter/View Contact Types** to display the **Contact Types** form.

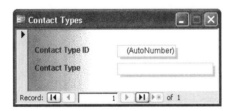

If the underlying Contact Types table contained any records, you could use this form to view them. The only action you can take now is to add a new record.

3 In the **Contact Type** box, type Supplier and press the ⌜Enter⌟ key.

Access supplies the entry for the Contact Type ID field. Access keeps track of this number and enters the next available number in this field whenever you add a new record.

4 Repeat the previous step to enter records for Customer and Shipper.

Close

5 Use the *Navigation buttons* at the bottom of the form to scroll through the records in the **Contact Types** table. Then click the **Close** button to close the form.

Important With most computer programs, *saving* your work often is important to avoid losing it if your computer crashes or the power goes out. With Access, it is not only *not* important to save your data, it is *not possible* to manually save it. When you move the insertion point out of a record after entering or editing information, Access saves that record. This mixed blessing means that you don't have to worry about losing your changes, but you do have to remember that any data entry changes you make are permanent and can be undone only by editing the record again.

6 Click **Return to Main Switchboard**.

7 Click **Enter/View Contacts**.

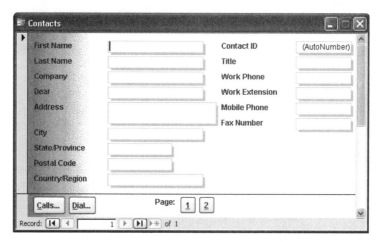

The Contacts form is displayed. You use this two-page form to enter records in the underlying Contacts table or to view records that are already there. The form has buttons at the bottom to switch between pages and to open other forms from which you can place calls (Dial) or where you can record information about communications you've had with the contact (Calls).

8 Enter some information on this form—your own first and last name will do— and notice that when you enter your name, Access provides a contact ID.

9 At the bottom of the form, click the **2** button to move to page 2, and then expand the list of contact types.

The list displays the three types you just entered in the Contact Types table through the Contact Types form.

10 Click one of the contact types.

11 Return to the first page, click in the **Work Phone** box to place the insertion point there, type 555-0100, and press [Enter].

12 Click in the **Work Phone** box again, and click **Dial**.

The AutoDialer dialog box appears, with the contents of the box that is currently selected on the form displayed as a potential number to dial.

Tip This dialog box is not part of Access; it is a Windows utility. When you click the Dial button, VBA code attached to the button calls the utility. If you were to click Setup, the Windows Phone And Modem Options dialog box would be displayed. (If you don't have a modem installed, the Install New Modem dialog box appears instead.)

13 Click **Cancel** to close the **AutoDialer** dialog box, and then click the **Calls** button.

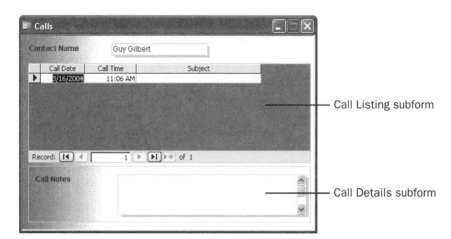

Call Listing subform

Call Details subform

The Calls form is displayed. This form includes the Call Listing subform, which lists any previous calls you have recorded, and the Call Details subform, which displays details of the selected call. You can record information about communications (phone calls, e-mail exchanges, and so on) that you've had with this contact.

14 Click in the **Subject** cell of the new record, and enter Order information as the subject.

Access adds a New Record line, where the Call Date and Call Time fields default to the current date and time.

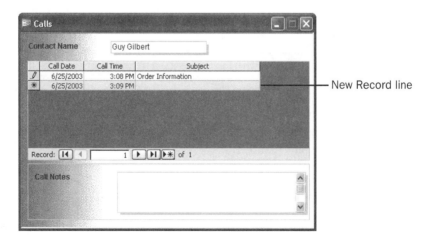

New Record line

15   Click in the **Call Notes** box, and type a short note.

16   Click the **Close** button to close the **Calls** form, and then close the **Contacts** form.

17   Click **Preview Reports** to display the Reports Switchboard window.

18   Preview the two short reports by clicking the button for each one, reading it, and then closing it.

When you preview the Weekly Call Summary report, you can enter a range of dates that you want included on the report. If you accept the default range of the current week, the summary of the call you just added is included in the report.

19   Click **Return to Main Switchboard**, and then click the **Close** button to close the Main Switchboard window without closing the database.

20   Double-click the database window's title bar to restore the window.

21   Explore all the objects in the database by clicking each type on the **Objects** bar and then opening the individual tables, forms, and reports.

You won't be able to open the Report Date Range form directly, because it is designed to be opened by VBA code that supplies the information that the form needs.

CLOSE the *Contacts* database.

Creating Tables the Simple Way

Microsoft Office Specialist

When you use the Database Wizard to create a contact management database, the database has all the *components* needed to store basic information about people. But suppose The Garden Company needs to store different types of information for different types of contacts. For example, it might want to maintain different types of information about employees, customers, and suppliers. In addition to the standard information—such as names, addresses, and phone numbers—the company might want to track these other kinds of information:

- Employee Social Security number, date of hire, marital status, deductions, and pay rate

- Customer order and account status

- Supplier contact, current order status, and discounts

While building the database, you could add a lot of extra fields to the Contacts table and then fill in just the ones it needs for each contact type, but cramming all this information into one table would soon get pretty messy. It's better to create a database with one table for each contact type: employee, customer, and supplier.

The Database Wizard doesn't offer exactly this combination of tables, so in this exercise, you will create a GardenCo database with an empty structure. You will then add several tables to the database by using the Table Wizard.

New

1 On the toolbar, click the **New** button to display the **New File** task pane.

2 In the **New** area of the **New File** task pane, click **Blank database**.

3 Navigate to the *My Documents\Microsoft Press\Access 2003 SBS\CreateNew \CreateGrdn* folder, in the **File name** box, replace *db1* with GardenCo, and then click **Create**.

Access displays a database window that contains no tables, queries, forms, or other database objects. (You can confirm that the database is empty by clicking each of the object types on the Objects bar.)

4 On the database window's toolbar, click the **New** button to display the **New Table** dialog box.

Tip Instead of clicking the New button, on the Database toolbar, you can click the down arrow to the right of the New Object button, and then click Table; or you can click Tables on the Objects bar, and then double-click "Create table by using wizard"; or you can click Table on the Insert menu, and then double-click Table Wizard.

5   Double-click **Table Wizard**.

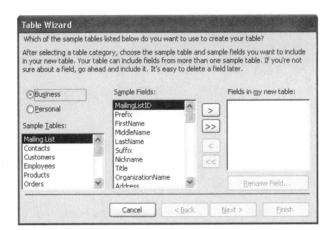

The wizard's first page appears. You can display a list of either business tables or personal tables. Although these categories are generally oriented toward business or personal use, depending on the nature of your business or preferences, you might find the sample table you want in either list.

6   Take a few minutes to browse through the business list, and then select the **Personal** option to see those sample tables.

Each category contains a list of sample tables. When you click an item in the Sample Tables list, the Sample Fields list displays all the fields available for that table. (If you need more fields, you can add them after creating the table.) Selecting an item in the Sample Fields list and then clicking the > button moves the selected field to the "Fields in my new table" list. Clicking the >> button moves all sample fields to the "Fields in my new table" list. The < and << buttons remove one or all fields from your new table list.

7   Select the **Business** option, and in the **Sample Tables** list, select **Customers**.

8   Click the **>>** button to copy all the fields to the **Fields in my new table** list, and then click **Next**.

The next page of the wizard is displayed, in which you can provide a name for your new table and specify whether the wizard should set a *primary key* for the table. A primary key consists of one or more fields that differentiate one record from another.

9   Accept **Customers** as the table name, click **No, I'll set the primary key**, and then click **Next**.

The wizard suggests *CustomerID* as the field that will uniquely identify records, and asks what type of data the field will contain.

10   Click **Numbers and/or letters I enter when I add new records**, and then click **Next**.

The last page of the wizard is displayed, in which you can select one of the three option buttons on this page to determine whether the table should open in Design view or in Datasheet view, or whether a wizard-generated form should open so that you can enter data.

11   Accept the default selection, **Enter data directly into the table**, and click **Finish** to create and open the **Customers** table.

12   Scroll horizontally through the table to view all the fields created by the wizard based on your selections on its first page. Then close the table.

The Customers table appears in the database window.

13   Start the **Table Wizard** again, this time by double-clicking **Create table by using wizard** in the database window.

14   Select the Business option, click **Employees**, and then move only the following fields to the **Fields in my new table** list, by selecting each field in the **Sample Fields** list and clicking the **>** button.

EmployeeID
FirstName
LastName
Title
Address
City
StateOrProvince
PostalCode
HomePhone
Birthdate
DateHired
Photograph
Notes

15   In the **Fields in my new table** list, select **StateOrProvince**, click the **Rename Field button**, change the name of the field to State, and click **OK**.

16 Click the **Next** button twice to move two pages forward, naming the table **Employees** and allowing Access to create a primary key.

Because one table already exists in the database, the wizard attempts to establish a relationship between the tables and displays a new page.

17 Click **Next**.

18 Click **Finish**, and then close the **Employees** table.

19 Repeat steps 13 through 18 to create a table called Suppliers that includes all the fields provided (don't forget to rename **StateOrProvince**). Click **Finish** to accept all the suggestions and defaults.

20 Close the **Suppliers** table.

Three tables are now listed in the Tables pane of the database window.

CLOSE the *GardenCo* database.

Refining How Data Is Displayed

Microsoft Office Specialist

When you use the Table Wizard to create tables and populate them with the fields you specify, it sets a variety of properties for each field. These *properties* determine what data can be entered in a field and how the data will look on the screen.

The field properties set by Access are a good starting place, and most of them are probably fine as they are. However, suppose some of the properties don't meet your needs. You can change some of them without affecting the data stored in the table; others might affect the data, so it pays to be cautious about making drastic changes until you have some experience working with Access.

In this exercise, you will review and edit a few of the property settings for one of the tables in the GardenCo database.

USE the *GardenCo* database in the practice file folder for this topic. This practice file is located in the *My Documents\Microsoft Press\Access 2003 SBS\CreateNew\Refine* folder and can also be accessed by clicking *Start/All Programs/Microsoft Press/Access 2003 Step by Step*.
OPEN the *GardenCo* database and acknowledge the safety warning, if necessary.

1 In the database window, double-click **Employees** in the **Tables** pane to open the table in Datasheet view.

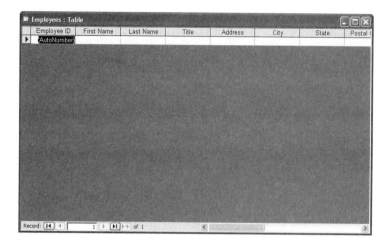

Tip   Your table window might be a different size than this one. Notice that any field name that is composed of two words (such as FirstName) has a space between the words, whereas the name you specified in the wizard had no space. Remember this when you are looking at the table later, in Design view.

Tip   As with other Microsoft Office applications, you can change the size of the window by moving the pointer to a corner and, when the pointer becomes a double-headed arrow, clicking and dragging to expand or reduce the size of the window.

View

2   On the toolbar, click the **View** button to display the table in Design view.

Primary key

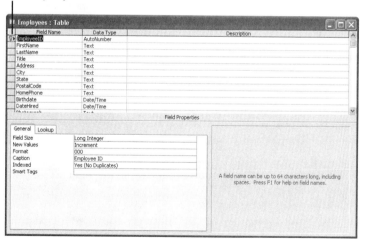

In Design view, the top portion of the window contains a list of the table's fields. The Field Name column contains the names you, or the wizard, specified when you created the table. Notice that there are no spaces in the names. The Data Type column specifies the type of data that the field can contain. The Description column can contain a description of the field.

Tip You can use field names that include spaces, but this can affect how queries and modules have to be written, so it is best not to do so.

Primary Key

Notice the Primary Key icon to the left of the EmployeeID field. The value in the primary key field is used to uniquely identify each record; that is, no two records can have the same value in this field. You can take responsibility for entering this value, or you can let Access help you with this chore. When the data type of a field is set to AutoNumber, Access fills this field in every new record with the next available number.

Tip If you no longer want the table to have a primary key, select the field designated as the primary key in the top portion of the window, and on the Edit menu, click Primary Key. If you want to assign a different field as the primary key, select that field, and click Primary Key on the Edit menu to toggle it off.

3 Click in the **Data Type** cell for the **EmployeeID** field—the one with **AutoNumber** in it—and then click the down arrow that appears.

The cell expands to show a list of all possible *data types*. Each data type cell contains this list, which you use to set the appropriate data type for each field. The data type setting restricts data entry to that specific type. If you try to enter data that is incompatible with that type, Access rejects it.

Tip For a description of all the data types, search for the *data type* topic in Access online Help.

4 Press the ⌨Esc key to close the list without changing the data type.

5 At the bottom of the table window, click in each box in the **Field Properties** section.

The number of properties in the Field Properties section varies with each data type. For example, the AutoNumber data type has six properties, four of which have drop down lists from which you can select settings. As you click each property, a description of that property appears in the area on the right.

Tip For more information about a particular property, click in its box, and press the ⌨F1 key to see the pertinent Access online Help topic.

Click this down arrow to see property options.

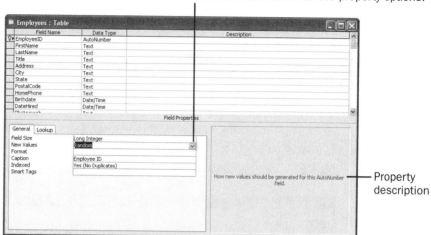

Property description

The Field Size property determines the size and type of value that can be entered in the field. For example, if this property is set to Long Integer, the field will accept entries from –2,147,483,648 to 2,147,483,647. If the data type is AutoNumber, the entries in this field will start with 1, so you could conceivably have over two billion employees before you outgrew this table.

The Increment setting for the New Values property specifies that Access should use the next available sequential number. The alternative (which you can see by expanding the list for this cell) is Random.

The Format property determines how data from the field is displayed on the screen and in print; it does not control how it is stored. Some data types have predefined formats, and you can also create custom formats.

Remember that when you displayed the table in Datasheet view, some of the field names had spaces in them? The way the field names are displayed in Datasheet view is controlled by the Caption property. If there is an entry for this property, it is used in place of the actual field name.

The Yes (No Duplicates) setting for the Indexed property indicates that the information in this field will be indexed for faster searching, and that duplicate values are not allowed. For the primary key field, this property is automatically set to Yes (No Duplicates), but a field can also be indexed without being a primary key.

New in Office 2003
Smart Tags

Tip   The ability to apply a Smart Tag to a field is a new feature with Office 2003. See the sidebar at the end of this chapter for more information about Smart Tags.

6 With the **EmployeeID** field still selected (as indicated by the arrow in the *row selector*), click in the **Format** box, and enter three zeros (000).

The ID number generated by Access will now be displayed as three digits. If the number isn't three digits long, it will be padded on the left with zeros.

7 Click the **Photograph** field, and change its data type from **OLE Object** to **Text**.

The Table Wizard included the Photograph field in this table and set this field's data type to OLE Object so that you can store a graphic in the field. But you will be storing the file name of a graphic, not the graphic itself, so Text is a more appropriate data type.

8 Click in the **HomePhone** field to display the field's properties.

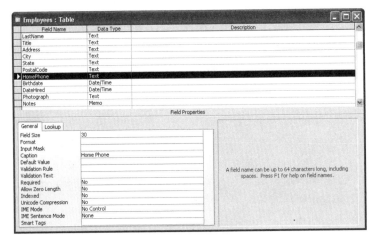

The data type for the HomePhone field is Text, even though the data will be a string of numbers. Because this type of entry can also contain parentheses, dashes, and spaces and is not the type of number that you would use in a calculation, Text is the appropriate data type.

Looking at the Field Properties section for this field, you can see that fields with this data type have more properties than fields with the AutoNumber data type.

The Field Size property for a field with the Text data type determines the number of characters that can be entered in the field. If you attempt to enter too many characters, Access displays a warning message, and you won't be able to leave the field until you reduce the number of characters to this many or fewer.

The Caption property is set to Home Phone. This name will be used at the top of the field's column in Datasheet view. The wizard supplies these descriptive names, but you can change them.

9 Click in the **DateHired** field to display the field's properties.

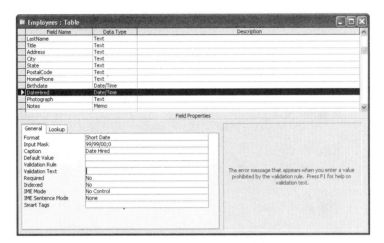

The Format property for this field is set to Short Date, which looks like this: 4/21/2003. If a valid date is entered in just about any standard format, such as 21 April 03, this property displays the date as 4/21/2003.

Important Exercises in this book that use the short date format assume that the year display is set to four digits (M/d/yyyy). This is set in the Regional and Language Settings dialog box in Microsoft Windows XP. To check or change this on your computer click Start, click Control Panel, click Date, Time, Language, and Regional Options, and then click the Regional and Language Options icon. The process is similar in earlier versions of Microsoft Windows, but some of the command names are a little different.

This field also has its Input Mask property set to 99/99/00;0. An *input mask* controls how data looks when you enter it and the format in which it is stored. Each 9 represents an optional numeral, and each 0 represents a required one. When you move to this field to enter a date in Datasheet view, you will see a mask that looks like this: __/__/__. The mask indicates that the date must be entered in the 4/21/01 format, but as soon as you press Enter to move to the next field, the date will change to whatever format is specified by the Format property.

Another interesting property is Validation Rule. None of the wizard-generated tables use *validation rules*, because the rules are too specific to the data being entered to anticipate, but let's take a quick look at how they work.

10 Click in the **Validation Rule** box, and enter <Now(). Then click in the **Validation Text** box and type "Date entered must be today or earlier."

A rule is created stating that the date entered must be before (less than) the current instant in time, as determined by the system clock of the computer where the database is stored. If you enter a date in the future, Access will not accept it and will display the validation text in an alert box.

Important The Format, Input Mask, and Validation Rule properties seem like great ways to be sure that only valid information is entered in your tables. But if you aren't careful, you can make data entry difficult and frustrating. Test your properties carefully before releasing your database for others to use.

View

11 Click the **View** button to return to Datasheet view, clicking **Yes** when prompted to save the table.

Tip When you try to switch from Design view to Datasheet view after making changes (and sometimes even if you haven't made any changes), you are presented with an alert box stating that you must save the table. If you click No, you remain in Design view. If you click Yes, Access saves your changes and switches to Datasheet view. If you want to switch views without saving changes that you have made inadvertently, click No, and then click the table's Close button. When Access displays another alert box, click No to close the table without saving any changes.

12 Enter a future date in both the **Birthdate** and **Date Hired** fields.

The Birthdate field, which has no validation rule, accepts any date, but the Date Hired field won't accept a date beyond the one set on your computer.

Close

13 Click **OK** to close the alert box, change the **Date Hired** value to a date in the past, and then click the **Close** button to close the **Employees** table.

14 In the database window, click **Suppliers**, and click the **Design** button to open the table in Design view.

15 Delete the **Country/Region**, **PaymentTerms**, **EmailAddress**, and **Notes** fields by clicking in the row selector and pressing the ⌫ key.

Tip Access alerts you that deleting the EmailAddress field requires deleting the field and all its indexes. Click Yes. (You will see this alert again in step 17; click Yes each time to delete the fields.)

16 Close the **Suppliers** table, clicking **Yes** to save your changes.

17 Open the **Customers** table in Design view, and delete the following fields: **CompanyName**, **CompanyOrDepartment**, **ContactTitle**, **Extension**, **FaxNumber**, **EmailAddress**, and **Notes**.

18 Click in the **CustomerID** field, and change the **Field Size** property from *4* to *5*.

19 Change the following fields and their captions (note that there is no space in the first two new field names, but there is a space between the words in their captions):

Original field name	New field name	New caption
ContactFirstName	FirstName	First Name
ContactLastName	LastName	Last Name
BillingAddress	Address	Address
StateOrProvince	Region	Region
Country/Region	Country	Country

20 Close the **Customers** table, clicking **Yes** to save it.

CLOSE the *GardenCo* database.

Manipulating Table Columns and Rows

When you refine a table's structure by adding fields and changing field properties in Design view, you are affecting the data that is stored in the table. But sometimes you will want to adjust the table itself to get a better view of the data. If you want to look up a phone number, for example, but the names and phone numbers are several columns apart, you will have to scroll the table window to get the information you need. You might want to rearrange columns or hide a few columns to be able to see the fields you are interested in at the same time.

You can manipulate the columns and rows of an Access table without in any way affecting the underlying data. You can size both rows and columns, and you can also hide, move, and freeze columns. You can save your table formatting so that the table will look the same the next time you open it, or you can discard your table adjustments without saving them.

In this exercise, you will open a table and manipulate its columns and rows. To make the value of table formatting more apparent, you will work with a version of the GardenCo database that has several tables containing many records.

USE the *GardenCo* database in the practice file folder for this topic. This practice file is located in the *My Documents\Microsoft Press\Access 2003 SBS\CreateNew\Manipulate* folder and can also be accessed by clicking *Start/All Programs/Microsoft Press/Access 2003 Step by Step*.
OPEN the *GardenCo* database and acknowledge the safety warning, if necessary.

1 On the **Objects** bar, click **Tables**.

2 Double-click the **Customers** table to open it in Datasheet view.

3 Drag the vertical bar at the right edge of the **Address** column header to the left until the column is about a half inch wide.

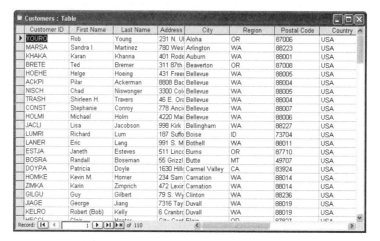

The column is too narrow to display the entire address.

4 Point to the vertical bar between the **Address** and **City** column headers, and double-click.

The column to the left of the vertical bar is the minimum width that will display all the text in that field in all records. This technique is particularly useful in a large table where you can't easily determine the length of a field's longest entry.

5 On the left side of the datasheet, drag the horizontal bar between any two record selectors downward to increase the height of all rows in the table.

6 On the **Format** menu, click **Row Height** to display the **Row Height** dialog box.

7 Select the **Standard Height** check box, and then click **OK**.

The height of all rows is returned to the default setting. (You can also set the rows to any other height in this dialog box.)

8 Click in the **First Name** column, and then on the **Format** menu, click **Hide Columns**.

The First Name column disappears, and the columns to its right shift to the left. If you select several columns before clicking Hide Columns, they all disappear.

Tip You can select adjacent columns by clicking in the header of one, holding down the Shift key, and then clicking in the header of another. The two columns and any columns in between are selected.

9 To restore the hidden field, on the **Format** menu, click **Unhide Columns** to display the **Unhide Columns** dialog box.

10 Select the **First Name** check box, and then click **Close**.

Access redisplays the First Name column.

11 Drag the right side of the database window to the left to reduce its size so that you cannot see all fields in the table.

12 Point to the **Customer ID** column header, hold down the mouse button, and drag through the **First Name** and **Last Name** column headers. Then with the three columns selected, on the **Format** menu, click **Freeze Columns**.

The first three columns will remain in view when you scroll the window horizontally to view columns that are off the screen to the right.

13 On the **Format** menu, click **Unfreeze All Columns** to restore the columns to their normal condition.

14 Close the table without saving your changes.

CLOSE the *GardenCo* database.

Smart Tags

New In
Office 2003
Smart Tags

A smart tag appears as a shortcut menu that displays options pertinent to a specific word, field, or type of content. For example, if Word determines that several words you typed might be a person's name, it will place a purple dotted line beneath them. If you move the mouse pointer over the underlined words, Word displays a Smart Tag Actions button. When you click this button Word displays a list of possible actions that includes sending e-mail, scheduling a meeting, and adding to contacts.

Smart tags were introduced as part of Windows XP and were supported in some Office XP programs. With Office 2003 they have been extended to Access.

When you create a table in Access, you can apply one or more smart tags to each field. When information from that field is displayed in a table, form, or query, and the mouse pointer is moved over the text, the Smart Tag Action button is displayed and some action can be taken that is appropriate for the kind of information.

There are not currently a lot of smart tags available for use in Access, but they are being created by third-party developers and made available on the Web.

For more information about smart tags, see *www.officesmarttags.com*.

Key Points

- Microsoft Office Access 2003 includes wizards to help you quickly and easily create databases and their objects, such as tables, queries, forms and reports.

- In Design view, you can modify any object you created with a wizard.

- Rather than storing all information in one table, you can create several different tables for each specific type of information, such as employee contact information, customer contact information, and supplier contact information.

- Properties determine what data can be entered in a field, and how the data will look on the screen. In Design view, you can change some properties without affecting the data stored in the table; but changing some might affect the data, so you must exercise caution when modifying properties.

- You can adjust the structure of a table—by manipulating or hiding columns and rows—without affecting the data stored in the table.

- When you create a table in Access, you can apply one or more smart tags to each field. When information from that field is displayed in a table, form, or query, and the mouse pointer is moved over the text, the Smart Tag Action button is displayed and some action can be taken that is appropriate for the kind of information.

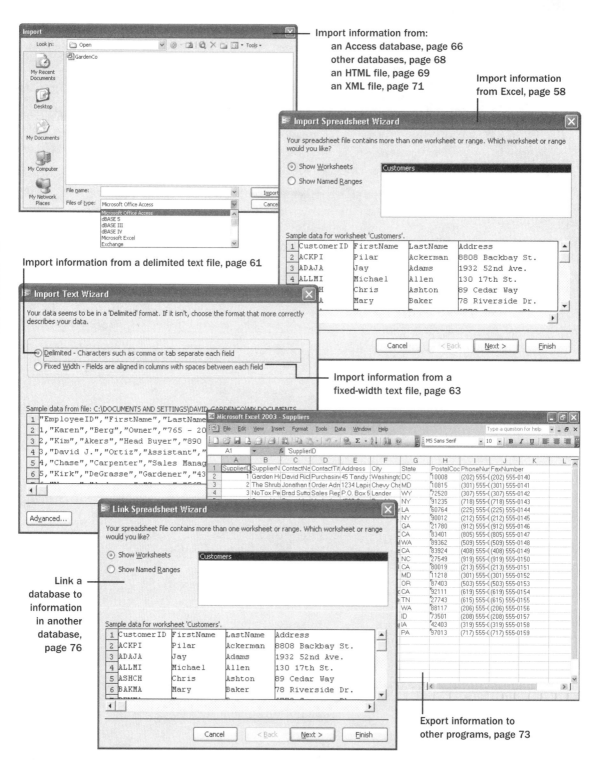

Import information from:
an Access database, page 66
other databases, page 68
an HTML file, page 69
an XML file, page 71

Import information from Excel, page 58

Import information from a delimited text file, page 61

Import information from a fixed-width text file, page 63

Link a database to information in another database, page 76

Export information to other programs, page 73

Chapter 3 at a Glance

3 Getting Information Into and Out of a Database

In this chapter you will learn to:

✔ Import information from Excel.

✔ Import information from a delimited text file.

✔ Import information from a fixed-width text file.

✔ Import information from an Access database.

✔ Import information from other databases.

✔ Import information from an HTML file.

✔ Import information from an XML file.

✔ Export information to other programs.

✔ Link a database to information in another database.

✔ Share Access data other ways.

Not many people enjoy typing information in a database, so one of your goals when designing a *relational database* is to structure the tables in such a way that the same information never has to be entered more than once. If, for example, you are designing a database to track customer orders, you don't want sales clerks to have to type the name of the customer in each order. So you need a customer table to hold all the pertinent information about each customer, and you can then simply reference a customer ID in each order. If information about a customer changes, you only have to update it in one place in the database: the customer table. In this way, the only item of customer information in the order records (the ID) remains accurate. An added benefit of this system is that you reduce the confusion that can result from typographical errors and from having the same information appear in different formats throughout the database.

Good database design saves keystrokes when you're entering new information and maintaining the database, but even more time and effort can be saved in another way. As part of The Microsoft Office System, Microsoft Office Access 2003 can easily share information with the other programs in The Microsoft Office System. It also makes it easy to populate a database by *importing* information in numerous other formats. If the information that you intend to store in an Access database has already been entered into almost any other electronic document, it is quite likely that you can move it into Access without retyping it.

57

If your information is still being actively maintained in another program and you want to bring it into Access to analyze it, create reports, or easily export it to another format, you should consider *linking* your Access database to the existing information in its original program rather than importing the information. When you link to data in another program, you can view and edit it in both programs, and what you see in Access is always up to date.

Many companies that store accounting, manufacturing, marketing, sales, and other information on their computers have discovered the advantages of sharing this information within the company through an *intranet,* or with the rest of the world through the Internet. With Access, you can speed up this process by *exporting* the information stored in a database as Hypertext Markup Language (HTML) and Extensible Markup Language (XML) pages.

Microsoft Office Specialist

In this chapter, you'll import information stored in various formats into the GardenCo database. You'll also export some of their data to several standard formats. After all this importing and exporting, you will experiment with viewing and updating information in another program by linking to it.

See Also Do you need only a quick refresher on the topics in this chapter? See the Quick Reference entries on pages xxxi–xxxiii.

Important Before you can use the practice files in this chapter, you need to install them from the book's companion CD to their default location. See "Using the Book's CD-ROM" on page xiii for more information.

Importing Information from Excel

Microsoft Office Specialist

Access works well with Microsoft Excel. You can import entire *worksheets* or a *named range* from a worksheet into either a new table (one that is created during the import) or an existing table. You can also import specific fields from a worksheet or range.

Excel is a good intermediate format to use when importing information that isn't set up quite right. For example, if you want to add or remove fields, combine or split fields, or use complex mathematical functions to manipulate data before importing it into Access, Excel is a great place to do it.

In this exercise, you will import information about The Garden Company's customers, which is stored in an Excel worksheet, into the Customers table in the GardenCo database.

BE SURE TO start Access before beginning this exercise.

USE the *GardenCo* database and the *Customers* worksheet in the practice file folder for this topic. These practice files are located in the *My Documents\Microsoft Press\Access 2003 SBS\Importing\ImportExcel* folder and can also be accessed by clicking *Start/All Programs/Microsoft Press/Access 2003 Step by Step*. OPEN the *GardenCo* database and acknowledge the safety warning, if necessary.

1   On the **File** menu, point to **Get External Data**, and then click **Import**.

2   In the **Files of type** list, click **Microsoft Excel**.

3   Navigate to the *My Documents\Microsoft Press\Access 2003 SBS\Importing \ImportExcel* folder, click **Customers**, and then click **Import**.

Access displays the first page of the Import Spreadsheet Wizard.

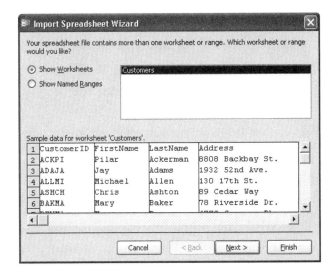

On this page, you can browse the contents of any worksheets or named ranges in the spreadsheet you just selected. You can scroll horizontally and vertically to view the worksheet's columns and rows, which are displayed in the lower pane.

4   With **Customers** selected in the list of worksheets, click **Next**.

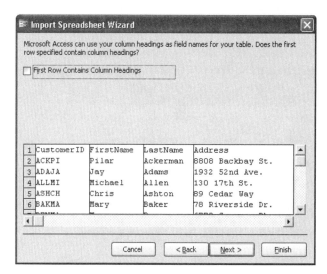

5 Select the **First Row Contains Column Headings** check box, and then click **Next**.

The background of the top row changes to gray, and when you scroll up and down, the top row no longer scrolls.

6 Click **In an Existing Table**, click **Customers** in the adjacent drop-down list, and then click **Next**.

Important When importing into an existing table, all the field names and data types must match exactly; otherwise, Access can't import the file and displays an error. If the structure matches but data in a field is too large or has some other minor problem, Access might import the record containing the field into an ImportError table, rather than into the desired one. You can fix the problem in the ImportError table, and then copy and paste the record into the correct table.

7 Click **Finish** to import the file.

Access informs you that the file was imported.

8 Click **OK** to close the message box, and then double-click **Customers** to open the table and confirm that Access imported the customer list.

9 Close the **Customers** table.

CLOSE the *GardenCo* database.

Importing Information from a Delimited Text File

Microsoft Office Specialist

Text files are the common denominator of documents. Almost every program that works with words and numbers can generate some kind of a text file, in addition to files in its *native format*. Access can import tabular data (tables and lists) from text files if the data has been stored in a recognizable format. The most common formats are called *delimited* and *fixed width* (which will be discussed later in this chapter).

In a *delimited text file*, each record ends in a carriage return, and each field is separated from the next by a comma or some other special character, called a *delimiter*. If a field contains one of these special characters, you must enclose the entire field in quotation marks. (Some people enclose all fields in quotation marks to avoid having to locate and enclose the special cases.)

In this exercise, you will import information about The Garden Company's employees, which is stored in a *comma-delimited text file*, into the Employees table in the GardenCo database.

USE the *GardenCo* database and the *Employees* text file in the practice file folder for this topic. These practice files are located in the *My Documents\Microsoft Press\Access 2003 SBS\Importing\ImportDText* folder and can also be accessed by clicking *Start/All Programs/Microsoft Press/Access 2003 Step by Step*. OPEN the *GardenCo* database and acknowledge the safety warning, if necessary.

1 On the **File** menu, point to **Get External Data**, and then click **Import**.

2 In the **Files of type** list, click **Text Files**.

> **Tip** Text files typically have an extension of *.txt*. However, some programs save delimited text files with a *.csv* or *.tab* extension. You will also occasionally see text files with an extension of *.asc* (for *ASCII*). Fixed-width files are sometimes stored with an extension of *.prn* (for *printer*), but Access doesn't recognize this extension, so you would have to rename it with one it does recognize. All acceptable extensions are treated the same way by Access.

3 Navigate to the *My Documents\Microsoft Press\Access 2003 SBS\Importing \ImportDText* folder, click **Employees**, and then click **Import**.

Access displays the first page of the Import Text Wizard.

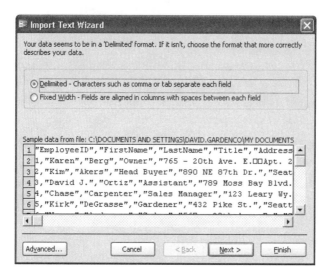

Each field is enclosed in quotation marks, and there is a comma between them. The selected file is delimited, so that option is selected.

4 Click the **Advanced** button to display the default import specifications for this file.

The Employees Import Specification dialog box appears, in which you can fine-tune the import process.

Tip If you want to import several files that deviate in some way from the default settings, you can specify the new settings and save them. Then as you open each of the other files, you can display this dialog box and click the Specs button to select and load the saved specifications.

5 Click **Cancel** to close the **Employees Import Specification** dialog box, and then click **Next**.

The wizard breaks the file into fields, based on its assumption that items are separated by commas. From the neat columns you see here, this assumption is obviously a good one. If the columns were jumbled, you could choose a different delimiter from the options at the top of this page.

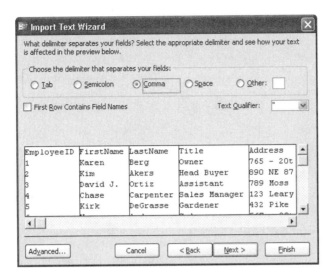

6 Select the **First Row Contains Field Names** check box, and then click **Next**.

The background of the first row is gray to indicate that these entries are field names.

7 Select the **In an Existing Table** option, click **Employees** in the drop-down list, and then click **Next**.

8 Click **Finish** to import the text file into the **Employees** table.

A message appears informing you that the file was imported.

9 Click **OK** to close the message box, and then double-click **Employees** to open the table and confirm that nine records were imported from the employees list.

10 Close the **Employees** table.

CLOSE the *GardenCo* database.

Importing Information from a Fixed-Width Text File

Microsoft Office Specialist The only way to get the data of many older programs into Access is to export the data to a *fixed-width text file* and then import that file into Access. In a fixed-width text file, the same field in every record contains exactly the same number of characters. If the actual data doesn't fill a field, the field is padded with spaces so that the starting point of the data in the next field is the same number of characters from the beginning of every record. For example, if the first field contains 12 characters, the second field always starts 13 characters from the beginning of the record, even if the actual data in the first field is only 4 characters.

Fixed-width text files used to be difficult to import into databases, because you had to carefully count the number of characters in each field and then specify the field sizes in the database layout or the import program. If the text in any field was even one character off, all records from that point on would be jumbled. That is no longer a problem with Access because the Import Text Wizard makes importing a fixed-width text file simple.

In this exercise, you will import a fixed-width text file into the Suppliers table in the GardenCo database.

USE the *GardenCo* database and the *Suppliers* text file in the practice file folder for this topic. These practice files are located in the *My Documents\Microsoft Press\Access 2003 SBS\Importing\ImportFText* folder and can also be accessed by clicking *Start/All Programs/Microsoft Press/Access 2003 Step by Step.* OPEN the *GardenCo* database and acknowledge the safety warning, if necessary.

1　On the **File** menu, point to **Get External Data**, and then click **Import**.

2　In the **Files of type** list, click **Text Files**.

3　Navigate to the *My Documents\Microsoft Press\Access 2003 SBS\Importing \ImportFText* folder, click **Suppliers**, and then click **Import** to display the first page of the **Import Text Wizard**.

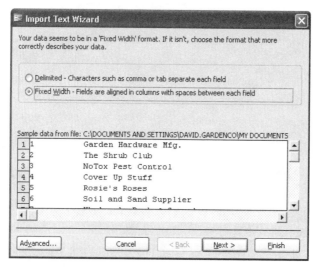

The text is displayed in Fixed Width format.

4　Click **Next** to display the second page of the wizard.

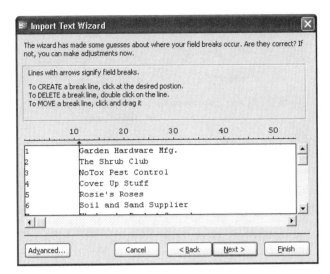

The wizard breaks the file into fields based on the assumption that a column of one or more spaces extending through all records marks the end of a field.

5 Use the horizontal scroll bar to scroll through the fields until you get to the two fields that contain phone numbers.

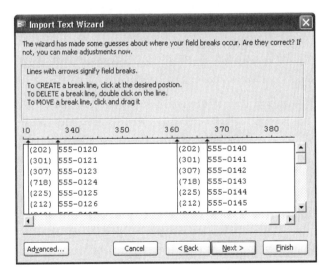

The wizard broke each phone number into two fields because a column of spaces separates the area code from the number. Breaking the numbers this way would be fine if you wanted to store the area codes in separate fields, but you don't want to do that in this database.

6 Double-click the dividing line at column 337 to remove it. Then repeat this step for the dividing line at column 367, and click **Next**.

Tip If necessary, you can also add or move lines in the table. Simply follow the wizard's directions.

7 Select the **In an Existing Table** option, click **Suppliers** in the drop-down list, and then click **Next**.

8 Click **Finish** to import the text file into the **Suppliers** table.

A message appears informing you that the file was imported.

9 Click **OK** to close the message box, and then double-click **Suppliers** to open the table and confirm that 20 records were imported from the suppliers list.

10 Close the **Suppliers** table.

CLOSE the *GardenCo* database.

Importing Information from an Access Database

Microsoft Office Specialist

Suppose you already have an Access database that includes tables of information about products and orders, and another that includes contact information. Now you wish you had just one database so that all the information you use on a regular basis is in one place. You had to create the existing databases by hand and then type in all the data, and you don't relish the thought of having to retype anything. You can take advantage of this earlier work by importing the product and orders information into the contacts database, rather than re-creating it all.

You can easily import one or more of the standard Access objects: tables, queries, forms, reports, pages, macros, and modules. When importing a table, you have the option of importing just the table definition (the structure that you see in Design view), or both the definition and the data. When importing a query, you can import it as a query or you can import the results of the query as a table.

When you import an Access object, the entire object is imported as an object of the same name in the active database. You don't have the option of importing selected fields or records. If the active database already has an object of the same name, Access imports the object with a number added to the end of its name.

Tip If you need only some of the fields or records from a table in another database, you can create a query in the other database to select just the information you need, and then import the results of the query as a table. Alternatively, you can import the table and then either edit it in Design view or use queries to clean it up.

In this exercise, you will import a couple of tables from a Products database into the GardenCo database.

USE the *GardenCo* and *Products* databases in the practice file folder for this topic. These practice files are located in the *My Documents\Microsoft Press\Access 2003 SBS\Importing\ImportAccess* folder and can also be accessed by clicking *Start/All Programs/Microsoft Press/Access 2003 Step by Step*.
OPEN the *GardenCo* database and acknowledge the safety warning, if necessary.

1   On the **File** menu, point to **Get External Data**, and then click **Import**.

2   In the **Files of type** list, make sure **Microsoft Office Access** is selected.

3   Navigate to the *My Documents\Microsoft Press\Access 2003 SBS\Importing \ImportAccess* folder, click **Products**, and then click **Import**.

The Import Objects dialog box appears, in which you can import any type of Access object from this database.

4   Click the **Options** button to expand the dialog box and display the import options.

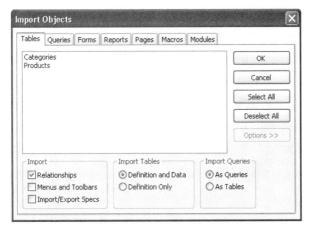

5   Click **Select All** to select the two tables listed.

6   Click **OK** to import the tables.

7   Open the new **Categories** and **Products** tables to confirm that records were imported.

8   Close the two tables.

CLOSE the *GardenCo* database.

Importing Information from Other Databases

Importing information from databases other than Access is usually an all-or-nothing situation, and quite often, what you get isn't in the exact format you need. You might find, for example, that *transaction records* include redundant information, such as the name of the product or purchaser, in every record. A database containing information about people might include the full name and address in one field, when you would like separate fields for the first name, last name, street address, and so on. You can choose to import information as it is and manipulate it in Access, or you can move it into some other program, such as Excel or Word, and manipulate it there before importing it into Access.

Access can import data from the following versions of dBASE, Lotus 1-2-3, and Paradox:

Program	Versions
dBASE	III, IV, 5, and 7
Lotus 1-2-3	WKS, WK1, WK3, W4
Paradox	3, 4, 5, 8

In this exercise, you will import information from a dBASE file into the Shippers table in the GardenCo database.

USE the *GardenCo* and *Shippers* databases in the practice file folder for this topic. These practice files are located in the *My Documents\Microsoft Press\Access 2003 SBS\Importing\ImportDbase* folder and can also be accessed by clicking *Start/All Programs/Microsoft Press/Access 2003 Step by Step*.
OPEN the *GardenCo* database and acknowledge the safety warning, if necessary.

1   On the **File** menu, point to **Get External Data**, and then click **Import** to open the **Import** dialog box.

2   In the **Files of type** list, click **dBASE 5**.

3   Navigate to the *My Documents\Microsoft Press\Access 2003 SBS\Importing \ImportDbase* folder, click **Shippers**, and then click **Import**.

A message box appears, informing you that the file was imported.

4   Click **OK** to close the message box, click **Close** to close the **Import** dialog box, and then double-click **Shippers** to open the table and confirm that five records were imported properly.

5   Close the table.

CLOSE the *GardenCo* database.

Importing Information from an HTML File

You might be familiar with the *Hypertext Markup Language (HTML)*, which is used to create Web pages. HTML uses *tags* to control the appearance and alignment of text when it is displayed in a Web browser. To display a table on a Web page, the table's elements—rows and cells—are enclosed in appropriate *HTML tags*. For example, a simple HTML table might look like this:

```
.
.
.
<table>
<tr>
   <td>LastName</td><td>FirstName</td>
</tr>
   <td>Anderson</td><td>Amy</td>
</tr>
</table>
.
.
.
```

Of course, a lot of other tags and text would appear above and below this little table, and few tables are this simple. But you can get the general idea. With an HTML document, it is the <table>, <tr> (table row), and <td> (table data) tags that make the data look like a table when viewed in a Web browser.

All Office 2003 programs can save a document in HTML format, and to a limited extent, they can read or import a document that was saved in HTML format by another program. If you attempt to import an HTML document into Access, it will *parse* the document and identify anything that looks like structured data. You can then look at what Access has found and decide whether to import it.

Important If you want to import data into an existing table but the structure of the data isn't the same as the table structure, it is often easier to import the data into Excel, manipulate it there, and then import it into Access.

In this exercise, you will import new customer information that is stored in an HTML document into the Customers table in the GardenCo database.

USE the *GardenCo* database and the *NewCust* HTML file in the practice file folder for this topic. These practice files are located in the *My Documents\Microsoft Press\Access 2003 SBS\Importing\ImportHTML* folder and can also be accessed by clicking *Start/All Programs/Microsoft Press/Access 2003 Step by Step*. OPEN the *GardenCo* database and acknowledge the safety warning, if necessary.

1   Open the **Customers** table, and notice that it contains 107 records. Close the table.

2 On the **File** menu, point to **Get External Data**, and then click **Import**.

3 In the **Files of type** list, click **HTML Documents**.

4 Navigate to the *My Documents\Microsoft Press\Access 2003 SBS\Importing \ImportHTML* folder, click **NewCust**, and then click **Import** to display the first page of the **Import HTML Wizard**.

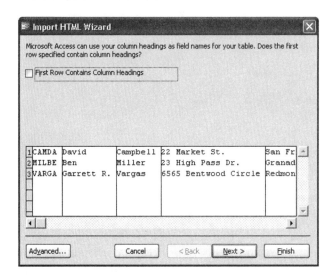

The wizard displays the contents of the NewCust file, divided into rows and columns. If a file contains multiple tables or lists, the wizard lists them here, and you can select the one you want to import.

5 Click **Next** to display the next page of the wizard.

6 Select the **In an Existing Table** option, click **Customers** in the drop-down list, and then click **Next**.

7 Click **Finish** to import the new customers into the **Customers** table.

8 In the message box that appears, click **OK** to close it, and then open the **Customers** table.

The table now contains 110 records.

9 Close the **Customers** table.

CLOSE the *GardenCo* database.

Importing Information from an XML File

Extensible Markup Language (XML) files are often used for exchanging information between programs, both on and off the Web. XML files are similar to HTML files in two ways: both are plain text files that use tags to format their content, and both use start and end tags. However, HTML tags describe how elements should look, whereas XML tags specify the structure of the elements in a document. Also, as its name implies, the XML tag set is extensible—there are ways to add your own tags. Here is an example of a simple XML file:

```
<?xml version="1.0"?>
<ORDER>
            <CUSTOMER>Nancy Davolio</CUSTOMER>
            <PRODUCT>
              <ITEM>Sterilized Soil</ITEM>
              <PRICE>$8.65</PRICE>
              <QUANTITY>1 bag</QUANTITY>
            </PRODUCT>
</ORDER>
```

This file describes an order that Nancy Davolio (the customer) placed for one bag (the quantity) of Sterilized Soil (the item) at a cost of $8.65 (the price). As you can see, when the data's *structure* is tagged rather than just its *appearance*, you can easily import the data into a database table.

In this exercise, you will import the Orders and Order Details XML documents into the GardenCo database.

USE the *GardenCo* database and the *Orders* and *OrderDetails* XML files in the practice file folder for this topic. These practice files are located in the *My Documents\Microsoft Press\Access 2003 SBS\Importing \ImportXML* folder and can also be accessed by clicking *Start/All Programs/Microsoft Press /Access 2003 Step by Step*.
OPEN the *GardenCo* database and acknowledge the safety warning, if necessary.

1 On the **File** menu, point to **Get External Data**, and then click **Import**.

2 In the **Files of type** list, click **XML**.

3 Navigate to the *My Documents\Microsoft Press\Access 2003 SBS\Importing \ImportXML* folder.

There is one file named *Orders* and two files named *Order Details*. Of the two Order Details files, one has the extension *.xml*, and the other has the extension *.xsd*. (You might not see the extensions unless your computer is set to display file extensions, but you can quickly view them by hovering over each file name.) XML consists of data and a *schema*, which describes the structure of the data. Programs that export to XML might combine the data and schema in one *.xsd* file, as with

Orders, or might create an *.xml* file to hold the data and an *.xsd* file to hold the schema, as with Order Details. If the program exports two separate files, you will have to have both files to import both the data and the structure into Access.

4 Click **Orders**, click **Import** to open the **Import XML** dialog box, and then click the **Options** button to display the import options.

New in
Office 2003
Transform

Tip   A powerful new feature in Access 2003 is the ability to apply a transform script to data as you import or export it. Transforms are a type of template that is used to convert XML data to other formats. When you apply a transform during import, the data is transformed before it enters the table, so you can adapt an XML file to a different table structure. For more information about using transforms, search for *transforms* in Access Help.

5 Click **OK** to accept the default to import structure and data.

The Orders file is imported and the Orders table is created.

6 Click **OK** to close the message that the import process is complete.

7 Repeat step 1 to open the **Import** dialog box.

8 Click **Order Details** (the *.xml* file), and then click **Import**.

9 Click **Order Details** and click **OK** to accept the default to import both structure and data.

The *Order Details.xml* and *Order Details.xsd* files are imported and the Order Details table is created.

10 Click **OK**, and then open and view the **Orders** and **Order Details** tables to confirm that the data and structure were imported.

The two date fields that were imported, OrderDate and ShippedDate, are displayed in the format yyyy-mm-dd. They were also imported as text rather than date values, which would make it difficult to use them in queries to find orders placed between specified dates.

11 Close the **Order Details** table. Leave the **Orders table** open.

View

12 Click the **View** button to switch to Design View.

13 Change the **Data Type** for OrderDate and ShippedDate to **Date/Time**.

14 Click the **Save** button to save your changes.

Save

15 Return to Datasheet view.

The dates are now displayed in a more conventional format, and can be manipulated as dates.

CLOSE the GardenCo database.

Exporting Information to Other Programs

Microsoft Office Specialist

You can export Access database objects in a variety of formats. The specific formats available depend on the object you are trying to export. Tables, for example, can be exported in pretty much the same formats in which they can be imported. Macros, on the other hand, can be exported only to another Access database.

The following table lists the export formats available for each object:

Object	Export formats
Table	Access, dBASE, Excel, HTML, Lotus 1-2-3, Paradox, Text, SharePoint Team Services , Active Server Pages (ASP), Microsoft Internet Information Server (IIS), Rich Text Format (RTF), Word Merge, XML, Open Database Connectivity (ODBC)
Query	Access, dBASE, Excel, HTML, Lotus 1-2-3, Paradox, SharePoint Team Services, Text, ASP, IIS, RTF, Word Merge, XML, ODBC
Form	Access, Excel, HTML, Text, ASP, IIS, RTF, XML
Report	Access, Excel, HTML, Text, RTF, Snapshot, XML
Page	Access, Data Access Page (DAP)
Macro	Access
Module	Access, Text

Tables and queries can be exported to most versions of the listed formats. Forms and reports are more limited, but even so, exporting to the formats you are most likely to use is pretty straightforward. The ones that get a little tricky are Active Server Pages (ASP), Microsoft Internet Information Server (IIS), and Open Database Connectivity (ODBC).

In this exercise, you will export the Suppliers table from the GardenCo database in a format that can be used by Excel. Then you'll export the Customers table to an XML document.

Tip   To complete this exercise, you will need to have Excel 97 or later installed on your computer.

USE the *GardenCo* database in the practice file folder for this topic. This practice file is located in the *My Documents\Microsoft Press\Access 2003 SBS\Importing\Export* folder and can also be accessed by clicking *Start/All Programs/Microsoft Press/Access 2003 Step by Step*.
OPEN the *GardenCo* database and acknowledge the safety warning, if necessary.

1   In the database window, click the **Suppliers** table.

2   On the **File** menu, click **Export** to display the **Export Table 'Suppliers' To** dialog box.

3   In the **Save as type** list, click **Microsoft Excel 97-2003**.

Access inserts the name of the table (*Suppliers*) in the File name box.

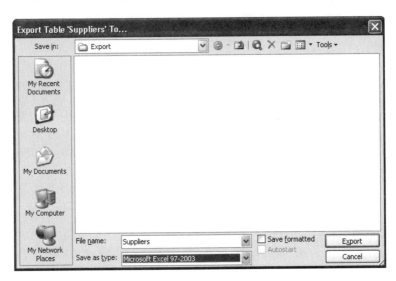

4   Click **Export**.

5   Navigate to the *My Documents\Microsoft Press\Access 2003 SBS\Importing\Export* folder, and double-click **Suppliers** to view the new worksheet in Excel.

Smart Tag

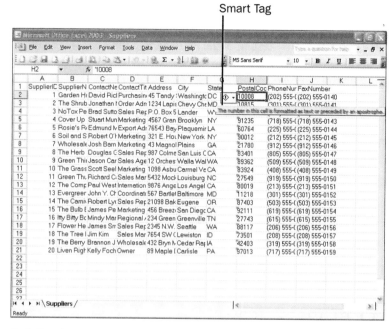

6   Quit Excel.

7   Click the title bar of the database window to activate it, and with the **Suppliers** table
    still selected, on the **File** menu, click **Export**.

8   Navigate to the *My Documents\Microsoft Press\Access 2003 SBS\Importing\Export*
    folder, click **XML** in the **Save as type** box, accept **Suppliers** as the file name, and
    then click the **Export** button to open the **Export XML** dialog box.

    Tip   Access 2003 has been updated to comply with the 2001 XML Schema
    recommendation described at *www.w3.org/2001/XMLSchema*. You can therefore
    export data from Access in an XML format that can be used by other applications
    that are also in compliance. This makes it possible for you to output XML data that
    can be used by Visual Studio .NET programs.

9   Make sure both **Data (XML)** and **Schema of the data** are selected, and then click **OK**.

*New in
Office 2003*
Transform

    Tip   Access 2003 supports the ability to apply a transform script to data
    as you export it. Export transforms are applied after the data is exported. For more
    information about using transforms, search for *transforms* in Access Help.

10 Press ⎇+⇥ to switch to Windows Explorer, and notice that Access exported
    the **Suppliers** table as both an *.xml* and an *.xsd* file.

> **Tip** You can combine the data and schema in one file by clicking the More Options button, clicking the Schema tab, and then selecting the appropriate option.

11 Repeat steps 8 and 9 and try exporting the **Suppliers** table in various other formats by changing the options in the **Save as Type** box. Then view the exported files to see the results.

> **Tip** If you export to an HTML file, you can view the table in a browser, such as Microsoft Internet Explorer. To see the tags that define the structure of the table, either view the source in the browser or open the file in a text editor.

CLOSE the *GardenCo* database and close Windows Explorer.

Linking a Database to Information in Another Database

*Microsoft
Office
Specialist*

Instead of importing data into an Access database from another program, you can leave the data in the other program and link to it. Although working with data that is stored in your own database is faster, safer, and more flexible, sometimes linking is preferable.

The most common reason for linking to data in another Access database or a different program is because you don't own the data. Perhaps another department in your organization maintains the data in a *SQL database*, and they are willing to give you permission to read the tables and queries but not to change them. Other reasons are security and ease of data distribution.

> **Important** If you link to a file on a *local area network (LAN)*, be sure to use a *universal naming convention (UNC) path*, rather than a *mapped network drive*. A UNC path includes the computer name as well as the drive letter and folder names, so it is less likely to change.

In this exercise, you will link a table in the GardenCo database to a table in another Access database and then link to a named range in an Excel worksheet.

USE the *GardenCo* and the *LinkDatabase* databases and the *LinkWorksheet* worksheet in the practice file folder for this topic. These practice files are located in the *My Documents\Microsoft Press\Access 2003 SBS \Importing\Link* folder and can also be accessed by clicking *Start/All Programs/Microsoft Press /Access 2003 Step by Step*.
OPEN the *GardenCo* database and acknowledge the safety warning, if necessary.

1 On the **File** menu, point to **Get External Data**, and then click **Link Tables**.

2 In the **Link** dialog box, navigate to the *My Documents\Microsoft Press \Access 2003 SBS\Importing\Link* folder.

3 Click the **LinkDatabase** file. Then click **Link** to display the **Link Tables** dialog box.

4 Click **Shippers** as the name of the table that you want to link to, and click **OK**.

The dialog box closes, and a table named *Shippers1* is added to the database window. (Access adds *1* to the table name because the GardenCo database already contains a table named *Shippers*.) Notice that the table's icon has an arrow to its left, indicating that its data is linked, rather than stored in the database.

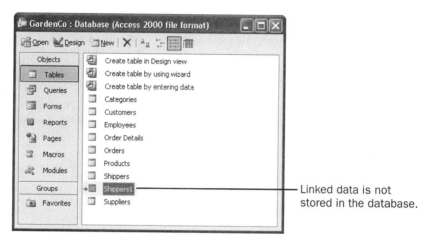

— Linked data is not stored in the database.

5 Open the table to confirm that it contains a list of shipping companies, and then close it.

6 Repeat step 1 to open the **Link** dialog box again.

7 In the **Files of type** list, click **Microsoft Excel**.

8 Navigate to the *My Documents\Microsoft Press\Access 2003 SBS\Importing\Link* folder, click **LinkWorksheet**, and then click **Link**.

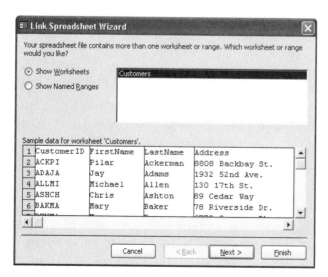

The first page of the Link Spreadsheet Wizard appears, in which you can browse through all the worksheets and named ranges in the selected spreadsheet.

9 Select the **Show Named Ranges option**, and in the list of ranges, click **SpecialCustomers**. Then click **Next**.

10 Leave the **First Row Contains Column Headings** check box cleared, because this particular named range doesn't have column headings, and then click **Next**.

11 Leave the default table name, click **Finish**, and then click **OK** when the message box appears.

A new table, named *SpecialCustomers*, is added to the database window. The table's icon has an arrow to its left to indicate that it is a linked table, but the icon itself has an Excel logo instead of an Access logo.

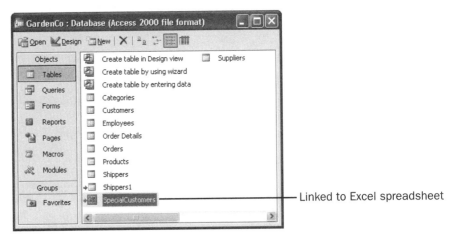
Linked to Excel spreadsheet

Delete

12 Click each linked table, click the **Delete** button, and then click **Yes** to confirm the deletion.

CLOSE the *GardenCo* database.

Other Ways to Share Access Data

All the methods of importing and exporting data described in this chapter work well, but they aren't the only ways to share information with other programs.

Sometimes the quickest and easiest way to get information into or out of a database is to just copy it and paste it where you want it. This technique works particularly well for getting data *out of* an Access table and into Word or Excel. If you paste into Word, the data becomes a Word table, complete with a header row containing the field captions as column headings. If you paste into Excel, the data is displayed in the normal row-and-column format on the worksheet.

Getting data *into* an Access table by using this technique is a little more complicated. The data you are pasting must meet all the criteria for entering it by hand (input mask, validation rules, field size, and so on), and you have to have the correct cells selected when you use the Paste command. If Access encounters a problem when you attempt to paste a group of records, it displays an error message and pastes the problem records into a Paste Errors table. You can then troubleshoot the problem in that table, fix whatever is wrong, and try copying and pasting again.

Tip   You can also copy an entire table from one Access database into another. Simply open both databases, copy the table from the source database to the Clipboard, and then paste it in the destination database. Access prompts you to give the new table a name, and you can choose to paste the table structure only, paste the structure and data, or append the data to an existing table.

Another quick way to share the information in an Access database with Word or Excel is through the OfficeLinks button on the toolbar. Clicking the down arrow to the right of this button displays a menu of three commands you can use to merge the data in the table with a Word mail merge document, to publish the table in a Word document, or to instantly export the table to an Excel worksheet.

In this exercise, you will experiment with copying records.

Tip   To complete this exercise, you will need to have Excel and Word installed on your computer.

USE the *GardenCo* database in the practice file folder for this topic. This practice file is located in the *My Documents\Microsoft Press\Access 2003 SBS\Importing\OfficeLink* folder and can also be accessed by clicking *Start/All Programs/Microsoft Press/Access 2003 Step by Step*.
OPEN the *GardenCo* database and acknowledge the safety warning, if necessary.

1   Open the **Customers** table.

Copy

2   Select about six records by pointing to the row selector of the first record you want to select (the pointer changes to a right arrow), holding down the left mouse button and dragging to the last record you want to select. Then on the toolbar, click the **Copy** button.

Paste

3   Start Excel, and with cell A1 of a new blank worksheet selected, click the **Paste** button on Excel's toolbar.

Toolbar Options

If the Paste button is not visible, click the Toolbar Options button to display a palette of additional buttons, and then click the Paste button on the palette.

The records are copied in Excel, complete with the same column headings. (You will have to widen the columns to see all the data.)

4   Press [Alt]+[Tab] to switch back to Access.

5   Select a block of cells in the middle of the table by moving the pointer over the left edge of the first one you want to select, and when the pointer changes to a thick cross, dragging until you have selected all the desired cells.

6   Click the **Copy** button (the **Clipboard** task pane and the Office Assistant might appear), press [Alt]+[Tab] to move back to Excel, click a cell below the records you pasted previously, and then click the **Paste** button.

Excel pastes in the new selection, again with column headings.

7   The data you copied is still on the Clipboard, so start Word, and on Word's toolbar, click the **Paste** button.

The selection is pasted into a nicely formatted table with the title *Customers*, reflecting the name of the table from which this data came.

8   Quit Word and Excel without saving your changes.

9   Close the **Clipboard** task pane, and then close the **Customers** table.

CLOSE the *GardenCo* database and quit Access.

Key Points

- Access 2003 makes it easy to import information in numerous formats from other programs. If the information is still being actively maintained in another program and you want to bring it into Access to work with it, you can link your Access database to the information in its original program.

- You can import entire Excel worksheets, or a named range from a worksheet into a new table or an existing table. You can also import specific fields from a worksheet or range.

- You can use the Import Wizard to import delimited and fixed-width text files into your Access database.

- You can easily import one or more of the standard Access objects: tables, queries, forms, reports, pages, macros, and modules.

- You can import data from certain versions of dBASE, Lotus 1-2-3, and Paradox into Access. You can choose to import information as it is and manipulate it in Access, or you can move it into some other program, such as Excel or Word, and manipulate it there before importing it into Access.

■ You can import a document saved in HTML format by another program into Access. If you attempt to import an HTML document into Access, it will parse the document and identify anything that looks like structured data. You can then look at what Access has found and decide whether or not to import it.

■ You can import Extensible Markup Language (XML) files into Access. XML consists of data and a schema, which describes the structure of the data. Programs that export to XML might combine the data and schema in one file, or might create two files. If the program exports two separate files, you will need both files to import both the data and the structure into Access.

■ You can export the information in your Access database in a variety of formats, depending on the object you are trying to export.

■ You can leave data in another program and link to it. You can also copy and paste data from your database into other programs. A quick way to share the information in an Access database with Word or Excel is through the OfficeLinks button on the toolbar. You can merge the data in the table with a Word mail merge document, publish the table in a Word document, or export the table to an Excel worksheet.

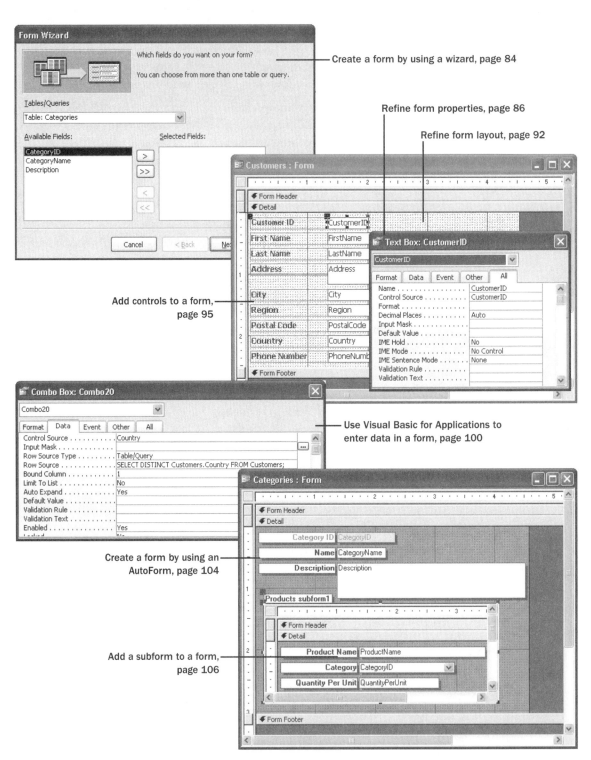

Create a form by using a wizard, page 84

Refine form properties, page 86

Refine form layout, page 92

Add controls to a form, page 95

Use Visual Basic for Applications to enter data in a form, page 100

Create a form by using an AutoForm, page 104

Add a subform to a form, page 106

Chapter 4 at a Glance

4 Simplifying Data Entry with Forms

In this chapter you will learn to:

✔ Create a form by using a wizard.

✔ Refine form properties.

✔ Refine form layout.

✔ Add controls to a form.

✔ Use Visual Basic for Applications to enter data in a form.

✔ Create a form by using an AutoForm.

✔ Add a subform to a form.

A database that contains the day-to-day records of an active company is useful only if it can be kept up to date and if particular items of information can be found quickly. Although Microsoft Office Access 2003 is fairly easy to use, entering, editing, and retrieving information in Datasheet view is not a task you would want to assign to someone who's not familiar with Access. Not only would these tasks be tedious and inefficient, but working in Datasheet view leaves far too much room for error, especially if details of complex transactions have to be entered into several related tables. The solution to this problem, and the first step in the conversion of this database to a *database application*, is to create and use forms.

A form is an organized and formatted view of some or all of the fields from one or more tables or queries. Forms work interactively with the tables in a database. You use *controls* in the form to enter new information, to edit or remove existing information, or to locate information. Like printed forms, Access forms can include *label controls* that tell users what type of information they are expected to enter, as well as *text box controls* in which they can enter the information. Unlike printed forms, Access forms can also include a variety of other controls, such as *option buttons* and *command buttons* that transform Access forms into something very much like a Microsoft Windows dialog box or one page of a wizard.

Tip Some forms are used to navigate among the features and functions of a database application and have little or no connection with its actual data. A *switchboard* is an example of this type of form.

As with other Access objects, you can create forms by hand or with the help of a wizard. Navigational and housekeeping forms, such as switchboards, are best created by hand in Design view. Forms that are based on tables, on the other hand, should always be created with a wizard and then refined by hand—not because it is difficult to drag the necessary text box controls onto a form, but because there is simply no point in doing it by hand.

In this chapter, you will create some forms to hide the complexity of the GardenCo database from the people who will be entering and working with its information. First you will discover how easy it is to let the Form Wizard create forms that you can then modify to suit your needs. You'll learn about the controls you can place in a form, and the properties that control its function and appearance. After you have created a form containing controls, you will learn how to tell Access what to do when a user performs some action in a control, such as clicking or entering text. You will also take a quick look at subforms (forms within a form).

See Also Do you need only a quick refresher on the topics in this chapter? See the Quick Reference entries on pages xxxiii–xxv.

Important Before you can use the practice files in this chapter, you need to install them from the book's companion CD to their default location. See "Using the Book's CD-ROM" on page xiii for more information.

Creating a Form by Using a Wizard

Microsoft Office Specialist

Before you begin creating a form, you need to know what table it will be based on and have an idea of how the form will be used. Having made these decisions, you can use the Form Wizard to help create the basic form. Remember though, that like almost any other object in Access, after the form is created you can always go into Design view to customize the form if it does not quite meet your needs.

In this exercise, you'll create a form that will be used to add new customer records to the Customers table of The Garden Company's database.

BE SURE TO start Access before beginning this exercise.

USE the *GardenCo* database in the practice file folder for this topic. This practice file
is located in the *My Documents\Microsoft Press\Access 2003 SBS\Forms\FormByWiz* folder and can also
be accessed by clicking *Start/All Programs/Microsoft Press/Access 2003 Step by Step*.

OPEN the *GardenCo* database and acknowledge the safety warning, if necessary.

1 On the **Objects** bar, click **Forms**.

2 Double-click **Create form by using wizard** to display the first page of the **Form Wizard**.

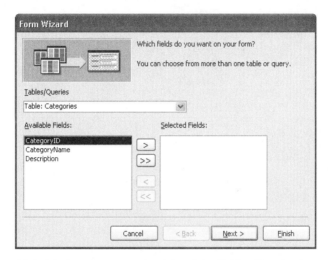

3 Click the down arrow to the right of the **Tables/Queries** box and click **Table: Customers**
to display the fields from that table in the **Available Fields** list.

4 Click the **>>** button to move all the fields from the **Available Fields** list to the **Selected
Fields** list, and then click **Next**.

The second page of the Form Wizard appears, in which you choose the layout of the
fields in the new form. When you select an option on the right side of the page,
the preview area on the left side shows what the form layout will look like with that
option applied.

5 If it is not already selected, select **Columnar**, and then click **Next**.

The third page of the wizard appears, in which you can select a style option to see
how the style will look when applied to the form.

6 Click the **Sumi Painting** style in the list, and click **Next**.

7 Because this form is based on the **Customers** table, Access suggests *Customers* as the form's title. Accept this suggestion, leave the **Open the form to view or enter information** option selected, and click **Finish**.

The new Customers form opens, displaying the first customer record in the Customers table.

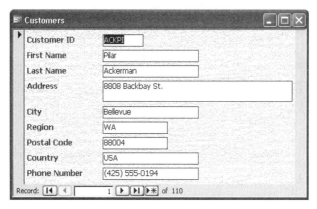

8 Use the navigation controls at the bottom of the form to scroll through a few of the records.

9 Close the form.

CLOSE the *GardenCo* database.

Refining Form Properties

Microsoft Office Specialist

As with tables, you can work with forms in multiple views. The two most common views are Form view, which you use to view or enter data, and Design view, which you use to add controls to the form or change the form's properties or layout.

When you use the Form Wizard to create a form in a column format, every field you select from the underlying table is represented by a text box control and its associated label control. A form like this one, which is used to enter or view the information stored in a specific table, is linked, or *bound*, to that table. Each text box—the box where data is entered or viewed—is bound to a specific field in the table. The table is the *record source*, and the field is the *control source*. Each control has a number of properties, such as font, font size, alignment, fill color, and border. The wizard assigns default values for these properties, but you can change them to improve the form's appearance.

In this exercise, you will edit the properties of the Customers form so that it suits the needs of the people who will be using it on a daily basis.

USE the *GardenCo* database and the *tgc_bkgrnd* graphic in the practice file folder for this topic. These practice files are located in the *My Documents\Microsoft Press\Access 2003 SBS\Forms\Properties* folder and can also be accessed by clicking *Start/All Programs/Microsoft Press/Access 2003 Step by Step*. OPEN the *GardenCo* database and acknowledge the safety warning, if necessary.

1 With **Forms** selected on the **Objects** bar, click **Customers** in the list of forms, and click the **Design** button to open the form in Design view.

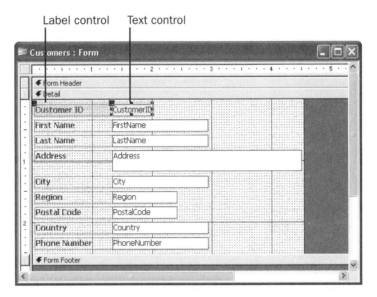

When a form is created, some of its properties are inherited from the table on which it is based. In this example, the names assigned to the text boxes (*FirstName*, *LastName*, and so on) are the field names from the Customers table, and the labels to the left of each text box reflect the Caption property of each field. The size of each text box is determined by the Field Size property.

Tip After a form has been created, its properties are not bound to their source. In previous versions of Access, changing the table's field properties had no impact on the corresponding form property, and vice versa. Now in Access 2003, when you modify an inherited field property in Table Design view, you can choose to update the property in all or some controls that are bound to the field.

2 Click the **Customer ID** label (not its text box). Then on the Formatting toolbar, click the down arrow to the right of the **Font** button, and click **Microsoft Sans Serif**. (If you don't see Microsoft Sans Serif, click **MS Sans Serif**.)

3 With the label still selected, click the down arrow to the right of the **Font Size** box, and click **8** to make the font slightly smaller.

4   Right-click the **CustomerID** text box (not its label), and click **Properties** on the shortcut menu to display the **Properties** dialog box for the **CustomerID** text box.

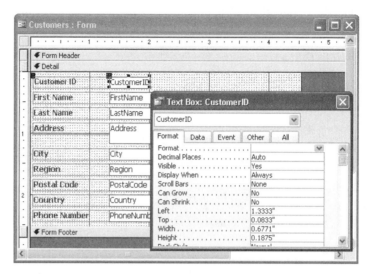

All the settings available on the toolbar (plus a few more) are also available in a Properties dialog box that is associated with each control. You can use this dialog box to display the properties of any object in the form, including the form itself: simply click the down arrow to the right of the box at the top of the dialog box, and click the object whose properties you want to display.

You can display related types of properties by clicking the appropriate tab: Format, Data, Event, or Other. You can also display all properties by clicking the All tab.

5   Click the **Format** tab, scroll to the **Font Name** property, and change it to **Microsoft Sans Serif** (or **MS Sans Serif**). Then set **Font Size** to **8**, and set **Font Weight** to **Bold**.

On the form behind the dialog box, you can see how these changes affect the CustomerID text in the text box (you might have to move the dialog box).

Tip   When you are working in Design view with the Properties dialog box open, you can drag the dialog box by its title bar to the side of the screen so that you can see the changes you're making to the form.

6   Click the down arrow to the right of the box at the top of the **Properties** dialog box, and click **FirstName_Label** box to select the label to the left of the **FirstName** text box.

7   Repeat step 5 to change the font settings for this control.

These different ways of selecting a control and changing its properties provide some flexibility and convenience, but you can see that it would be a bit tedious to apply any of them to a few dozen controls in a form. The next two steps provide a faster method.

8 Click anywhere in the form, and then press Ctrl+A to select all the controls in the **Detail** section of the form.

> **Tip** You can also select all the controls in a form by opening the Edit menu and clicking Select All, or by dragging a rectangle over some portion of all the controls.

Small black handles appear around all the controls to indicate that they are selected. The title bar of the Properties dialog box now displays *Multiple selection*, and the Objects list is blank. Only the Format settings that have the same settings for all the selected controls are displayed. Because the changes you made in the previous steps are not shared by all the selected controls, the Font Name, Font Size, and Font Weight settings are now blank.

9 To apply the settings to all the selected controls, set the **Font Name**, **Font Size**, and **Font Weight** properties as you did in step 5.

10 With all controls still selected, on the **Format** tab, click **Back Style**, and set it to **Normal**.

The background of the labels will no longer be transparent.

11 Click **Back Color**, and then click the ... button at the right end of the box to display the **Color** dialog box.

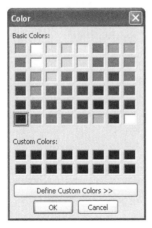

12 Click pale yellow (the second option in the top row), click **OK**, and then press Enter to accept the change.

The background of all the controls changes to pale yellow.

Tip If you don't see a color you want to use, click Define Custom Colors, work with the various settings until you have specified the desired color, and then click Add to Custom Colors.

13 Set **Special Effect** to **Shadowed**, and set **Border Color** to a shade of green.

You can either click the ... button and make a selection, or type a color value such as 32768 in the Border Color box.

14 Click the **Detail** section in the form to deselect all the controls.

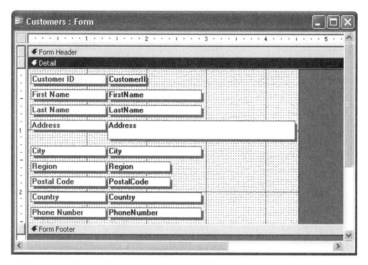

15 Click the label to the left of **FirstName**, and in the **Properties** dialog box, scroll up to the **Caption** box and change *First Name* to Name.

16 Repeat step 15 to change *Phone Number* to Phone.

Tip You can edit the Caption property of a label or the Control Source property of a text box by selecting it, clicking its text, and then editing the text as you would in any other Windows program. However, take care when editing the Control Source property, which defines where the content of the text box comes from.

17 Remove the label to the left of **LastName** by clicking it and then pressing the [Del] key.

18 Select all the labels, but not their corresponding text boxes, by holding down the [Shift] key as you click each of them. Then in the **Properties** dialog box, scroll down and set the **Text Align** property to **Right**.

19 On the **Format** menu, point to **Size**, click **To Fit** to size the labels to fit their contents, and then click anywhere in the form, but outside the controls, to deselect them.

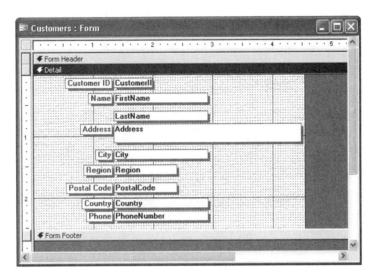

Tip The order in which you make formatting changes, such as the ones you just made, can have an impact on the results. If you don't see the expected results, click the Undo button or press Ctrl + Z to step back through your changes, and then try again.

20 Hold down the Shift key while clicking each text box to select all the text boxes but not their corresponding labels, and in the **Properties** dialog box, change the **Left** setting to **1.5"** to insert a little space between the labels and the text boxes.

21 Change the **Font Weight** property to **Normal**, and then click anywhere in the form, but outside the controls, to deselect them.

22 To change the background to one that better represents The Garden Company, click the down arrow to the right of the box at the top of the **Properties** dialog box, click **Form**, click the **Picture** property—which shows *(bitmap)*—and then click the **...** button to open the **Insert Picture** dialog box.

23 Navigate to the *My Documents\Microsoft Press\Access 2003 SBS\Forms\Properties* folder, and double-click **tgc_bkgrnd**. (If you don't see this file listed, change the **Files of type** setting to **Graphics Files**.)

The form's background changes, and the path to the graphic used for the new background is displayed in the Picture property box.

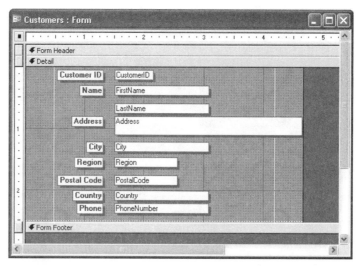

Save

24 Click the **Save** button to save the design of your **Customers** form.

25 Close the form. (The **Properties** dialog box closes when you close the form.)

CLOSE the *GardenCo* database.

Refining Form Layout

Microsoft Office Specialist

The forms created by a wizard are functional, not fancy. However, it's fairly easy to customize the layout to suit your needs. You can add and delete labels, move both labels and text controls around the form, add logos and other graphics, and otherwise improve the layout of the form to make it attractive and easy to use.

As you work with a form's layout, it is important to pay attention to the shape of the pointer, which changes to indicate the manner in which you can change the selected item. Because a text box and its label sometimes act as a unit, you have to be careful to notice the pointer's shape before making any change. This table explains what action each shape indicates:

Pointer	Shape	Action
🖑	Hand	Drag to move both controls together, as one.
👆	Pointing finger	Drag to move just the control.
↕	Vertical arrows	Drag the top or bottom border to change the height.

Pointer	Shape	Action
↔	Horizontal arrows	Drag the right or left border to change the width.
↘	Diagonal arrows	Drag the corner to change both the height and width.

In this exercise, you will rearrange the label and text box controls in the Customers form to make them more closely fit the way people will work with them.

USE the *GardenCo* database in the practice file folder for this topic. This practice file is located in the *My Documents\Microsoft Press\Access 2003 SBS\Forms\Layout* folder and can also be accessed by clicking *Start/All Programs/Microsoft Press/Access 2003 Step by Step*.
OPEN the *GardenCo* database and acknowledge the safety warning, if necessary.

1 Open the **Customers** form in Design view.

2 If necessary, drag the lower-right corner of the Form window down and to the right until you can see the form footer at the bottom of the form and have an inch or so of blank area to the right of the background.

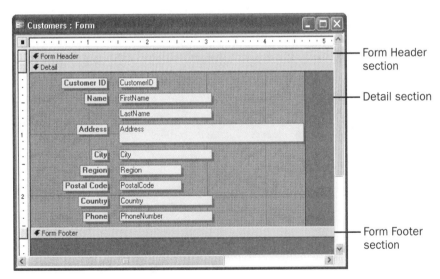

The form is divided into three sections: Form Header, Detail, and Form Footer. Only the Detail section currently has anything in it.

3 Point to the right edge of the **Detail** background, and when the pointer changes to a two-way arrow, drag the edge of the background to the right until you can see about five full grid sections.

4 Click the **LastName** text box, and then slowly move the pointer around its border, from black handle to black handle, noticing how it changes shape.

5 Move the pointer over the **LastName** text box and when it changes to a hand, drag it up and to the right of the **FirstName** text box.

6 One by one, select each control, resize it, and move it to the location shown in the following graphic. (Don't worry if you don't get everything aligned exactly as shown here.)

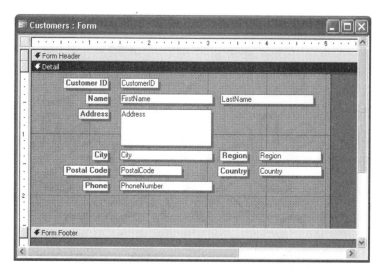

Tip To fine-tune the position of a control, click it and then hold down the Ctrl key while pressing the appropriate arrow key—←, ↓, ↑, or →—to move the control in small increments. To fine-tune the size of a control, use the same process but hold down the Shift key.

7 On the **Format** menu, click **AutoFormat** to display the **AutoFormat** dialog box.

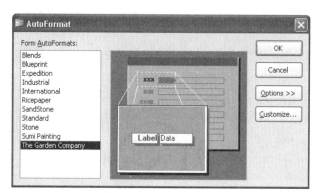

8 Click the **Customize** button to display the **Customize AutoFormat** dialog box.

9 Click **Create a new AutoFormat based on the Form 'Customers'**, and then click **OK**.

New in
Office 2003
Support for
Windows XP
Theming

> **Tip** Form controls inherit whatever theme is set in the operating system. To change the theme, open the Control Panel, click Display, click the Themes tab, select a new theme, and then click OK.

10 In the **New Style Name** dialog box, type The Garden Company as the name of the new style, and then click **OK**.

Back in the AutoFormat database, the new style appears in the Form AutoFormats list. From now on, this style will be available in any database you open on this computer.

11 Click **OK** to close the **AutoFormat** dialog box.

> **Tip** Access saves data automatically as you enter it, but layout changes to any object must be manually saved.

Save

12 Click the **Save** button.

13 Close the form.

CLOSE the *GardenCo* database.

Adding Controls to a Form

Microsoft
Office
Specialist

Every form has three basic sections: Form Header, Detail, and Form Footer. When you use a wizard to create a form, the wizard adds a set of controls for each field that you select from the underlying table to the Detail section and leaves the Form Header and Form Footer sections blank. Because these sections are empty, Access collapses them, but you can size all the sections by dragging their *selectors*. Although labels and text box controls are perhaps the most common controls found in forms, you can also enhance your forms with many other types of controls. For example, you can add groups of option buttons, check boxes, and list boxes to present people with choices instead of making them type entries in text boxes.

The most popular controls are stored in the Toolbox. Clicking the More Controls button displays a list of all the other controls on your computer. The controls displayed when you click the More Controls button are not necessarily associated with Access or even with another Microsoft Office program. The list includes every control that any program has installed and registered on your computer.

Important Some controls, such as the Calendar Control, can be very useful. Others might do nothing when you add them to a form, or might do something unexpected and not entirely pleasant. If you feel like experimenting, don't do so in an important database.

In this exercise, you will add a graphic and a caption to the Form Header section of the Customers form from the GardenCo database. You will also replace the Country text box control in the Detail section with a combo box control.

USE the *GardenCo* database and the *tgc_logo2* graphic in the practice file folder for this topic. This practice file is located in the *My Documents\Microsoft Press\Access 2003 SBS\Forms\Controls* folder and can also be accessed by clicking *Start/All Programs/Microsoft Press/Access 2003 Step by Step*.
OPEN the *GardenCo* database and acknowledge the safety warning, if necessary.

1. Open the **Customers** form in Design view.

2. Point to the horizontal line between the **Form Header** section selector and the **Detail** section selector, and when the pointer changes to a double-headed arrow, drag the **Detail** section selector down a little over an inch.

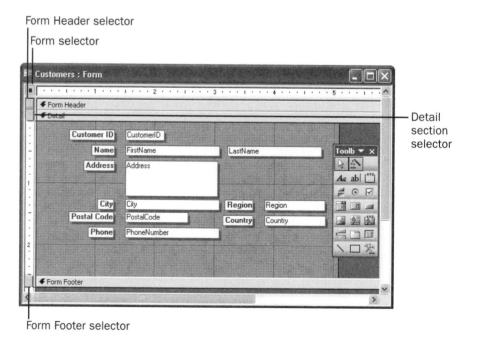

Toolbox

3   If the Toolbox isn't displayed, click the **Toolbox** button on the Form Design toolbar.

You can also open the View menu and select the Toolbox check box. To keep the Toolbox open but out of the way, you can drag it off to the side, and dock it on one edge of the screen.

4   To get an idea of the controls that are available, move the pointer over the buttons in the Toolbox, pausing just long enough to display each button's ScreenTip.

Image

5   Click the **Image** control in the Toolbox, and then drag a rectangle about 1 inch high and 3 inches wide at the left end of the **Form Header** section.

When you release the mouse button, Access displays the Insert Picture dialog box, in which you can select an image to insert in the control.

6   Navigate to the *My Documents\Microsoft Press\Access 2003 SBS\Forms\Controls* folder, and double-click **tgc_logo2**. (If you don't see this file listed, change the **Files of type** setting to **Graphics Files**.)

The Garden Company logo appears inside the image control.

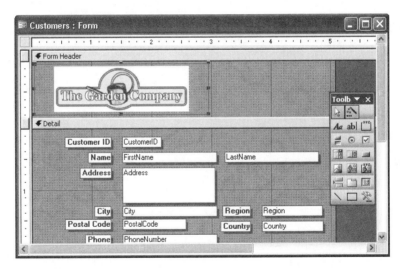

Tip   If the control isn't large enough, the image is cropped. You can enlarge the control to display the entire image. (You might also have to enlarge the Form Header section.)

Aa
Label

7   To add a caption to the header, click the **Label** control in the Toolbox, and then drag another rectangle in the header section.

Access inserts a label control containing the insertion point, ready for you to enter a caption.

8 Type the caption Customers, and press [Enter].

The Customers label takes on the formatting of the other labels.

9 With the **Customers** label selected, press the [F4] key to display the **Properties** dialog box.

10 Change the **Font Size** property to **18**, and change the **Text Align** property to **Center**. Then close the **Properties** dialog box.

11 On the **Format** menu, point to **Size**, and then click **To Fit**.

12 Adjust the size and position of the two controls you added so that they are side-by-side.

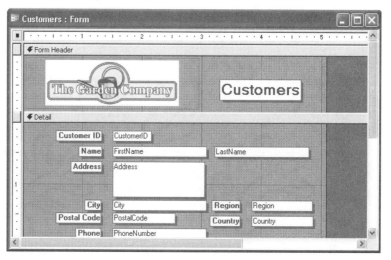

Control Wizards

13 If the **Control Wizards** button is active (orange) in the toolbox, click it to deactivate it.

With the Control Wizards button turned off, you can create a control with all the default settings without having to work through the wizard's pages.

Combo Box

14 Insert a combo box in the **Details** section by clicking the **Combo Box** control in the Toolbox and then dragging a rectangle just below the current **Country** text box.

When you release the mouse button, Access displays a combo box control, which is *unbound* (not attached to a field in the Customers table).

Troubleshooting Access provides a number for each control as it is created, so don't be concerned if the number displayed in your control is different from what you see in the graphics in this book.

Format Painter

15 Copy the formatting of the **Country** text box to the new combo box control by clicking the **Country** text box, clicking the **Format Painter** button on the Form Design toolbar, and then clicking the combo box control.

Both the combo box control and its label take on the new formatting.

16 Right-click the combo box and click **Properties** on the shortcut menu to display the **Properties** dialog box.

17 Click the **Data** tab, set the **Control Source** property to **Country**, and then type the following in the **Row Source** box:

```
SELECT DISTINCT Customers.Country FROM Customers;
```

(Note that there is no space between *Customers* and *Country*; there is only a period. There is also a semi-colon at the end of the text.)

This line is a query that extracts one example of every country in the Country field of the Customers table and displays the results as a list when you click the box's down arrow.

(You might have to widen the Properties dialog box to display the whole query.)

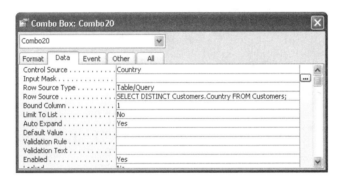

Tip If you need to add a new customer from a country that is not in the list, you can type the new country's name in the combo box. After the record is added to the database, that country shows up when the combo box list is displayed.

18 If necessary, set the **Row Source Type** to **Table/Query**.

19 Click the label to the left of the combo box (if necessary, drag the **Properties** dialog box to see the combo box label). Then click the dialog box's **Format** tab, change the caption to **Country**, and close the dialog box.

20 Delete the original **Country** text box and its label, and move the new combo box and label into their place, resizing them as needed.

View

21 Click the **View** button to see your form.

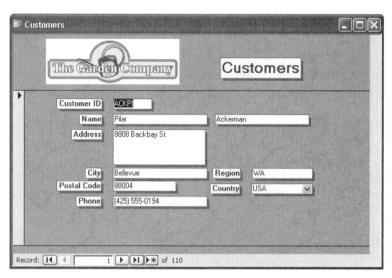

22 Scroll through a couple of records, and display the combo box's list to see how you can select a country.

23 You don't need the *record selector*—the gray bar along the left edge of the form—so return to Design view, and display the **Properties** dialog box for the entire form by clicking the **Form** selector (the box at the junction of the horizontal and vertical rulers) and pressing ⌹. Then on the **Format** tab, change **Record Selectors** to **No**. While you're at it, change **Scroll Bars** to **Neither**. Then close the **Properties** dialog box.

24 Save the form's new design, and switch to Form view for a final look.

25 Close the form.

CLOSE the *GardenCo* database.

Using Visual Basic for Applications to Enter Data in a Form

As you might have suspected by now, almost everything in Access, including the Access program itself, is an object. One of the characteristics of objects is that they can recognize and respond to *events*, which are essentially actions. Different objects recognize different events. The basic events, recognized by almost all objects, are Click, Double Click, Mouse Down, Mouse Move, and Mouse Up. Most objects recognize quite a few other events. A text control, for example, recognizes about 17 different events; a form recognizes more than 50.

Tip You can see the list of events recognized by an object by looking at the Event tab on the object's Properties dialog box.

While you use a form, objects are signaling events, or *firing events*, almost constantly. However, unless you attach a *macro* or *Microsoft Visual Basic for Applications (VBA) procedure* to an event, the object is really just firing blanks. By default, Access doesn't do anything obvious when it recognizes most events. So without interfering with the program's normal behavior, you can use an event to specify what action should happen. You can even use an event to trigger the running of a macro or a VBA procedure that performs a set of actions.

Sound complicated? Well, it's true that events are not things most casual Access users tend to worry about. But because knowing how to handle events can greatly increase the efficiency of objects such as forms, you should take a glimpse at what they're all about while you have a form open.

For example, while looking at customer records in the GardenCo database, you might have noticed that the CustomerID is composed of the first three letters of the customer's last name and the first two letters of his or her first name, all in capital letters. This technique will usually generate a unique ID for a new customer. If you try to enter an ID that is already in use, Access won't accept the new entry, and you'll have to add a number or change the ID in some other way to make it unique. Performing trivial tasks, such as combining parts of two words and then converting the results to capital letters, is something a computer excels at. So rather than typing the ID for each new customer record that is added to The Garden Company's database, you can let VBA do it instead.

In this exercise, you will write a few lines of VBA code, and attach the code to the After Update event in the LastName text box in the Customers form. When you change the content of the text box and attempt to move somewhere else in the form, the Before Update event is fired. In response to that event, Access updates the record in the source table, and then the After Update event is fired. This is the event you are going to work with. This is by no means an in-depth treatment of VBA, but this exercise will give you a taste of VBA's power.

USE the *GardenCo* database and the *AftUpdate* text file in the practice file folder for this topic. This practice file is located in the *My Documents\Microsoft Press\Access 2003 SBS\Forms\Events* folder and can also be accessed by clicking *Start/All Programs/Microsoft Press/Access 2003 Step by Step*.
OPEN the *GardenCo* database and acknowledge the safety warning, if necessary.

1   With **Forms** selected on the **Objects** bar, click **Customers** in the list of forms, and click the **Design** button.

2   Click the **LastName** text box to select it, and if necessary, press ⟨F4⟩ to open the **Properties** dialog box.

3 Click the **Event** tab to see the options.

This tab lists the events to which the LastName text box control can respond to.

4 Click **After Update** in the list, and then click the ... button.

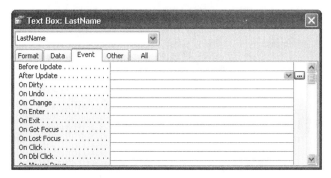

The Choose Builder dialog box appears, offering you the options of building an expression, a macro, or VBA code.

5 Click **Code Builder**, and then click **OK** to open the VBA Editor.

Project Explorer   Sub statement

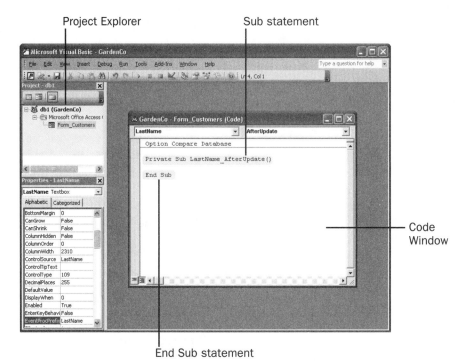

Code Window

End Sub statement

The Project Explorer pane lists any objects you have created to which you can attach code; in this case, only the Customers form (Form_Customers) is listed. As you create more forms and reports, they will appear here.

The Code window displays a placeholder for the procedure that Access will use to handle the After Update event for the LastName text control. This procedure is named *Private Sub LastName_AfterUpdate()*, and at the moment it contains only the Sub and End Sub statements that mark the beginning and end of any procedure.

6 Launch a text editor, such as Microsoft Notepad, navigate to the *My Documents \Microsoft Press\Access 2003 SBS\Forms\Events* folder, open the *AftUpdate* practice file, and copy the following lines of text to the Clipboard. Then ⎡Alt⎤+⎡Tab⎤ back to the Code window and paste the text between the Private Sub LastName_AfterUpdate() and End Sub statements:

```
'Create variables to hold first and last names
' and customer ID
Dim fName As String
Dim lName As String
Dim cID As String

'Assign the text in the LastName text box to
' the lName variable.
lName = Forms!customers!LastName.Text

'You must set the focus to a text box before
' you can read its contents.
Forms!customers!FirstName.SetFocus
fName = Forms!customers!FirstName.Text

'Combine portions of the last and first names
' to create the customer ID.
cID = UCase(Left(lName, 3) & Left(fName, 2))

'Don't store the ID unless it is 5 characters long
' (which indicates both names filled in).
If Len(cID) = 5 Then
   Forms!customers!CustomerID.SetFocus

   'Don't change the ID if it has already been
   ' entered; perhaps it was changed manually.
   If Forms!customers!CustomerID.Text = "" Then
      Forms!customers!CustomerID = cID
   End If
End If

'Set the focus where it would have gone naturally.
Forms!customers!Address.SetFocus
```

Important   When a line of text is preceded by an apostrophe, the text is a comment that explains the purpose of the next line of code. In the VBA Editor, comments are displayed in green.

View Microsoft
Access

7 Save the file, click the **View Microsoft Access** button to return to the Access window, and then close the **Properties** dialog box.

New Record

8 Switch to Form view and size the window as necessary. Then on the **Navigation** bar, click the **New Record** button to create a new record.

9 Press the ⎄ key to move the insertion point to the text box for the **FirstName** field, type John, press ⎄ to move to the text box for the **LastName** field, type Coake, and then press ⎄ again.

If you entered the VBA code correctly, *COAJO* appears in the CustomerID text box.

10 Change the first and last name to something else and notice that the **CustomerID** text box doesn't change even if the names from which it was derived do change.

11 Press the ⎋ key to remove your entry, and then try entering the last name first, followed by the first name.

Access does not create a Customer ID. The code does what it was written to do but not necessarily what you want it to do, which is to create an ID regardless of the order in which the names are entered. There are several ways to fix this problem. You could write a similar procedure to handle the After Update event in the FirstName text box, or you could write one procedure to handle both events and then jump to it when either event occurs. You won't do either in these exercises, but if you are interested, you can look at the code in the database file for the next exercise to see the second solution.

12 Press ⎋ to clear your entries, and then close the **Customers** form.

13 Press ⎇+⎄ to switch to the VBA Editor, which is still open, and close the editor.

CLOSE the *GardenCo* database.

Creating a Form by Using an AutoForm

Microsoft
Office
Specialist

Although a form doesn't have to include all the fields from a table, when it is used as the primary method of creating new records, it usually does include all of them. The quickest way to create a form that includes all the fields from one table is to use an *AutoForm*. And as with the forms created by a wizard, you can easily customize these forms.

In this exercise, you will create an AutoForm that displays information about each of the products carried by The Garden Company.

USE the *GardenCo* database in the practice file folder for this topic. This practice file is located in the *My Documents\Microsoft Press\Access 2003 SBS\Forms\AutoForm* folder and can also be accessed by clicking *Start/All Programs/Microsoft Press/Access 2003 Step by Step.*
OPEN the *GardenCo* database and acknowledge the safety warning, if necessary.

1   On the **Objects** bar, click **Forms**.

2   On the database window's toolbar, click the **New** button to display this **New Form** dialog box, which lists all the ways you can create a form.

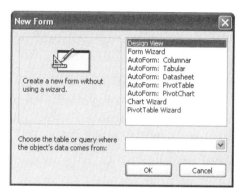

3   Click **AutoForm: Columnar** in the list of choices, click the down arrow to the right of the box at the bottom of the dialog box, click **Categories**, and then click **OK**.

The dialog box closes, and after a moment a new Categories form is displayed in Form view.

Save

4   Click the **Save** button, accept the default name of *Categories* in the **Save As** dialog box, and click **OK** to view the form.

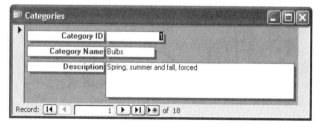

Tip   When AutoForm creates a form, Access applies the background style you selected the last time you used the Form Wizard (or the default style, if you haven't used the wizard). If your form doesn't look like this one, switch to Design view, and on the Format menu, click AutoFormat. You can then select The Garden Company style from the list displayed.

5 This form looks pretty good as it is, but switch to Design view so that you can make a few minor changes.

6 Delete the word *Category* from the **Category Name** label.

7 The **CategoryID** value is provided by Access and should never be changed, so you need to disable that text box control. Click the control and if necessary, press `F4` to display the control's **Properties** dialog box.

8 On the **Data** tab, change **Enabled** to **No**, and close the dialog box.

Disabling the CategoryID text box changes it, and the label text, to gray.

9 Switch to Form view, and scroll through a few categories. Try to edit entries in the **Category ID** field to confirm that you can't.

10 You don't need scroll bars or a record selector in this form, so return to Design view, and display the form's **Properties** dialog box by clicking the **Form** selector and pressing `F4`. On the **Format** tab, change **Scroll Bars** to **Neither** and **Record Selectors** to **No**, and then close the dialog box.

11 Save and close the **Categories** form.

CLOSE the *GardenCo* database.

Adding a Subform to a Form

Microsoft Office Specialist

A form can display information (fields) from one or more tables or queries. If you want to display fields from several tables or queries in one form, you have to give some thought to the *relationships* that must exist between those objects.

In Access, a relationship is an association between common fields in two tables, and you can use it to relate the information in one table to the information in another table. For example, in the GardenCo database a relationship can be established between the Categories table and the Products table because both tables have a CategoryID field. Each product is in only one category, but each category can contain many products, so this type of relationship—the most common—is known as a *one-to-many relationship*.

As you create forms and queries, Access might recognize some relationships between the fields in the underlying tables. However, it probably won't recognize all of them without a little help from you.

Other Types of Relationships

In addition to one-to-many relationships, you can create *one-to-one relationships* and *many-to-many relationships*, but they are not as common.

In a one-to-one relationship, each record in one table can have one and only one related record in the other table. This type of relationship isn't commonly used because it is easier to put all the fields in one table. However, you might use two related tables instead of one to break up a table with many fields, or to track information that applies to only some of the records in the first table.

A many-to-many relationship is really two one-to-many relationships tied together through a third table. For example, the GardenCo database contains Products, Orders, and Order Details tables. The Products table has one record for each product sold by The Garden Company, and each product has a unique ProductID. The Orders table has one record for each order placed with The Garden Company, and each record in it has a unique OrderID. However, the Orders table doesn't specify which products were included in each order; that information is in the Order Details table, which is the table in the middle that ties the other two tables together. Products and Orders each have a one-to-many relationship with Order Details. Products and Orders therefore have a many-to-many relationship with each other. In plain language, this means that every product can appear in many orders, and every order can include many products.

In this exercise, you will first define the relationship between the Categories and Products tables in the GardenCo database. You will then add a *subform* to a form. For each category displayed in the main form, this subform will display all the products in that category.

USE the *GardenCo* database in the practice file folder for this topic. This practice file is located in the *My Documents\Microsoft Press\Access 2003 SBS\Forms\Subform* folder and can also be accessed by clicking *Start/All Programs/Microsoft Press/Access 2003 Step by Step*.
OPEN the *GardenCo* database and acknowledge the safety warning, if necessary.

Relationships

1   On the Database toolbar, click the **Relationships** button to open the Relationships window.

Show Table

2   If the **Show Table** dialog box isn't displayed, on the toolbar, click the **Show Table** button. Then double-click **Categories** and **Products** in the list displayed. Close the **Show Table** dialog box to view the Relationships window.

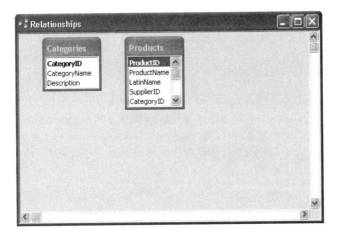

3   Click **CategoryID** in one table, and drag it on top of **CategoryID** in the other table.

Access displays the Edit Relationships dialog box, which lists the fields you have chosen to relate and offers several options.

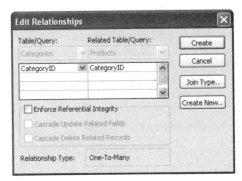

4   Select the **Enforce Referential Integrity** check box, select the other two check boxes, and then click **Create**.

Tip   Access uses a system of rules called *referential integrity* to ensure that relationships between records in related tables are valid, and that you don't accidentally delete or change related data. When the Cascade Update Related Fields check box is selected, changing a primary key value in the primary table automatically updates the matching value in all related records. When the Cascade Delete Related Records check box is selected, deleting a record in the primary table deletes any related records in the related table.

Access draws a line representing the one-to-many relationship between the CategoryID fields in each of the tables.

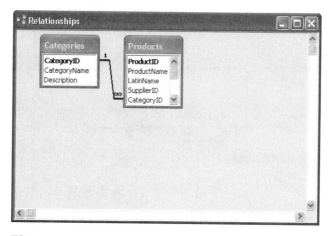

Tip   You can edit or delete a relationship by right-clicking the line and clicking the appropriate command on the shortcut menu.

5   Close the Relationships window, and click **Yes** when prompted to save the window's layout.

6   Open the **Categories** form in Design view.

7   Enlarge the Form window, and drag the **Form Footer** section selector down about 1 inch to give yourself some room to work.

Toolbox

8   If the Toolbox isn't displayed, click the **Toolbox** button.

Control Wizards

9   Make sure the **Control Wizards** button in the Toolbox is active (orange).

Subform/
Subreport

10   Click the **Subform/Subreport** button, and drag a rectangle in the lower portion of the **Details** section.

A white object appears in the form, and the first page of the Subform Wizard opens.

Tip   If prompted, follow the instructions to install this wizard.

11   Leave **Use existing Tables and Queries** selected, and click **Next**.

12   In the **Tables/Queries** list, click **Table: Products**.

13 Add the **ProductName**, **CategoryID**, **QuantityPerUnit**, **UnitPrice**, and **UnitsInStock** fields to the **Selected Fields** list by clicking each one and then clicking the **>** button.

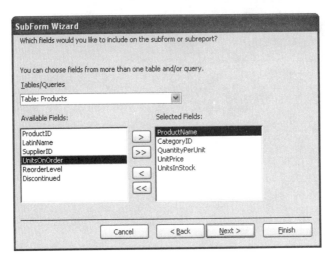

14 Click **Next** to display the third page of the wizard.

Because the Category ID field in the subform is related to the Category ID field in the main form, the wizard selects "Show Products for each record in Categories using CategoryID" as the "Choose from a list" option.

Tip If the wizard can't figure out which fields are related, it selects the "Define my own" option and displays list boxes in which you can specify the fields to be related.

15 Click **Next** to accept the default selection, and then click **Finish**, to accept the default name for the subform and complete the process.

Access displays the Categories form in Design view, with an embedded Products subform. The size and location of the subform is determined by the original rectangle you dragged in the form.

16 Adjust the size and location of the objects in your form as needed to view the entire subform.

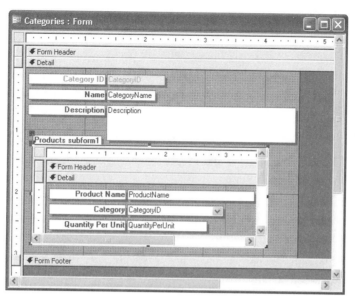

17 Notice the layout of the subform in Design view, and then click **View** to switch to Form view.

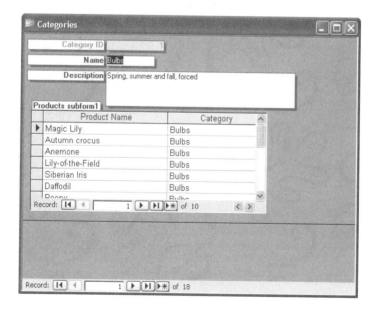

The format of the subform has totally changed. In Design view, it looks like a simple form, but in Form view, it looks like a datasheet.

18 Switch back to Design view, make any necessary size adjustments, and if necessary, open the **Properties** dialog box.

19 Click the **Form** selector in the upper-left corner of the subform twice.

The first click selects the Products subform control, and the second click selects the form. A small black square appears on the selector.

20 On the **Format** tab of the **Properties** dialog box, change both **Record Selectors** and **Navigation Buttons** to **No**.

While on this tab, notice the Default View property, which is set to Datasheet. You might want to return to this property and try the other options after finishing this exercise.

21 Close the **Properties** dialog box, switch back to Form view, and drag the dividers between column headers until you can see all the fields.

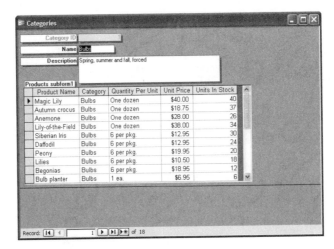

Tip You can quickly adjust the width of columns to fit their data by double-clicking the double arrow between column headings.

First Record

22 Click the navigation buttons to scroll through several categories. When you are finished, click the **First Record** button to return to the first category (Bulbs).

As each category is displayed at the top of the form, the products in that category are listed in the datasheet in the subform.

23 Click the category name to the right of the first product.

The arrow at the right end of the box indicates that this is a combo box.

24 Click the arrow to display the list of categories, and change the category to **Cacti**.

Next Record

25 Click the **Next Record** navigation button to move to the next category (Cacti).

You can see that the first product is now included in this category.

26 Display the list of categories, and then restore the first product to the **Bulbs** category.

27 You don't want people to be able to change a product's category, so return to Design view. Then in the subform, click the **CategoryID** text box control, and press [Del].

The CategoryID text box and its label are deleted.

Important You included the CategoryID field when the wizard created this subform because it is the field that relates the Categories and Products tables. The underlying Products table uses a combo box to display the name of the category instead of its ID number, so that combo box also appears in the subform.

28 Save the form, switch back to Form view, and then adjust the width of the subform columns and the size of the Form window until you can clearly see the fields.

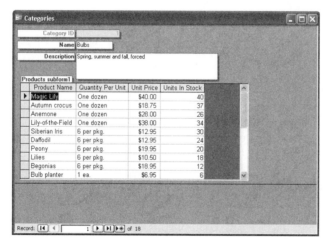

29 Close the **Categories** form, saving your changes to both the form and the subform.

CLOSE the *GardenCo* database.

Creating a Form and Subform by Using a Wizard

If you know when you create a form that you are going to add a subform, you can do the whole job with the Form Wizard, like this:

1 To create the form in your database, on the **Objects** bar, click **Forms**, and then click the **New** button on the database window's toolbar.

2 Click **Form Wizard**, select the form's base table from the list at the bottom of the page, and then click **OK**.

3 Verify that the table you selected is shown in the **Table/Queries** list, and then click the **>>** button to include all the fields in the new form.

4 To create the subform, display the **Tables/Queries** list, and click the name of the subform's base table.

5 Double-click the desired fields to add them to the list of selected fields, and then click **Next**.

6 Accept the default options, and click **Next**.

7 Accept the default **Datasheet** option, and click **Next**.

8 Click **Finish** to create the form and subform.

You can then clean up the form to suit your needs, just as you did in the previous exercise.

Key Points

- A form is an organized and formatted view of some or all of the fields from one or more tables or queries. Forms work interactively with the tables in a database. You use controls in the form to enter new information, to edit or remove existing information, or to locate information.

- When you know what table to base your form on, and have an idea of how the form will be used, you can use the Form Wizard to quickly create a form. You can make modifications to the form in Design view.

- The two most common views to use in forms are Form view, in which you view or enter data, and Design view, in which you add controls, change form properties, and change the form layout.

- In a form, each text box (the box where data is entered or viewed) is bound—or linked—to a specific field in the form's underlying table. The table is the record source and the field is the control source. Each control has a number of properties, such as font style, size and color, which you can change to improve a form's appearance.

■   In Design view, you can resize any of the three basic sections of a form: the Form Header, Detail, and Form Footer. You can customize any section of your form's layout by adding and deleting labels, moving labels and text controls, and adding logos and other graphics. The most popular controls are stored in the Toolbox.

■   The objects in your form can recognize and respond to events, which are essentially actions. But without a macro or VBA procedure attached to it, an event doesn't actually do anything. Knowing how to handle events can greatly increase the efficiency of objects, such as forms. For example, as you enter the first and last names of a new customer, your form could respond to one (or more) events to create an ID based on the customer's first and last name.

■   The quickest way to create a form that includes all the fields from one table is to use an AutoForm, which can easily be customized later in Design view.

■   If you want to display fields from several tables or queries in one form, you have to give some thought to the relationships that must exist between those objects. In Access, a relationship is an association between common fields in two tables, and you can relate the information in one table to the information in another table. There are three types of relationships that Access recognizes: one-to-one, one-to-many, and many-to-many.

■   After you define a relationship between tables, you can add subforms to your forms. For example, for each category displayed in your main form, you might have a subform that displays all the products in that category.

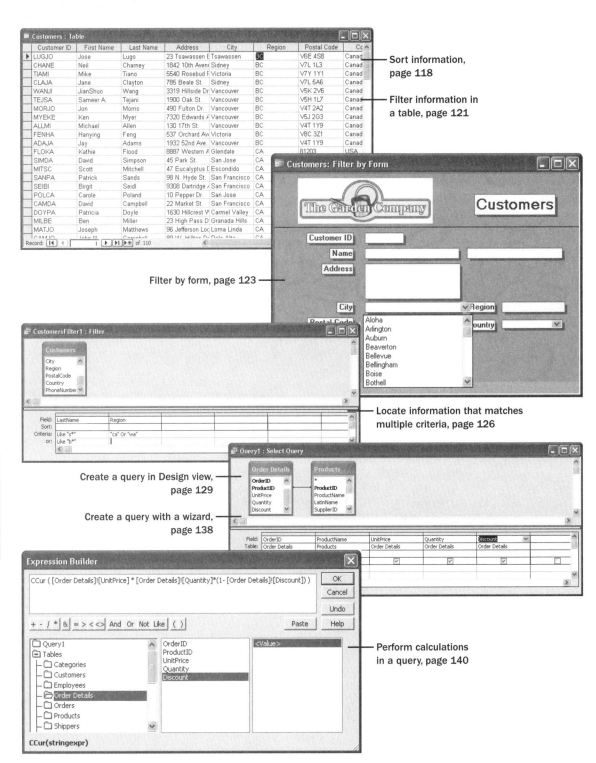

Sort information, page 118

Filter information in a table, page 121

Filter by form, page 123

Locate information that matches multiple criteria, page 126

Create a query in Design view, page 129

Create a query with a wizard, page 138

Perform calculations in a query, page 140

Chapter 5 at a Glance

5 Locating Specific Information

In this chapter you will learn to:

✔ Sort information.

✔ Filter information in a table.

✔ Filter by form.

✔ Locate information that matches multiple criteria.

✔ Create a query in Design view.

✔ Create a query with a Wizard.

✔ Perform calculations in a query.

A database is a repository for information. It might hold a few records in one table or thousands of records in many related tables. No matter how much information is stored in a database, it is useful only if you can locate the information you need when you need it. In a small database you can find information simply by scrolling through a table until you spot what you are looking for. But as a database grows in size and complexity, locating specific information becomes more difficult.

Microsoft Office Access 2003 provides a variety of tools you can use to organize the display of information in a database and to locate specific items of information. Using these tools, you can focus on just part of the information by quickly sorting a table based on any field (or combination of fields), or you can filter the table so that information containing some combination of characters is displayed (or excluded from the display). With a little more effort, you can create queries to display specific fields from specific records from one or more tables. You can even save these queries so that you can use them over and over again, as the information in the database changes.

A query can do more than simply return a list of records from a table. You can use functions in a query that perform calculations on the information in the table to produce the sum, average, count, and other mathematical values.

Working with the GardenCo database, in this chapter you will learn how to pinpoint precisely the information you need in a database using sorting and filtering tools, and queries. Note that you cannot continue with the database from the last chapter; you must use the practice files on the companion CD-ROM.

See Also Do you need only a quick refresher on the topics in this chapter? See the Quick Reference entries on pages xxxv–xxxvii.

Important Before you can use the practice files in this chapter, you need to install them from the book's companion CD to their default location. See "Using the Book's CD-ROM" on page xiii for more information.

Sorting Information

Microsoft Office Specialist

Information stored in a table can be sorted in either ascending or descending order, based on the values in one or more fields in the table. You could, for example, sort a customer table alphabetically based first on the last name of each customer and then on the first name. Such a sort would result in this type of list, which resembles those found in telephone books:

Last	First
Smith	Denise
Smith	James
Smith	Jeff
Thompson	Ann
Thompson	Steve

Occasionally you might need to sort a table to group all entries of one type together. For example, to qualify for a discount on postage, The Garden Company might want to sort customer records on the postal code field to group the codes before printing mailing labels.

If a field with the Text data type contains numbers, you can sort the field numerically by padding the numbers with leading zeros so that all entries are the same length. For example, 001, 011, and 101 are sorted correctly even if the numbers are defined as text.

How Access Sorts

The concept of sorting seems pretty intuitive, but sometimes your computer's approach to such a concept is not so intuitive. Sorting numbers is a case in point. In Access, numbers can be treated as text or as numerals. Because of the spaces, hyphens, and punctuation typically used in street addresses, postal codes, and telephone numbers, the numbers in these fields are usually treated as text, and sorting them follows the logic applied to sorting all text. Numbers in a price or quantity field, on the other hand, are typically treated as numerals.

When Access sorts text, it sorts first on the first character in the selected field in every record, then on the next character, then on the next, and so on—until it runs out of characters. When Access sorts numbers, it treats the contents of each field as a single value, and sorts the records based on that value. This tactic can result in seemingly strange sort orders. For example, sorting the list in the first column of the following table as text produces the list in the second column. Sorting the same list as numerals produces the list in the third column:

Original	Sort as text	Sort as number
1	1	1
1234	11	2
23	12	3
3	1234	4
11	2	5
22	22	11
12	23	12
4	3	22
2	4	23
5	5	1234

In this exercise, you will learn several ways to sort the information in a datasheet or a form.

BE SURE TO start Access before beginning this exercise.

USE the *GardenCo* database in the practice file folder for this topic. This practice file is located in the *My Documents\Microsoft Press\Access 2003 SBS\Queries\Sort* folder and can also be accessed by clicking *Start/All Programs/Microsoft Press/Access 2003 Step by Step*.

OPEN the *GardenCo* database and acknowledge the safety warning, if necessary.

1   On the **Objects** bar, click **Tables**.

2   Double-click **Customers** to open the table in Datasheet view.

Sort Ascending

3   To sort by Region, click anywhere in the **Region** column, and then click the **Sort Ascending** button.

> **Tip**   You can also use the Sort Ascending or Sort Descending commands by pointing to Sort on the Records menu; or you can right-click the column in the datasheet and click either command on the shortcut menu.

The records are rearranged in order of region.

Sort Descending

4   To reverse the sort order, while still in the **Region** column, click the **Sort Descending** button.

The records for the state of Washington (WA) are now at the top of your list. In both sorts, the region was sorted alphabetically, but the City field was left in a seemingly random order. What you really want to see is the records arranged by city within each region.

> **Tip**   Access can sort on more than one field, but it sorts consecutively from left to right. So the fields you want to sort must be adjacent, and they must be arranged in the order in which you want to sort them.

5   To move the **Region** field to the left of the **City** field, click its header to select the column, and then click the header again and drag the column to the left until a dark line appears between **Address** and **City**.

6   Because **Region** is already selected, hold down the ⇧shift key and click the **City** header to extend the selection so that both the **Region** and **City** columns are selected.

7   Click the **Sort Ascending** button to arrange the records with the regions in ascending order and the city names also in ascending order within each region (or in this case, each state).

> **Tip**   You can sort records while viewing them in a form. Click the box of the field on which you want to base the sort, and then click one of the Sort buttons. However, you can't sort on multiple fields in Form view.

8 The order of the columns in the **Customers** table doesn't really matter, so close the **Customers** table without saving changes.

CLOSE the *GardenCo* database.

Filtering Information in a Table

Microsoft Office Specialist

Sorting the information in a table organizes it in a logical manner, but you still have the entire table to deal with. If your goal is to locate all records containing information in one or more fields that match a particular pattern, one of the available Filter commands will satisfy your needs. For example, you could quickly create a filter to locate every customer of The Garden Company who lives in Seattle, or everyone who placed an order on January 13, or all customers who live outside of the United States.

You can apply simple filters while viewing information in a table or a form. These filters are applied to the contents of a selected field, but you can apply another filter to the results of the first one to further refine your search.

Tip The Filter commands you will use in this exercise are available by pointing to Filter on the Records menu; by clicking buttons on the toolbar; and by looking at the shortcut menu. However, not all Filter commands are available in each of these places.

Wildcards

When you don't know or aren't sure of a character or set of characters, you can use *wildcard characters* as placeholders for those unknown characters in your search criteria. The most common wildcards are listed in this table:

Character	Description	Example
*	Match any number of characters.	*Lname = Co** returns Colman and Conroy
?	Match any single alphabetic character.	*Fname = eri?* returns Eric and Erik
#	Match any single numeric character.	*ID = 1##* returns any ID from 100 through 199

In this exercise, you will practice several methods of filtering information in a table.

USE the *GardenCo* database in the practice file folder for this topic. This practice file is located in the *My Documents\Microsoft Press\Access 2003 SBS\Queries\FilterDS* folder and can also be accessed by clicking *Start/All Programs/Microsoft Press/Access 2003 Step by Step*.
OPEN the *GardenCo* database and acknowledge the safety warning, if necessary.

Filter By
Selection

1 Open the **Customers** table in Datasheet view.

2 Click any instance of **Sidney** in the **City** field, and then click the **Filter By Selection** button.

The number of customers displayed in the table changes from *110* to *2,* because only two customers live in Sidney.

Important When you filter a table, the records that don't match the filter aren't removed from the table; they are simply not displayed.

3 Click the **Remove Filter** button to redisplay the rest of the customers.

Remove Filter

4 What if you want a list of all customers who live anywhere that has a postal code starting with *V7L*? Find an example of this type of postal code in the table, select the characters **V7L**, and then click the **Filter By Selection** button again.

Only the two records with postal codes starting with *V7L* are now visible.

5 Click **Remove Filter**.

6 What if this table is enormous and you aren't sure if it contains even one *V7L*? Right-click any postal code, click **Filter For** on the shortcut menu, type V7L* in the cell, and press ⌨Enter to see the same results.

The asterisk (*) is a wildcard that tells Access to search for any entry in the postal code field that starts with *V7L*.

7 To find out how many customers live outside the United States, remove the current filter, right-click the **Country** field in any USA record, and click **Filter Excluding Selection** on the shortcut menu.

You see all customers from other countries (in this case, only Canada).

8 To experiment with one more filtering technique, remove the filter, save and close the **Customers** table, and double-click **Orders** to open the table in Datasheet view.

9 To find all orders taken by Michael Emanuel on January 23, right-click **Emanuel, Michael** in the **EmployeeID** field, and click **Filter By Selection** on the shortcut menu.

Troubleshooting If you do not see employee names listed in the EmployeeID field, it is because you continued with the database from the previous exercise. You must use the practice database supplied for this exercise. For instructions on installing the practice files, see "Using the Book's CD-ROM" on page xiii.

10 Right-click **1/23/2003** in the **OrderDate** field, and again click **Filter By Selection** on the shortcut menu.

You now have a list of Michael's orders on the 23rd of January. You could continue to refine this list by filtering on another field, or you could sort the results by clicking in a field and then clicking one of the Sort buttons.

Tip After you have located just the information you want and have organized it appropriately, you can display the results in a form or report. Click the New Object button on the toolbar, and follow the directions.

11 Remove the filters by clicking the **Remove Filter** button.

12 Save and close the **Orders** table.

CLOSE the *GardenCo* database.

Tip You can use the Filter commands to filter the information in a table when you are viewing it in a form. The Filter For command is often useful with forms because you don't have to be able to see the desired selection.

Filtering by Form

Microsoft Office Specialist

The Filter By Form command provides a quick and easy way to filter a table based on the information in several fields. If you open a table and then click the Filter By Form button, what you see looks like a simple datasheet. However, each of the blank cells is a combo box with a scrollable drop-down list of all the entries in that field.

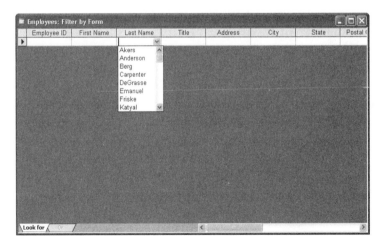

You can make a selection from the list and click the Apply Filter button to display only the records containing your selection.

Using Filter By Form on a table that has only a few fields, such as this one, is easy. But using it on a table that has a few dozen fields gets a bit cumbersome. Then it's easier to use Filter By Form in the form version of the table. If you open a form and then click Filter By Form, you see an empty form. Clicking in any box and then clicking its down arrow displays a list of all the entries in the field.

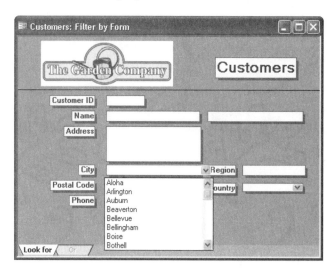

If you make a selection and click the ApplyFilter button, clicking the Next Record navigation button displays the first record that meets your selection criteria, then the next, and so on.

Tip Filter By Form offers the same features and techniques whether you are using it in a form or a table. Because defining the filter is sometimes easier in a form and viewing the results is sometimes easier in a table, you might consider using AutoForm to quickly create a form for a table. You can then use the form with Filter By Form rather than the table, and then switch to Datasheet view to look at the results.

In this exercise, you will try to track down a customer whose last name you have forgotten. You're pretty sure the name starts with S and the customer is from California or Washington, so you're going to use Filter By Form to try to locate the customer's record.

USE the *GardenCo* database in the practice file folder for this topic. This practice file is located in the *My Documents\Microsoft Press\Access 2003 SBS\Queries\FilterForm* folder and can also be accessed by clicking *Start/All Programs/Microsoft Press/Access 2003 Step by Step*.
OPEN the *GardenCo* database and acknowledge the safety warning, if necessary.

1 Click **Forms** on the **Objects** bar, and double-click **Customers** to open the **Customers** form in Form view.

2 Click the **Filter By Form** button on the toolbar.

Filter By Form

The Customers form, which displays the information from one record, is replaced by its Filter By Form version, which has a blank box for each field and the "Look for" and "Or" tabs at the bottom.

3 Click the second **Name** box (last name), type s*, and press Enter to tell Access to display all last names starting with S.

Access converts your entry to the proper format, or *syntax*, for this type of expression: *Like "s*"*.

4 Click the **Region** box, and click **CA** in the drop-down list.

5 Click the **Apply Filter** button to see only the customers living in California whose last names begin with S.

Apply Filter

Access replaces the filter window with the regular Customers form, and the navigation bar at the bottom of the form indicates that three filtered records are available.

6 Click the **Filter By Form** button to switch back to the filter.

Your filter criteria are still displayed. When you enter filter criteria using any method, they are saved as a form property and are available until they are replaced by other criteria.

7 To add the customers from another state, click the **Or** tab.

This tab has the same blank cells as the "Look for" tab. You can switch back and forth between the two tabs to confirm that your criteria haven't been cleared.

Tip When you display the "Or" tab, a second "Or" tab appears so that you can include a third state if you want.

8 Type s* in the **LastName** box, type or click **WA** in the **Region** box, and then click the **Apply Filter** button.

You can scroll through the filtered Customers form to view the six matched records.

9 Close the **Customers** form.

CLOSE the *GardenCo* database.

Locating Information that Matches Multiple Criteria

*Microsoft
Office
Specialist*
Filter By Selection, Filter For <input>, and Filter By Form are quick and easy ways to hone in on the information you need, as long as your filter criteria are fairly simple. But suppose The Garden Company needs to locate all the orders shipped to Midwest states between specific dates by either of two shippers. When you need to search a single table for records that meet multiple criteria or that require complex expressions as criteria, you can use the Advanced Filter/Sort command.

You work with the Advanced Filter/Sort command in the design grid. You can use this *design grid* to work with only one table.

Table field list   Design grid

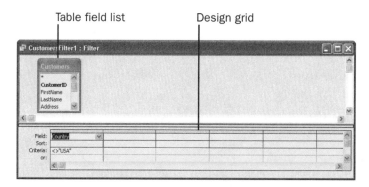

Tip If you create a simple query in the filter window that you think you might like to use again, you can save it as a query. Either click Save As Query on the File menu; click the Save As Query button on the toolbar; or right-click in the filter window, and then on the shortcut menu, click Save As Query.

In this exercise, you will create a filter to locate customers in two states using the Advanced Filter/Sort command. After locating the customers, you will experiment a bit with the design grid to get a better understanding of its filtering capabilities.

USE the *GardenCo* database in the practice file folder for this topic. This practice file is located in the *My Documents\Microsoft Press\Access 2003 SBS\Queries\AdvFilter* folder and can also be accessed by clicking *Start/All Programs/Microsoft Press/Access 2003 Step by Step*.
OPEN the *GardenCo* database and acknowledge the safety warning, if necessary.

1 Click **Tables** on the **Objects** bar, and double-click **Customers** to open the **Customers** table in Datasheet view.

2 On the **Records** menu, point to **Filter**, and then click **Advanced Filter/Sort**.

Tip   Remember, if you don't see the command on the menu, you can hover over a short menu to display the long menu, or click the double-chevrons at the bottom of the menu.

Access opens the filter window with the Customers field list in the top area.

3   If the design grid is not blank, on the **Edit** menu, click **Clear Grid**.

4   Double-click **LastName** to copy it to the **Field** cell in the first column of the design grid.

5   Click in the **Criteria** cell under **LastName**, type s*, and press ⌷Enter⌷.

Access changes the criterion to *"Like "s*""*.

6   Scroll to the bottom of the **Customers** field list, and double-click **Region** to copy it to the next available column of the design grid.

7   Click in the **Criteria** cell under **Region**, type ca or wa, and press ⌷Enter⌷.

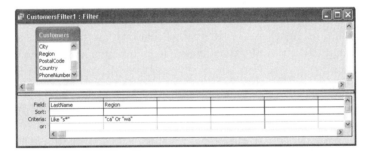

Your entry has changed to *"ca" Or "wa"*. The filter will now match customers with a last name beginning with s who live in California or Washington.

8   On the **Filter** menu, click **Apply Filter/Sort** to view the records that match the criteria.

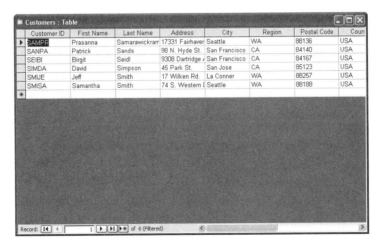

> **Tip** You can keep an eye on both the filter window and the table window if you reduce both in size.

9 On the **Records** menu, click **Filter** and then **Advanced Filter/Sort** to return to the filter window.

10 Click in the **or** cell in the **LastName** column, type b*, and press Enter.

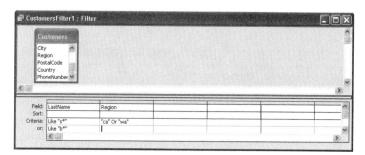

11 On the **Filter** menu, click **Apply Filter/Sort**.

The result includes records for all customers with last names that begin with *s* or *b*, but some of the *b* names live in Montana and Oregon. If you look again at the design grid, you can see that the filter is formed by combining the fields in the Criteria row with the *And* operator, combining the fields in the "Or" row with the *And* operator, and then using the *Or* operator to combine the two rows. So the filter is searching for customers with names beginning with *s* who live in California or Washington, or customers with names beginning with *b*, regardless of where they live.

12 Return to the filter window, type ca or wa in the **or** cell under **Region**, and press Enter.

13 Apply the filter again to see only customers from California and Washington.

14 Close the **Customers** table without saving your changes.

CLOSE the *GardenCo* database.

Expressions

The word *expressions*, as used in Access, is synonymous with *formulas*. An expression is a combination of *operators*, *constants*, *functions*, and *control properties* that evaluates to a single value. Access builds formulas using the format *a=b+c*, where *a* is the result and *=b+c* is the expression. An expression can be used to assign properties to tables or forms, to determine values in fields or reports, as part of queries, and in many other places.

The expressions you use in Access combine multiple *criteria* to define a set of conditions that a record must meet before Access will select it as the result of a filter or query. Multiple criteria are combined using logical, comparison, and arithmetic operators. Different types of expressions use different operators.

The most common *logical operators* are *And*, *Or*, and *Not*. When criteria are combined using the *And* operator, a record is selected only if it meets them all. When criteria are combined using the *Or* operator, a record is selected if it meets any one of them. The *Not* operator selects all records that don't match its criterion.

Common *comparison operators* include < (less than), > (greater than), and = (equal). These basic operators can be combined to form <= (less than or equal to), >= (greater than or equal to), and <> (not equal to). The *Like* operator is sometimes grouped with the comparison operators and is used to test whether or not text matches a pattern.

The common *arithmetic operators* are + (add), - (subtract), * (multiply), and / (divide), which are used with numerals. A related operator, & (a text form of +) is used to concatenate—or put together—two text strings.

Creating a Query in Design View

When you want to work with more than one table, you need to move beyond filters and into the realm of queries. The most common type of query selects records that meet specific conditions, but there are several other types, as follows:

■ A *select query* retrieves data from one or more tables and displays the results in a datasheet. You can also use a select query to group records and calculate sums, counts, averages, and other types of totals. You can work with the results of a select query in Datasheet view to update records in one or more related tables at the same time.

   ■ A *duplicate query* is a form of select query that locates records that have the same information in one or more fields that you specify. The Find Duplicates Query Wizard guides you through the process of specifying the table and fields to use in the query.

■ An *unmatched query* is a form of select query that locates records in one table that don't have related records in another table. For example, you could use this to locate people in the customer table who don't have an order in the order table. The Find Unmatched Query Wizard guides you through the process of specifying the tables and fields to use in the query.

■ A *parameter query* prompts you for information to be used in the query— for example, a range of dates. This type of query is particularly useful if the query is the basis for a report that is run periodically.

■ A *crosstab query* calculates and restructures data for easier analysis. It can calculate a sum, average, count, or other type of total for data that is grouped by two types of information—one down the left side of the datasheet and one across the top. The cell at the junction of each row and column displays the results of the query's calculation.

■ An *action query* updates or makes changes to multiple records in one operation. It is essentially a select query that performs an action on the results of the selection process. Four types of actions are available: *delete queries*, which delete records from one or more tables; *update queries*, which make changes to records in one or more tables; *append queries*, which add records from one or more tables to the end of one or more other tables; and *make-table queries*, which create a new table from all or part of the data in one or more tables.

Tip   Access also includes SQL queries, but you won't be working with this type of query in this book.

Filters and Sorts vs. Queries

The major differences between using filtering or sorting and using a query are:

■ The Filter and Sort commands are usually faster to implement than queries.

■ The Filter and Sort commands are not saved, or are saved only temporarily. A query can be saved permanently and run again at any time.

■ The Filter and Sort commands are applied only to the table or form that is currently open. A query can be based on multiple tables and other queries, which don't have to be open.

You can create a query by hand or by using a wizard. Regardless of how you create the query, what you create is a statement that describes the conditions that must be met for records to be matched in one or more tables. When you run the query, the matching records appear in a datasheet in Datasheet view.

In this exercise, you will create an order entry form that salespeople can fill in as they take orders over the phone. The form will be based on a select query that combines information from the Order Details table and the Products table. The query will create a datasheet listing all products ordered with the unit price, quantity ordered, discount, and extended price. Because the extended price isn't stored in the database, you will calculate this amount directly in the query.

USE the *GardenCo* database in the practice file folder for this topic. This practice file is located in the *My Documents\Microsoft Press\Access 2003 SBS\Queries\QueryDes* folder and can also be accessed by clicking *Start/All Programs/Microsoft Press/Access 2003 Step by Step*.
OPEN the *GardenCo* database and acknowledge the safety warning, if necessary.

1 On the **Objects** bar, click **Queries**.

2 Double-click **Create query in Design view**.

Access opens the query window in Design view and then opens the Show Table dialog box.

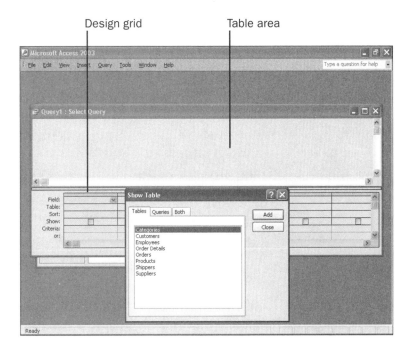

Design grid   Table area

You can use the Show Table dialog box to specify which tables and saved queries to include in the current query.

3 With the **Tables** tab active, double-click **Order Details** and **Products** to add both tables to the query window. Then close the dialog box.

Each table you added is represented in the top portion of the window by a small field list window with the name of the table—in this case, Order Details and Products—in its title bar.

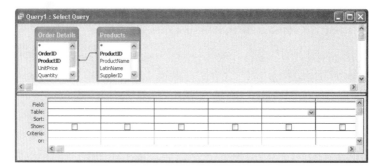

At the top of each list is an asterisk, which represents all the fields in the list. Primary key fields in each list are bold. The line from ProductID in the Order Details table to ProductID in the Products table indicates that these two fields are related.

Tip To add more tables to a query, reopen the Show Tables dialog box by right-clicking the top portion of the query window and clicking Show Table on the shortcut menu; or by clicking the Show Table button on the toolbar.

The lower area of the query window is taken up by a design grid where you will build the query's criteria.

4 To include fields in the query, you drag them from the lists at the top of the window to consecutive columns in the design grid. Drag the following fields from the two lists:

From table	Field
Order Details	OrderID
Products	ProductName
Order Details	UnitPrice
Order Details	Quantity
Order Details	Discount

Tip You can quickly copy a field to the next open column in the design grid by double-clicking the field. To copy all fields to the grid, double-click the title bar above the field list to select the entire list, and then drag the selection over the grid. When you release the mouse button, Access adds the fields to the columns in order. You can drag the asterisk to a column in the grid to include all the fields in the query, but you also have to drag individual fields to the grid if you want to sort on those fields or add conditions to them.

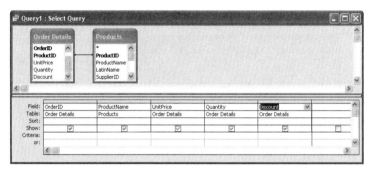

Run

5 Click the **Run** button to run the query and display the results in Datasheet view.

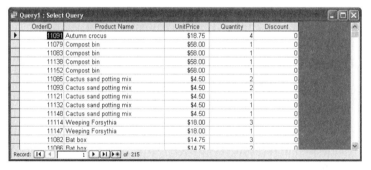

The results show that the query is working so far. There are two things left to do: sort the results on the OrderID field and add a field for calculating the extended price, which is the unit price times the quantity sold minus any discount.

View

6 Click the **View** button to return to Design view.

The third row in the design grid is labeled Sort. If you click in the Sort cell in any column, you can specify whether to sort in ascending order, descending order, or not at all.

133

7 Click in the **Sort** cell in the **OrderID** column, click the down arrow, and click **Ascending**.

Neither of the tables includes an extended price field. There is no point in entering this information in a table, because you will use the Expression Builder to insert an expression in the design grid that computes this price from existing information.

8 Right-click the **Field** row of the first blank column in the design grid (the sixth column), and on the shortcut menu, click **Build** to open the **Expression Builder** dialog box.

Operator buttons   Expression box

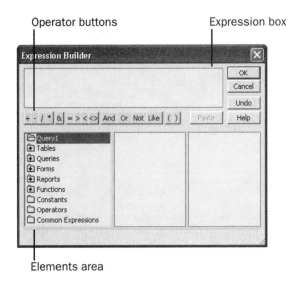

Elements area

Here is the expression you will build:

```
<CCur([Order Details].[UnitPrice]*[Quantity]*(1-[Discount]))>
```

The only part of this expression that you probably can't figure out is the CCur function, which converts the results of the math inside its parentheses to currency format.

9 Double-click the **Functions** folder in the first column of the elements area, and then click **Built-In Functions**.

The categories of built-in functions are displayed in the second column.

10 Click **Conversion** in the second column to limit the functions in the third column to those in that category. Then double-click **Ccur** in the third column.

134

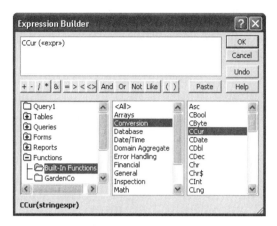

You've inserted the currency conversion function in the expression box. The *<<expr>>* inside the parentheses represents the other expressions that will eventually result in the number Access should convert to currency format.

11 Click **<<expr>>** to select it so that the next thing you enter will replace it.

12 The next element you want in the expression is the **UnitPrice** field from the Order Details table. Double-click the **Tables** object, click **Order Details**, and then double-click **UnitPrice**.

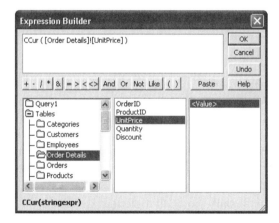

Your last action left the insertion point after UnitPrice, which is exactly where you want it.

13 Now you want to multiply the amount in the **UnitPrice** field by the amount in the **Quantity** field. Start by clicking the * (asterisk) button in the row of operator buttons below the expression box.

Access inserts the multiplication sign and another *<<Expr>>* placeholder.

14 Click **<<Expr>>** to select it, and then insert the **Quantity** field by double-clicking it in the second column.

What you have entered so far multiplies the price by the number ordered, which results in the total cost for this item. However, The Garden Company offers discounts on certain items at different times of the year. The amount of the discount is entered by the sales clerk and stored in the Order Details table. In the table, the discount is expressed as the percentage to deduct—usually 10 to 20 percent. But it is easier to compute the percentage the customer will pay—usually 80 to 90 percent of the regular price—than it is to compute the discount and then subtract it from the total cost.

15 Type *(1-, then double-click **Discount**, and type), and then widen the window to see the whole expression.

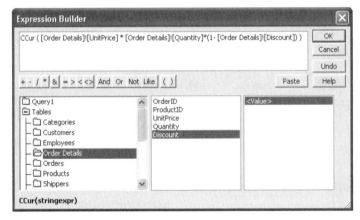

Remember that the discount is formatted in the datasheet as a percentage, but it is stored as a decimal number between 0 and 1. When you look at it you might see 10%, but what is actually stored in the database is 0.1. So if the discount is 10 percent, the result of *(1-Discount) is *.9. In other words, the formula multiplies the unit price by the quantity and then multiplies that result by 0.9.

16 Click **OK**.

Access closes the Expression Builder and copies the expression to the design grid.

17 Press Enter to move the insertion point out of the field, which completes the entry of the expression.

Tip   You can quickly make a column in the design grid as wide as its contents by double-clicking the line in the gray selection bar that separates the column from the column to its right.

18   Access has given the expression the name *Expr1*. This name isn't particularly meaningful, so rename it by double-clicking **Expr1** and then typing ExtendedPrice.

19   Click the **View** button to see the results in Datasheet view.

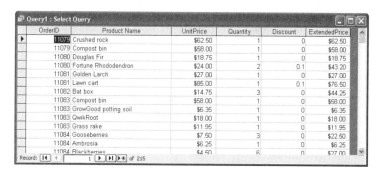

The orders are now sorted on the OrderID field, and the extended price is calculated in the last field.

20   Scroll down to see a few records with discounts.

If you check the math, you will see that the query calculates the extended price correctly.

21   Close the query window, and when prompted to save the query, click **Yes**. Type Order Details Extended to name the query, and click **OK** to close it.

CLOSE the *GardenCo* database.

Expression Builder

When an expression is a valid filter or query option, you can usually either type the expression or use the Expression Builder to create it. You open the Expression Builder by either clicking Build on a shortcut menu or clicking the ... button (sometimes referred to as the Build button) at the right end of a box that can accept an expression.

The Expression Builder isn't a wizard; it doesn't lead you through the process of building an expression. But it does provide a hierarchical list of most of the elements that you can include in an expression. After looking at the list, you can either type your expression in the expression box, or you can select functions, operators, and other elements to copy them to the expression box, and then click OK to transfer them to the filter or query.

Creating a Query with a Wizard

Microsoft Office Specialist

The process used to create a simple select query with the Query Wizard is almost identical to that for creating a form with the Form Wizard. With the Query Wizard, you can add one or more fields from existing tables or queries to the new query.

For Access to work effectively with multiple tables, it must understand the relationships between the fields in those tables. You have to create these relationships before using the Query Wizard, by clicking the Relationships button and then dragging a field in one table over the identical field in another table (the field names don't have to be the same in each table, but the field contents must represent the same information).

In this exercise, you will use the Query Wizard to create a new query that combines information from the Customers and Orders tables to provide information about each order. These tables are related through their common CustomerID fields. (This relationship has already been established in the GardenCo database files used in this chapter.)

USE the *GardenCo* database in the practice file folder for this topic. This practice file is located in the *My Documents\Microsoft Press\Access 2003 SBS\Queries\QueryWiz* folder and can also be accessed by clicking *Start/All Programs/Microsoft Press/Access 2003 Step by Step*.
OPEN the *GardenCo* database and acknowledge the safety warning, if necessary.

1 On the **Objects** bar, click **Queries**, and then double-click **Create query by using wizard**.

The first page of the Simple Query Wizard opens.

Tip You can also start the Query Wizard by clicking Query on the Insert menu or clicking the arrow to the right of the New Object button list, and then double-clicking Simple Query Wizard.

2 In the **Tables/Queries** list, click **Table: Orders**.

3 Click the **>>** button to move all available fields in the **Available Fields** list to the **Selected Fields** list.

4 Select **Table: Customers** from the **Tables/Queries** list.

5 In the **Available Fields** list, double-click the **Address**, **City**, **Region**, **PostalCode**, and **Country** fields to move them to the **Selected Fields** list, and then click **Next**.

Tip If the relationship between two tables hasn't already been established, you will be prompted to define it and then start the wizard again.

6 Click **Next** again to accept the default option of showing details in the results of the query.

7 Change the query title to Orders Qry, leave the **Open the query to view information** option selected, and then click **Finish**.

Access runs the query and displays the results in Datasheet view. You can scroll through the results and see that information is displayed for all the orders.

View Design

8 Click the **View** button to view the query in Design view.

Notice that the Show box is, by default, selected for each of the fields used in the query. If you want to use a field in a query—for example, to sort on, to set criteria for, or in a calculation—but don't want to see the field in the results datasheet, you can clear its Show check box.

View

9 Clear the **Show** check box for **OrderID**, **CustomerID**, and **EmployeeID**, and then click the **View** button to switch back to Datasheet view.

The three fields have been removed from the results datasheet.

10 Click the **View** button to return to Design view.

This query returns all records in the Orders table. To have this query match the records for a range of dates, you will convert it to a parameter query, which asks for the date range each time you run it.

11 In the **OrderDate** column, click in the **Criteria** cell, and type the following, exactly as shown:

Between [Type the beginning date:] And [Type the ending date:]

12 Click the **Run** button to run the query.

13 In the dialog box displayed, type 1/1/03, and press [Enter].

14 In the second **Enter Parameter Value** dialog box, type 1/31/03, and press [Enter] again.

The datasheet is displayed again, this time listing only orders between the parameter dates.

15 Close the datasheet, clicking **Yes** to save the query.

CLOSE the *GardenCo* database.

Performing Calculations in a Query

Microsoft
Office
Specialist

You typically use a query to locate all the records that meet some criteria. But sometimes you are not as interested in the details of all the records as you are in summarizing them in some way. As an example, you might want to know how many orders have been placed this year or the total dollar value of all orders placed. The easiest way to get this information is to create a query that groups the necessary fields and does the math for you. To do this, you use *aggregate functions* in the query.

Access queries support the following aggregate functions:

Function	Calculates
Sum	Total of the values in a field
Avg	Average of the values in a field
Count	Number of values in a field, not counting Null (blank) values
Min	Lowest value in a field
Max	Highest value in a field
StDev	Standard deviation of the values in a field
Var	Variance of the values in a field

In this exercise, you will create a query that calculates the total number of products in The Garden Company's inventory, the average price of all the products, and the total value of the inventory.

USE the *GardenCo* database in the practice file folder for this topic. This practice file is located in the *My Documents\Microsoft Press\Access 2003 SBS\Queries\Aggregate* folder and can also be accessed by clicking *Start/All Programs/Microsoft Press/Access 2003 Step by Step*.
OPEN the *GardenCo* database and acknowledge the safety warning, if necessary.

1   On the **Objects** bar, click **Queries**, and then double-click **Create query in Design view**.

Access first opens the query window in Design view and then displays the Show Table dialog box.

2   In the **Show Table** dialog box, double-click **Products**, and click **Close**.

Access adds the Products table to the query window and closes the Show Table dialog box.

3 In the list of fields in the **Products** table, double-click **ProductID** and then **UnitPrice**.

Access moves both fields to the design grid.

Σ
Totals

4 Click the **Totals** button on the toolbar.

A row named *Total* is added to the design grid.

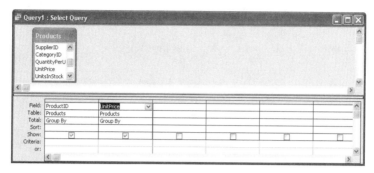

5 Click in the **Total** cell of the **ProductID** column, click the down arrow, and click **Count** in the drop-down list.

Access enters the word *Count* in the Total cell. When you run the query, this function will return a count of the number of records containing a value in the ProductID field.

6 In the **UnitPrice** column, set the **Total** cell to **Avg**.

When you run the query, this function will return the average of all the UnitPrice values.

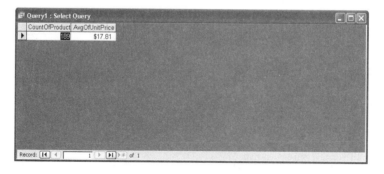
Run

7 Click the **Run** button.

The result of the query is a single record containing the count and the average price.

141

View

8 Click the **View** button to return to Design view.

9 In the **Field** cell of the third column, type **UnitPrice*UnitsInStock** and press ⏎ Enter.

The text you typed is changed to *Expr1: [UnitPrice]*[UnitsInStock]*. This expression will multiply the price of each product by the number of units in stock.

10 Set the **Total** cell of the third column to **Sum** to return the sum of all the values calculated by the expression.

11 Select **Expr1:**, and type **Value of Inventory:**.

12 Run the query again.

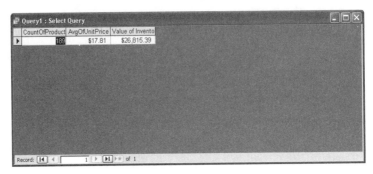

13 Close the query window, clicking **No** when prompted to save the query.

CLOSE the *GardenCo* database.

Key Points

■ Microsoft Office Access 2003 provides a variety of tools you can use to organize the display of information in a database and to locate specific items of information, making it easy to search through and find information in your database, even as it grows in size and complexity.

■ You can sort through a table in either ascending or descending order, based on the values in any field (or combination of fields). In Access, numbers can be treated as text or numerals.

■ You can filter a table so that information containing some combination of characters is displayed (or excluded from the display). You can apply simple filters while viewing information in a table or a form. These filters are applied to the contents of a selected field, but you can apply another filter to the results of the first one to further refine your search.

■ You can use the Filter By Form command to filter a table or form based on the information in several fields. Since defining a filter is often easier in a form and viewing the results is easier in a table, you can use AutoForm to quickly create a form for a table. You can use the form with Filter By Form, and then switch to Datasheet view to see the results.

■ When you need to search a single table for records that meet multiple criteria or that require complex expressions as criteria, you can use the Advanced Filter/Sort command.

■ You can create queries to display specific fields from specific records from one or more tables, even designing the query to perform calculations for you. You can then save your queries for later use.

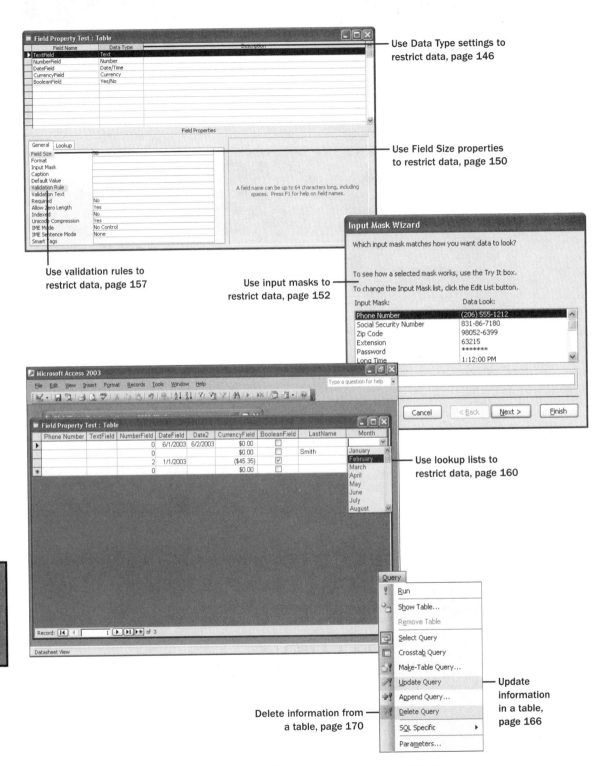

Use Data Type settings to restrict data, page 146

Use Field Size properties to restrict data, page 150

Use validation rules to restrict data, page 157

Use input masks to restrict data, page 152

Use lookup lists to restrict data, page 160

Update information in a table, page 166

Delete information from a table, page 170

Chapter 6 at a Glance

6 Keeping Your Information Accurate

In this chapter you will learn to:

✔ Use Data Type settings to restrict data.

✔ Use Field Size properties to restrict data.

✔ Use input masks to restrict data.

✔ Use validation rules to restrict data.

✔ Use lookup lists to restrict data.

✔ Update information in a table.

✔ Delete information from a table.

Depending on how much information you have and how organized you are, you might compare a database to an old shoebox or a file cabinet, into which you toss items such as photographs, bills, receipts, and a variety of other paperwork for later retrieval. However, neither a shoebox nor a file cabinet restricts what you can place in it (other than how much can fit in it) or imposes any order on its content. It is up to you to decide what you store there and to organize it properly so that you can find it when you next need it.

When you create a database with Microsoft Office Access 2003, you can set *properties* that restrict what can be entered in it, thereby keeping the database organized and useful. For example, The Garden Company wouldn't want its employees to enter text into *fields* that should contain numbers, such as price fields. Similarly, they wouldn't want to encourage employees to enter a long text description in a field when a simple "yes" or "no" answer would work best. The *field properties* that control input are: Required, Allow Zero Length, Field Size, Input Mask, and Validation Rule. The Required and Allow Zero Length properties are fairly obvious. If the Required property is set to *Yes*, the field can't be left blank. However, if Allow Zero Length is set to *Yes*, you can enter an empty *string* (two quotation marks with nothing in between), which looks like an empty field. The other properties are more complex, so you'll focus on them in the exercises in this chapter.

Tip Each property has many options. For more information about how to use properties, search for *field property* in Access online Help.

To ensure the ongoing accuracy of a database, you can create and run *action queries* that quickly update information or delete selected records from a table. For example, The Garden Company might decide to increase the price of all products in one category, or to remove one entire product line. This type of updating is easy to do with an action query. Not only does using a query save time, but it avoids human-input errors.

The exercises in this chapter demonstrate how to use the *data type* setting and some of the field properties to restrict the data that can be entered in a table or form. It is difficult to experiment with field properties in a table that is already filled with information because changing a field's data type or properties can destroy or alter the data. For that reason, the first few exercises in this chapter use a new database that you will create just for the purpose of experimenting with data types and properties. Then you will resume working with sample GardenCo database files provided on the book's companion CD.

See Also Do you need only a quick refresher on the topics in this chapter? See the Quick Reference entries on pages xxxvii–xxxix.

Important Before you can use the practice files in this chapter, you need to install them from the book's companion CD to their default location. See "Using the Book's CD-ROM" on page xiii for more information.

Using Data Type Settings to Restrict Data

Microsoft Office Specialist

The Data Type setting restricts entries to a specific type of data: text, numbers, dates, and so on. If, for example, the data type is set to Number and you attempt to enter text, Access refuses the entry and displays a warning.

In this exercise, you will create a new blank database, add fields of the most common data types, and experiment with how the Data Type setting and Field Size property can be used to restrict the data entered into a table.

BE SURE TO start Access before beginning this exercise.

1. In the **New File** task pane, click **Blank Database** in the **New** section to display the **File New Database** dialog box.

   If the New File task pane does not appear, on the toolbar, click the New button.

New

2   In the **File name** box, type *FieldTest*, navigate to the *My Documents\Microsoft Press \Access 2003 SBS\Accurate\DataType* folder, and then click **Create**.

Access opens the database window for the new database.

3   Double-click **Create table in Design view**.

A blank Table window opens in Design view so that you can define the fields that categorize the information in the table. You will define five fields, one for each of the data types: *Text*, *Number*, *Date/Time*, *Currency*, and *Yes/No*.

4   Click in the first **Field Name** cell, type *TextField*, and press ⌷ to move to the **Data Type** cell.

5   The data type defaults to **Text**, which is the type you want. Press ⌷ twice to accept the default data type and move the insertion point to the next row.

6   Type *NumberField*, and press ⌷ to move to the **Data Type** cell.

7   Click the down arrow to expand the list of data types, click **Number**, and then press ⌷ twice.

> **Tip**   Rather than displaying the list of data types and clicking one, you can type the first character of the desired type, and it will be entered in the cell.

8   Repeat steps 4 through 7 to add the following fields:

Field	Data type
DateField	Date/Time
CurrencyField	Currency
BooleanField	Yes/No

> **Tip**   The data type referred to as Yes/No in Access is more commonly called *Boolean* (in honor of George Boole, an early mathematician and logistician). This data type can hold either of two mutually exclusive values, often expressed as *yes/no*, *1/0*, *on/off*, or *true/false*.

Save

9   Click the **Save** button, type *Field Property Test* to name the table, and then click **OK**.

Access displays a dialog box recommending that you create a primary key.

10 You don't need a primary key for this exercise, so click **No**.

11 Click the row selector for **TextField** to select the first row.

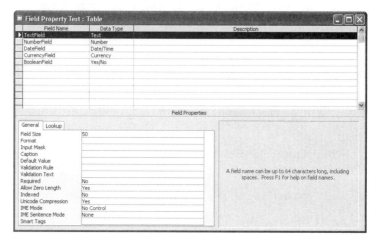

The properties of the selected field are displayed in the lower portion of the dialog box.

View

12 Click in each field and review its properties, and then click the **View** button to display the table in Datasheet view.

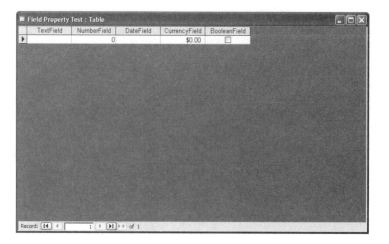

13   The insertion point should be in the first field. Type This entry is 32 characters long, and press ⟨Tab⟩ to move to the next field.

14   Type Five hundred, and press ⟨Tab⟩.

The data type for this field is Number. Access displays an alert box refusing your text entry.

15   Click **OK**, replace the text with the number 500, and press ⟨Tab⟩.

16   Type a number or text (anything but a date) in the date field, and press ⟨Tab⟩. When Access refuses it, click **OK**, type Jan 1, and press ⟨Tab⟩.

The date field accepts almost any entry that can be recognized as a date, and displays it in the default date format. Depending on the format on your computer, Jan 1 might be displayed as *1/1/2003* or *1/1/03*.

Tip   If you enter a month and day but no year in a date field, Access assumes the date is in the current year. If you enter a month, day, and two-digit year from 00 through 29, Access assumes the year is 2000 through 2029. If you enter a two-digit year that is greater than 29, Access assumes you mean 1930 through 1999.

17   Type any text or a date in the currency field, and press ⟨Tab⟩. When Access refuses the entry, click **OK**, type –45.3456 in the field, and press ⟨Tab⟩.

Access stores the number you entered but displays ($45.35), the default format for displaying negative currency numbers.

Tip   Access uses the regional settings in the Microsoft Windows Control Panel to determine the display format for date, time, currency, and other numbers. If you intend to share database files with people in other countries, you might want to create custom formats to ensure that the correct currency symbol is always displayed with your values. Otherwise, the numbers won't change, but displaying them as dollars, pounds, pesos, or euros will radically alter their value.

18   Enter text or a number in the **Boolean** field. Then click anywhere in the field to toggle the check box between **Yes** (checked) and **No** (not checked), finishing with the field in the checked state.

This field won't accept anything you type; you can only switch between two predefined values.

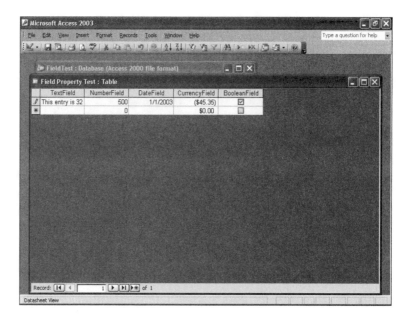

Tip In Design view, you can open the Properties dialog box, and on the Lookup tab, set the Boolean field to display as a check box, text box, or combo box. You can also set the Format property on the General tab to use True/False, Yes/No, or On/Off as the displayed values in this field (though the stored values will always be -1 and 0).

19 Close the table.

CLOSE the *FieldTest* database.

Using Field Size Properties to Restrict Data

Microsoft Office Specialist

You can set the Field Size property for the Text, Number, and AutoNumber data types. This property restricts the number of characters that you can enter in a text field and the size of numbers that can be entered in a number or AutoNumber field. For text fields, the Field Size property can be set to any number from 0 to 255. AutoNumber fields are automatically set to Long Integer. Number fields can be set to any of the following values:

Setting	Description
Byte	Stores numbers from 0 to 255 (no fractions).
Integer	Stores numbers from −32,768 to 32,767 (no fractions).
Long Integer	(The default.) Stores numbers from −2,147,483,648 to 2,147,483,647 (no fractions).

Setting	Description
Single	Stores numbers from –3.402823E38 to –1.401298E–45 for negative values and from 1.401298E–45 to 3.402823E38 for positive values.
Double	Stores numbers from –1.79769313486231E308 to –4.94065645841247E–324 for negative values and from 1.79769313486231E308 to 4.94065645841247E–324 for positive values.
Decimal	Stores numbers from -10^28 -1 through 10^28 -1.

By setting the Field Size property to a value that allows the largest valid entry, you prevent the user from entering certain types of invalid information. If you try to type more characters in a text field than the number allowed by the Field Size setting, Access beeps and refuses to accept the entry. Likewise, a value that is below or above the limits of a number field is rejected when you try to move out of the field.

In this exercise, you will change the Field Size property for several fields to see the impact this has on data already in the table and on new data that you enter.

USE the *FieldTest* database in the practice file folder for this topic. This practice file is located in the *My Documents\Microsoft Press\Access 2003 SBS\Accurate\FieldSize* folder and can also be accessed by clicking *Start/All Programs/Microsoft Press/Access 2003 Step by Step*.
OPEN the *FieldTest* database.

1 Open the **Field Property Test** table in Design view.

2 Click in the **TextField** row, and in the **Field Properties** area, change the **Field Size** property from *50* to **12**.

3 Click in the **NumberField** row, click the **Field Size** property, click its down arrow, and change the setting from *Long Integer* to **Byte**.

The number of characters that can be entered in the text field is restricted to 12, and the values that can be entered in the number field are restricted to the range 0 to 255.

View

4 Click the **View** button to return to Datasheet view, clicking **Yes** when prompted to save the table.

The table contains data that doesn't fit these new property settings, so Access displays a warning that some data might be lost.

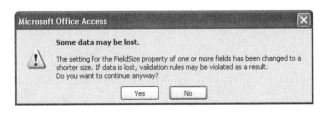

5   Click **Yes** to acknowledge the risk, and click **Yes** again to accept the deletion of the contents of one field.

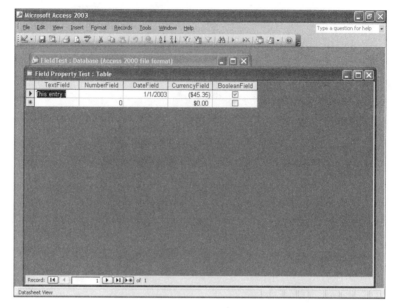

TextField now contains only 12 characters, rather than the 32 you entered. The other 20 characters have been permanently deleted. NumberField is empty because it is now limited to whole numbers from *0* through *255*, and the value of *500* that you entered was deleted.

6   Type **2.5** as the **NumberField** entry, and press [Enter].

The number is rounded to the nearest whole number.

7   Close the table.

CLOSE the *FieldTest* database.

Using Input Masks to Restrict Data

Microsoft Office Specialist

When you use *masks* in tables or forms, people entering information can see at a glance the format in which they should make entries and how long they should be. You can use the InputMask property to control how data is entered in text, number, date/time, and currency fields. This property has three sections, separated by semi-colons, like the mask for a telephone number, shown here:

!\(000") "000\-0000;1;#

The first section contains characters that are used as placeholders for the information to be typed, as well as characters such as parentheses and hyphens. Together, all these characters control the appearance of the entry. The following list explains the purpose of the most common input mask characters:

Character	Description
0	Required digit (0 through 9).
9	Optional digit or space.
#	Optional digit or space; blank positions are converted to spaces; plus and minus signs are allowed.
L	Required letter (A through Z).
?	Optional letter (A through Z).
A	Required letter or digit.
a	Optional letter or digit.
&	Required character (any kind) or a space.
C	Optional character (any kind) or a space.
<	All characters that follow are converted to lowercase.
>	All characters that follow are converted to uppercase.
!	Characters typed into the mask fill it from left to right. You can include the exclamation point anywhere in the input mask.
\	Character that follows is displayed as a literal character.
Password	Creates a password entry box. Any character typed in the box is stored as the character but displayed as an asterisk (*).

Any characters not included in this list are displayed as literal characters. If you want to use one of the special characters in this list as a literal character, precede it with the \ (backslash) character.

The second and third sections of the input mask are optional. Including a 1 or leaving nothing in the second section tells Access to store only the characters entered; including a 0 tells it to store both the characters entered and the mask characters. The character in the third section is displayed in a new record as the placeholder for the characters to be typed. This placeholder defaults to an underscore if the section is omitted.

The input mask !\(000") "000\-0000;1;# creates this display in a field in both a table and a form:

(###) ###-####

In this example, you are restricting the entry to ten digits—no more and no less. Access stores just the digits entered, not the parentheses, space, and dash (though those characters could be displayed in your table, form, or report if you set the correct format property).

In this exercise, you will use the Input Mask Wizard to apply a predefined telephone input mask to a text field, forcing entered numbers into the (206) 555-0001 format. You will then create a custom mask to force the first letter of an entry to be uppercase (a capital letter).

USE the *FieldTest* database in the practice file folder for this topic. This practice file is located in the *My Documents\Microsoft Press\Access 2003 SBS\Accurate\InputMask* folder and can also be accessed by clicking *Start/All Programs/Microsoft Press/Access 2003 Step by Step*.
OPEN the *FieldTest* database.

1 Open the **Field Property Test** table in Design view.

2 In the first blank **Field Name** cell, type PhoneField, and leave the data type set to *Text*.

3 Click the row selector to select the row, and then drag the new field to the top of the field list so that it will appear at the left end of the table.

4 Save the table design, and with **PhoneField** still selected, click **Input Mask** in the **Field Properties** area.

5 Click the ... button to the right of the cell to start the **Input Mask Wizard** and display the first page of the wizard. (Click **Yes** if you are prompted to install this feature.)

Tip You can create an input mask by hand for text, number, date, or currency fields, or you can use this wizard to apply one of several standard masks for text and date fields.

6 With **Phone Number** selected in the **Input Mask** list, click **Next**.

The second page of the wizard displays the input mask and gives you the opportunity to change the placeholder character that will indicate what to type. The exclamation point causes Access to fill the mask from left to right with whatever is typed. The parentheses and hyphen are characters that Access will insert in the speci-fied places. The 9s represent optional digits, and the 0s represent required digits, so you can enter a telephone number with or without an area code.

Tip Because Access fills the mask from left to right, you would have to press the Right Arrow key to move the insertion point past the first three placeholders to enter a telephone number without an area code.

7 Change 999 to 000 to require an area code, and then change the placeholder character to #.

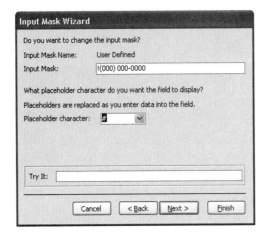

8 Click **Next**.

On the third page of the wizard, you specify whether you want to store the symbols with the data. If you store the symbols, the data will always be displayed in tables, forms, and reports in this format. However, the symbols take up space, meaning that your database will be larger.

9 Accept the default selection—to store data without the symbols—by clicking **Finish**.

Access closes the wizard and displays the edited mask as the Input Mask property.

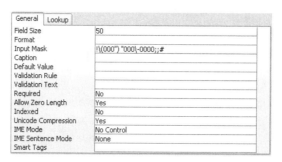

10 Press ⬚Enter⬚ to accept the mask.

Access changes the format of the mask to *!\(000") "000\-0000;;#*. Notice the two semicolons that separate the mask into its three sections. Because you told Access to store data without the symbols, nothing is displayed in the second section of the mask.

New in Office 2003
Property Update Options

Tip   When you press ⬚Enter⬚, a button is added in front of the Input Mask. This is the Property Update Options button, and if you click it, a list of options is displayed. In this case, the only option is to apply the input mask everywhere PhoneField is used. This button disappears when you edit any other property or change to a different field.

View

11 Save your changes, and click the **View** button to return to Datasheet view.

12 Press the ⬚↓⬚ key to move to the new record, and type a series of at least ten digits and then some letters to see how the mask works.

Any letters you type are ignored. The first ten digits are formatted as a telephone number. If you type more than ten digits, they are also ignored. If you type fewer than ten digits and press Tab or Enter, Access warns you that your entry doesn't match the input mask.

Tip   An input mask can contain more than just the placeholders for the data to be entered. If, for example, you type "The number is" in front of the telephone number in the Input Mask property, the default entry for the field is *The number is (###) ###-####*. Then if you place the insertion point to the left of *The* and start typing numbers, the numbers replace the # placeholders, not the text. The Field Size setting is not applied to the characters in the mask, so if this setting is *15*, the entry is not truncated even though the number of displayed characters (including spaces) is 28.

13 Return to Design view, and add a new field below **BooleanField**. Name it LastName. Leave the **Data Type** setting as the default **Text**.

14 Select the new field, click **Input Mask**, type >L<?????????????????? (18 question marks), and press ⌷Enter⌷.

The > forces all following text to be uppercase. The *L* requires a letter. The < forces all following text to be lowercase. Each *?* allows any letter or no letter, and there is one fewer question mark than the maximum number of letters you want to allow in the field (19, including the leading capital letter). The Field Size setting must be greater than this maximum.

15 Save your changes, return to Datasheet view, type smith in the **LastName** field of one of the records, and press ⌷Tab⌷. Try entering SMITH, and then McDonald.

As you can see, only the first letter is capitalized, no matter how you try to type the name, so this type of mask has its limitations. But it can be useful in many situations.

16 Close the table.

CLOSE the *FieldTest* database.

Using Validation Rules to Restrict Data

A *validation rule* is an *expression* that can precisely define the information that will be accepted in one or several fields in a record. You might use a validation rule in a field containing the date an employee was hired to prevent a date in the future from being entered. Or if you make deliveries to only certain local areas, you could use a validation rule on the phone field or ZIP code field to refuse entries from other areas.

You can type validation rules in by hand, or you can use the *Expression Builder* to create them. At the field level, Access uses the rule to test an entry when you attempt to leave the field. At the table level, Access uses the rule to test the content of several fields when you attempt to leave the record. If an entry doesn't satisfy the rule, Access rejects the entry and displays a message explaining why.

In this exercise, you will create and test several field validation rules and one table validation rule.

USE the *FieldTest* database in the practice file folder for this topic. This practice file is located in the *My Documents\Microsoft Press\Access 2003 SBS\Accurate\ValRules* folder and can also be accessed by clicking *Start/All Programs/Microsoft Press/Access 2003 Step by Step*.
OPEN the *FieldTest* database.

1 Open the **Field Property Test** table in Design view.

2 To add a validation rule to **PhoneField** that will prevent the entry of an area code other than 206 or 425, select **PhoneField**, and click in the **Validation Rule** box.

A ... button appears at the end of the Validation Rule box. You can click this button to use the Expression Builder to create an expression, or you can type an expression in the box.

3 Type the following in the **Validation Rule** box, and press ⌨Enter⌨:

Like "206*" Or Like "425*"

Troubleshooting Be sure to include the asterisk after the 206 and 425.

4 In the **Validation Text** box, type Area code must be 206 or 425.

A rule for the first three digits typed in the PhoneField field is set including the text that Access should display if someone attempts to enter an invalid phone number.

5 Click in the **Caption** box, and type Phone Number.

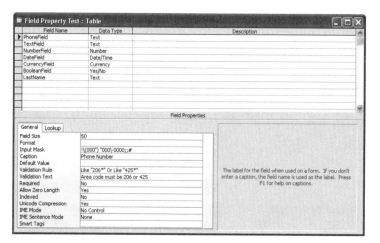

6 Save the table.

Access warns you that data integrity rules have changed. The table violates the new rule because it contains blank phone number fields.

7 Click **No** to close the message box without testing the data.

Tip You can test the validation rules in a table at any time by right-clicking the title bar of the table and clicking Test Validation Rules on the shortcut menu.

8 Return to Datasheet view, where the caption for the first field is now *Phone Number*.

9 Place the insertion point to the left of the first # of any **Phone Number** field, type 3605550009, and press [Enter].

> **Tip** To select the entire field, move the pointer to the left end of the Phone Number field, and when the pointer changes to a thick cross, click the field. The insertion point is then at the start of the area code when you begin typing.

The Validation Rule setting causes Access to display an alert box, warning you that the area code must be either 206 or 425.

10 Click **OK** to close the alert box, type a new phone number with one of the allowed area codes, and press [Enter].

11 Return to Design view, and add another date field. Type Date2 as the field name, set the data type to **Date/Time**, and drag the new field to just below **DateField**.

12 Right-click the table window, and click **Properties** on the shortcut menu to open the **Table Properties** dialog box.

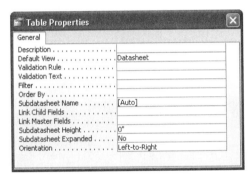

> **Tip** This dialog box is not the same one displayed when you right-click the table in the database window and click Properties. The only point in common between the two is the Description property, which you can enter in either dialog box.

13 Click in the **Validation Rule** box, type [DateField]<[Date2], and press [Enter].

14 Type Date2 must be later than DateField, and close the dialog box.

A table validation rule is added that ensures that the second date is always later than the first one.

15 Save the table (click **No** to close the data-integrity alert box), and return to Datasheet view.

16 In any record, type 6/1/03 in **DateField** and 5/1/03 in **Date2**, and then click in another record.

Access displays the Validation Text setting from the Table Properties dialog box, reminding you that Date2 must be later than DateField.

17 Click **OK**, change **Date2** to 6/2/2003, and click in another record.

18 Close the table.

CLOSE the *FieldTest* database.

Using Lookup Lists to Restrict Data

It is interesting how many different ways people can come up with to enter the same items of information in a database. Asked to enter the name of their home state, for example, residents of the state of Washington will type *Washington*, *Wash*, or *WA*, plus various typos and misspellings. If you ask a dozen sales clerks to enter the name of a specific product, customer, and shipper in an invoice, the probability that all of them will type the same thing is not very high. In cases like this, in which the number of correct choices is limited (to actual product name, actual customer, and actual shipper), providing the option to choose the correct answer from a list will improve your database's consistency.

Minor inconsistencies in the way data is entered might not be really important to someone who later reads the information and makes decisions. Most people know that *Arizona* and *AZ* refer to the same state. But a computer is very literal, and if you tell it to create a list so that you can send catalogs to everyone living in *AZ*, the computer won't include anyone whose state is listed in the database as *Arizona*.

You can limit the options for entering information in a database in several ways:

- For only two options, you can use a Boolean field represented by a check box. A check in the box indicates one choice, and no check indicates the other choice.

- For several mutually exclusive options on a form, you can use *option buttons* to gather the required information.

- For more than a few options, a *combo box* is a good way to go. When you click the down arrow at the end of a combo box, a list of choices is displayed. Depending on the properties associated with the combo box, if you don't see the option you want, you might be able to type something else, adding your entry to the list of possible options displayed in the future.

■ For a short list of choices that won't change often, you can have the combo box look up the options in a list that you provide. Although you can create a lookup list by hand, it is a lot easier to use the *Lookup Wizard.*

In this exercise, you will use the Lookup Wizard to create a list of months from which the user can choose.

USE the *FieldTest* database in the practice file folder for this topic. This practice file is located in the *My Documents\Microsoft Press\Access 2003 SBS\Accurate\Lookup* folder and can also be accessed by clicking *Start/All Programs/Microsoft Press/Access 2003 Step by Step.*
OPEN the *FieldTest* database.

1 Open the **Field Property Test** table in Design view.

2 Add a new field below **LastName**. Name it Month, and set the data type to **Lookup Wizard.**

The first page of the Lookup Wizard appears.

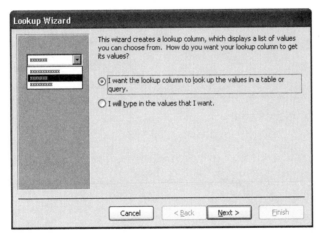

You can use this wizard to create a combo box that provides the entry for a text field. The combo box list can come from a table or query, or you can type the list in the wizard.

Tip If a field has a lot of potential entries, or if they will change often, you can link them to a table. (You might have to create a table expressly for this purpose.) If the field has only a few items and they won't change, typing the list in the wizard is easier.

3 Select the **I will type in the values that I want option**, and then click **Next**.

4 Leave the number of columns set to *1*, and click in the **Col1** box.

5 Enter the 12 months of the year (January, February, and so on), pressing ⎯Tab⎯ after each one to move to a new row. Then click **Next**.

6 Accept the Month default label, and click **Finish**.

7 In the **Field Properties** area, click the **Lookup** tab to view the Lookup information for the **Month** field.

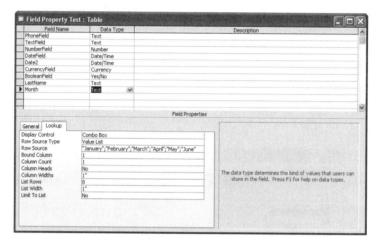

The wizard entered this information, but you could easily figure out what you would have to enter to create a lookup list by hand.

View

8 Click the **View** button to change to Datasheet view, clicking **Yes** to save your changes.

9 Adjust the column widths so that you can see all the fields, by dragging the vertical bars between columns in the header.

> **Tip** You can drag the vertical bars between the columns to make them smaller than the text in them. You can also double-click the vertical bars to automatically size the columns to fit the text in them.

10 Click in the **Month** field of a record, and then click the down arrow to display the list.

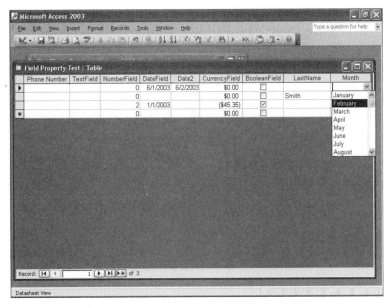

11 Click **February** to enter it in the field.

12 Click in the next **Month** field, type Jan, and press [Enter].

As soon as you type the *J*, the combo box displays *January*. If you had typed *Ju*, the combo box would have displayed *June*.

13 In the next **Month** field, type jly, and press [Enter].

Even though the entry isn't in the list, it is accepted just as you typed it. Although there might be times when you want to allow the entry of information other than the items in the list, this isn't one of those times, so you need to change the field properties to limit what can be entered.

14 Return to Design view.

The last property on the Lookup tab is "Limit To List". It is currently set to *No*, which allows people to enter information that isn't in the list.

15 Change **Limit To List** to **Yes**.

16 Save the table, return to Datasheet view, type jly in a new **Month** field, and press [Enter].

Access informs you that the text you entered is not in the list, and refuses the entry.

17 Click **OK**, and then click **July** in the list.

A list of the names of months is convenient for people, but if your computer has to deal with this information in some mathematical way, a list of the numbers associated with each month is easier for it to use. There is a solution that will work for both humans and machines.

18 Return to Design view, create a new field named Month2, and again set the data type to **Lookup Wizard**.

19 Select the **I will type in the values that I want** option, and click **Next**.

20 Type 2 to add a second column, and then click in the **Col1** box.

Access adds a second column, labeled *Col2*.

21 Enter the following numbers and months in the two columns, pressing ⬚ᵀᵃᵇ to move from column to column:

Number	Month	Number	Month
1	January	7	July
2	February	8	August
3	March	9	September
4	April	10	October
5	May	11	November
6	June	12	December

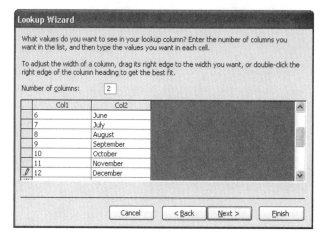

22 Click **Next** to move to the next page.

23 Accept the default selection of **Col1** as the column whose data you want to enter when a selection is made from the list, and click **Finish**.

You return to the table, and the Field Properties area displays the Lookup information.

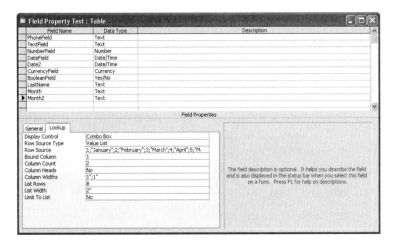

The wizard has inserted your column information into the Row Source box and set the other properties according to your specifications.

24 Change **Limit To List** to **Yes**.

25 Save your changes, switch to Datasheet view, and then click the down arrow in a **Month2** field to display the list.

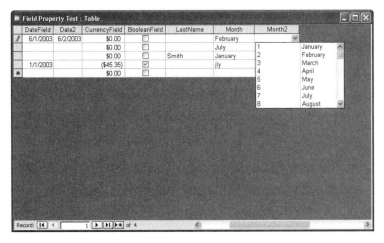

26 Click **January**.

Access displays the number _1_ in the field, which is useful for the computer. However, people might be confused by the two columns and by seeing something other than what they clicked or typed.

27 Switch back to Design view, and in the **Column Widths** box—which appears as *1";1"*—change the width for the first column to 0 (you don't have to type the symbol for inches) to prevent it from being displayed.

28 Save your changes, return to Datasheet view, and as a test, in the remaining records set **Month2** to **February** in two records and to **March** in one record.

Only the name of the month is now displayed in the list, and when you click a month, that name is displayed in the field. However, Access actually stores the associated number from the list's first column.

29 Right-click in the **Month2** column, click **Filter For** on the shortcut menu, type 2 in the box, and press Enter.

Only the two records with February in the **Month2** field are now displayed.

Remove Filter

30 Click the **Remove Filter** button, and then repeat the previous step, this time typing 3 in the box to display the one record with March in the **Month2** field.

CLOSE the *FieldTest* database, saving your changes.

Updating Information in a Table

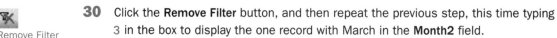
Microsoft Office Specialist

As you use a database and as it grows, you might discover that errors creep in or that some information becomes out of date. You can tediously scroll through the records looking for those that need to be changed, but it is more efficient to use a few of the tools and techniques provided by Access for that purpose.

If an employee has consistently misspelled the same word, you can use the Find and Replace commands on the Edit menu to locate each instance of the misspelled word and replace it with the correct spelling. This command works much like the same commands in Microsoft Office Word or Microsoft Office Excel.

However, if you decide to increase the price of some products or replace the content of a field only under certain circumstances, you need the power of an *update query*, which is a select query that performs an action on the query's results.

In this exercise, you will open the GardenCo database and use an update query to increase the price of all bulbs and cacti by 10 percent.

USE the *GardenCo* database in the practice file folder for this topic. This practice file is located in the *My Documents\Microsoft Press\Access 2003 SBS\Accurate\QueryUp* folder and can also be accessed by clicking *Start/All Programs/Microsoft Press/Access 2003 Step by Step*.
OPEN the *GardenCo* database and acknowledge the safety warning, if necessary.

1 On the **Objects** bar, click **Queries**.

2 In the **Queries** pane, double-click **Create query by using wizard**.

3 In the **Tables/Queries** list, select **Table: Categories**.

4 Double-click **CategoryName** to move it from the **Available Fields** list to the **Selected Fields** list.

5 In the **Tables/Queries** list, select **Table: Products**.

6 Double-click **ProductName** and **UnitPrice** to move them from the **Available Fields** list to the **Selected Fields** list.

7 Click **Finish** to accept all defaults and create the query.

Access displays the query results in a datasheet. Only the Category Name, Product Name, and Unit Price fields are displayed.

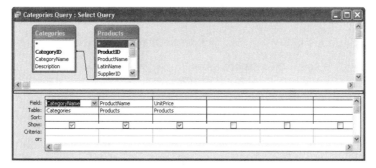

View

8 Click the **View** button to display the query in Design view.

This query displays the products in all categories. You want to raise the prices of only the bulbs and cacti, so your first task is to change this query so that it selects just those categories.

9 In the **Criteria** row under **CategoryName**, type **bulbs,** and then type **cacti** in the **or** row.

Run

10 Click the **Run** button to run the query and confirm that only bulbs and cacti are listed, and then return to Design view.

A select query that selects just the records you want to change is created. But to actually make a change to the records, you have to use an update query.

11 Click the **Query** menu to display the commands that apply to a query.

The four available action queries are listed toward the middle of the menu, with exclamation points in their icons.

Tip You can't create an action query directly; you must first create a select query and then change the query to one of the action types. With an existing select query open, you can find the command to convert it to an action query either on the Query menu, in the list that appears when you click the Query Type button's arrow, or on the shortcut menu that appears when you right-click the query and point to Query Type.

12 On the **Query** menu, click **Update Query**.

The select query is converted to an update query. The only noticeable changes to the design grid are that the Sort and Show rows have been removed and an Update To row has been added.

13 In the **Update To** row under **UnitPrice**, type [UnitPrice]*1.1.

Tip   You enclose UnitPrice in brackets to indicate that it is an Access object. If you use the Expression Builder to insert this expression, it looks like this: *[Products]![UnitPrice]*1.1*. Because this description of the field includes the table in which it is found, this expression can be inserted in other tables.

When you run an update query, you make changes to the table that can't be undone. Because of this, you should create a backup copy of the table before running the query. For the purposes of this exercise, however, before running the query you will perform one simple check.

You can quickly create a backup copy of a table by displaying the Tables pane in the database window, clicking the table you want to back up, and then pressing [Ctrl]+[C] followed by [Ctrl]+[V]. In the dialog box that appears, provide a name for the backup table, and click OK.

View

14   Click the **View** button.

In a select query, clicking the View button is the same as clicking the Run button. But in an update query, clicking the View button simply displays a list of the fields that will be updated. In this case, you see a list of unit prices that matches the ones shown earlier in the select query.

15   Return to Design view, and then click the **Run** button.

Access displays a rather firm warning.

16   Click **Yes** to acknowledge the warning, and then click the **View** button again to display the **UnitPrice** field, where all the prices have been increased by 10 percent.

17   Save and close the query.

CLOSE the *GardenCo* database.

Deleting Information from a Table

Microsoft Office Specialist

Over time, some types of information in a database can become obsolete. The Products table in The Garden Company database, for example, maintains a list of all the products the company currently offers for sale or has sold in the past. When a product is no longer available for sale, a check mark is placed in the Discontinued field. Discontinued products aren't displayed in the catalog or pushed by salespeople, but they are kept in the database for a while in case it becomes practical to sell them again. A similar situation could exist with customers who haven't placed an order in a long time or who have asked to be removed from a mailing list but might still place orders.

Eventually, the time comes to clean house and discard some records. You could do this by scrolling through the tables and deleting records by hand, but if all the records to be deleted match some pattern, you can use a *delete query* to quickly get rid of all of them.

Important Keep in mind several things when deleting records from a database. First, there is no quick recovery of deleted records. Second, the effects of a delete query can be more far-reaching than you intend. If the table in which you are deleting records has a relationship with another table, and the "Cascade Delete Related Records" option for that relationship is set, records in the second table will also be deleted. Sometimes this is what you want, but sometimes it isn't. For example, you don't want to delete the records of previous sales just because you're deleting discontinued products. There are two solutions to this problem: back up your database before deleting the records; or create a new table (perhaps named *Deleted<file name>*), and then move the records you want to delete to the new table.

In this exercise, you will create a delete query to remove all discontinued products from the Products table of the GardenCo database.

USE the *GardenCo* database in the practice file folder for this topic. This practice file is located in the *My Documents\Microsoft Press\Access 2003 SBS\Accurate\QueryDel* folder and can also be accessed by clicking *Start/All Programs/Microsoft Press/Access 2003 Step by Step*.
OPEN the *GardenCo* database and acknowledge the safety warning, if necessary.

1   On the **Objects** bar, click **Queries**.

2   Double-click **Create query in Design view** to open both the query window and the **Show Table** dialog box.

3   Double-click **Products** to add that table to the list area of the query window, and then click **Close** to close the **Show Table** dialog box.

4 Double-click the asterisk at the top of the list of fields to include all the fields in the query.

Products.* appears in the Field row of the first column of the design grid, and *Products* appears in the Table row.

Tip Double-clicking the asterisk in the field list is a quick way to move all the fields in the table to the query, without having each field appear in its own column. However, when you do it that way you can't set Sort, Show, and Criteria values for individual fields. To set these values, you have to add the specific fields to the design grid, thereby adding them twice. To avoid displaying the fields twice, clear the check mark in the Show row of the duplicate individual fields.

5 Scroll to the bottom of the field list, and double-click **Discontinued** to copy it to the next available column in the design grid.

6 On the **Query** menu, click **Delete Query** to convert this select query to a delete query.

Tip You might have to hover over the short menu or click the double–chevrons to see the Delete Query command on the long menu.

In the design grid, the Sort and Show rows have disappeared, and a Delete row has been added. In the first column, which contains the reference to all fields in the Products table, the Delete row contains the word *From*, indicating that this is the table from which records will be deleted. When you add individual fields to the remaining columns, as you did with the Discontinued field, the Delete row displays *Where*, indicating that this field can include deletion criteria.

7 Type Yes in the **Criteria** row under **Discontinued**.

The Discontinued field is set to the Boolean data type, which is represented in the datasheet as a check box that has a check mark to indicate Yes and no check mark to indicate No. To locate all discontinued products, you need to identify records with the Discontinued field set to Yes.

View

8 To check the accuracy of the query, click the **View** button.

Access displays a list of 18 discontinued products that will be deleted, but it hasn't actually changed the table yet. Scroll to the right to verify that all records display a check in the Products.Discontinued field.

View

9 Click the **View** button to return to Design view.

Tip Before actually deleting records, you might want to display the Relationships window by clicking Relationships on the Tools menu. If the table you are deleting from has a relationship with any table containing order information that shouldn't be deleted, right-click the relationship line, click Edit Relationship on the shortcut menu, and make sure that Enforce Referential Integrity is selected and Cascade Delete Related Records is *not* selected.

Run

10 Click the **Run** button to run the delete query.

Access displays a warning to remind you of the permanence of this action.

11 Click **Yes** to delete the records.

12 Click the **View** button to see that all the records were deleted.

Save

13 If you think you might run the same delete query in the future, click the **Save** button, and name the query. Then close the query.

Tip If you are concerned that someone might accidentally run a delete query and destroy records you weren't ready to destroy, change the query back to a select query before saving it. You can then open the select query in Design view and change it to a delete query when you want to run it again.

14 Close the query.

CLOSE the *GardenCo* database.

Key Points

- When you create a database with Microsoft Office Access 2003, you can set properties that restrict what can be entered in it.

- To ensure the ongoing accuracy of a database, you can create and run action queries that quickly update information or delete selected records from a table.

- The Data Type setting restricts entries to a specific type of data: text, numbers, dates, and so on. For example, if the data type is set to Number and you try to enter text, Access refuses your entry and displays a warning.

- You can set the Field Size property for the Text, Number, and AutoNumber data types. This property restricts the number of characters allowed in a text field, and the size of numbers that can be entered in a number or AutoNumber field.

- The input mask property controls the format in which data can be entered, and restricts the number of characters that can be entered in a field. For example, the mask for a telephone number can be set to have three sections separated by semicolons, so someone entering information can see at a glance the format for ten numbers in that particular field.

- You can use a validation rule to precisely define the information that will be accepted in one or several fields in a record. At the field level, Access uses the rule to test an entry when you attempt to leave the field, and does not accept entries that don't meet the rule. At the table level, Access uses the rule to test the content of several fields when you attempt to leave the record, rejecting an entry that doesn't satisfy the rule.

■ For fields in which the number of correct entries is limited, you can use a lookup field to ensure that users enter the right information. This helps prevent inconsistencies in how data is entered and makes it easier and more efficient to sort and perform searches on your data.

■ You can use an update query to quickly perform an action based on the results of a query. For example, you can search and replace the contents of a field under certain circumstances, which are defined in the update query.

■ You can use a delete query to quickly delete records that have become obsolete. You should always back up your database before running a delete query, and you must exercise caution when deleting records in this way. The effects of a delete query can be far-reaching, and there is no quick recovery of deleted records.

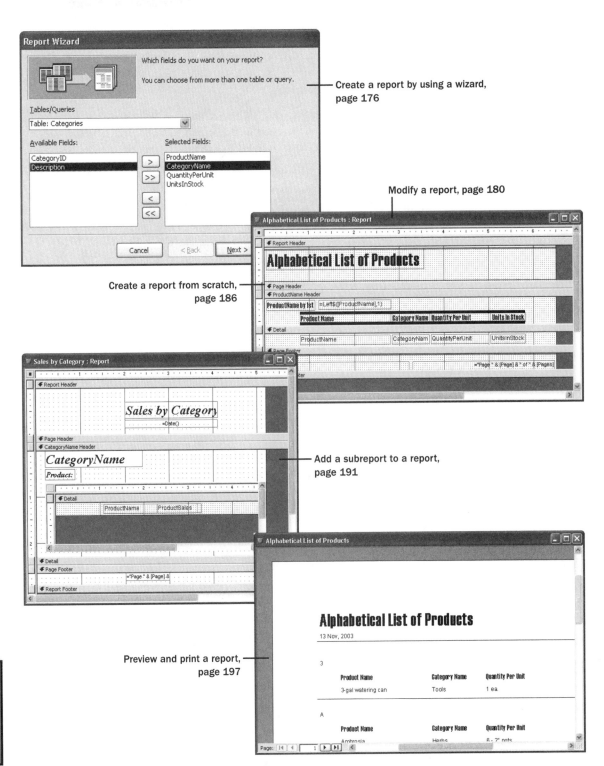

Create a report by using a wizard, page 176

Modify a report, page 180

Create a report from scratch, page 186

Add a subreport to a report, page 191

Preview and print a report, page 197

7 Working with Reports

In this chapter you will learn to:

✔ Create a report by using a wizard.

✔ Modify a report.

✔ Create a report from scratch.

✔ Add a subreport to a report.

✔ Preview and print a report.

People generally think of *reports* as summaries of larger bodies of information. For example, The Garden Company's database might hold detailed information about thousands of orders. If you want to edit those orders or enter new ones, you do so directly in the table or with a form. If you want to summarize those orders to illustrate the rate of growth of the company's sales, you use a report.

Like a book report or the annual report of a company's activities, a report created in Microsoft Office Access 2003 is typically used to summarize and organize information to express a particular point of view to a specific audience. When designing a report, it is important to consider the point you are trying to make, the intended audience, and the level of information they will need.

In many ways, reports are like forms. You can use similar wizards to create them, and the design environment is much the same. Just as with a form, you can add label, text box, image, and other controls, and you can set their properties. You can display information from one or more records from one or more tables or queries, and you can have multiple sets of headers and footers.

Microsoft Office Specialist

In this chapter, you will use the GardenCo database to learn how to generate and print reports that extract specific information from a database and format it in an easy-to-read style.

See Also   Do you need only a quick refresher on the topics in this chapter? See the Quick Reference entries on pages xxxix–xlii.

 Important   Before you can use the practice files in this chapter, you need to install them from the book's companion CD to their default location. See "Using the Book's CD-ROM" on page xiii for more information.

Creating a Report by Using a Wizard

Microsoft Office Specialist The content of an Access report can be divided into two general categories: information derived from records in one or more tables, and everything else. The *everything else* category includes the title, page headers and footers, introductory and explanatory text, logo, background and graphics, and calculations based on database content.

You can use a wizard to get a jump-start on a report. The wizard creates a basic layout, attaches styles, and adds a text box control and its associated label for each field you specify. Depending on the report you want to produce, you might be able to do almost all the work in the wizard, or you might have to refine the report in Design view.

Forms vs. Reports

Forms and reports have one purpose in common: to give people easy access to the information stored in a database. The main differences between forms and reports are the following:

■ Forms are used to enter, view, and edit information. Reports are used only to view information.

■ Forms are usually displayed on the screen. Reports can be previewed on the screen, but they are usually printed.

■ Forms generally provide a detailed look at records and are usually for the people who actually work with the database. Reports are often used to group and summarize data, and are often for people who don't work with the database but who use its information for other business tasks.

Forms and reports are sufficiently alike that you can save a form as a report when you want to take advantage of additional report refinement and printing capabilities.

In this exercise, you will use the Report Wizard to create a simple report that displays an alphabetical list of The Garden Company's products.

BE SURE TO start Access before beginning this exercise.
USE the *GardenCo* database in the practice file folder for this topic. This practice file is located in the *My Documents\Microsoft Press\Access 2003 SBS\Reports\RepByWiz* folder and can also be accessed by clicking *Start/All Programs/Microsoft Press/Access 2003 Step by Step*.
OPEN the *GardenCo* database and acknowledge the safety warning, if necessary.

1 On the **Objects** bar, click **Tables**, and then click the **Products** table to select it.

2 On the **Insert** menu, click **Report** to display the **New Report** dialog box.

Notice in the New Report dialog box that Products is already selected as the table on which to base the new report.

Tip   If you select a table or query before starting the Report Wizard, that table or query becomes the basis for the report.

3   Double-click **Report Wizard**.

The first page of the Report Wizard appears.

Tip   You can also start the Report Wizard by displaying the New Object button's list and clicking Report, or by double-clicking "Create report by using wizard" in the Report pane of the database window.

4   Double-click **ProductName**, **QuantityPerUnit**, and **UnitsInStock** to move them from the **Available Fields** list to the **Selected Fields** list.

Tip   Fields appear in a report in the same order as they are listed in the wizard's Selected Fields list. You can save yourself the effort of rearranging the fields in the report if you enter them in the desired order in the wizard.

5   Select **Tables:Categories** in the **Tables/Queries** list to display the fields from the Categories table.

6   Click **ProductName** in the **Selected Fields** list to select it.

The next field you add will be inserted below the selected field.

7   Double-click **CategoryName**.

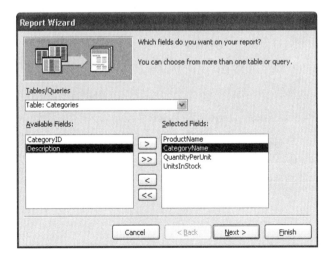

Tip   If you are using more than two tables in a form or report, or if you will be using the same combination of tables in several places, you can save time by creating a query based on those tables, and using that query as the basis for the form or report.

8   Click **Next** to display the wizard's second page.

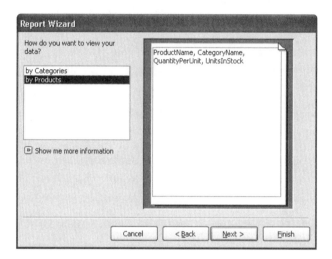

When you include more than one table in a report, the wizard evaluates the relationships between the tables, and offers to group the records in any logical manner available. In this example, you can group them by category or by product. You can click either option to see it depicted in the right pane.

Important   If the relationships between the tables aren't already established in the Relationships window, you have to cancel the wizard and establish them.

9   Accept the default to group **by Products**, and click **Next**.

On this page, you can specify the fields to establish *grouping levels*.

10   Double-click **ProductName** to move it to the top of the simulated report on the right.

11   Click the **Grouping Options** button at the bottom of the page to display the **Grouping Intervals** dialog box.

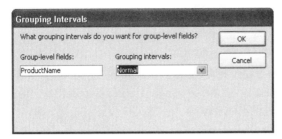

12 Click the down arrow to the right of the **Grouping intervals** box, click **1st Letter**, and then click **OK**.

13 Click **Next** to display a page on which you can specify the sort order and summary options.

14 Click the down arrow in the first field, and click **ProductName** in the drop-down list as the first **Ascending** sort field.

You can use this page to specify up to four fields by which to sort. If any fields include numeric information, the Summary Options button becomes available. You can click it to display a list of the numeric fields, each with Sum, Avg (average), Min (minimum), and Max (maximum) check boxes. The only numeric field in this report is UnitsInStock, and there is no need to summarize it.

15 Click **Next** to display the next page of the wizard.

A page displaying the options in the Layout group appears. None of them is exactly what you are looking for, but Outline 1 is close.

16 Click **Outline 1**, leave the **Portrait** orientation option selected, leave the **Adjust the field width so all fields fit on a page** option selected, and then click **Next** to display a list of predefined styles.

17 Click **Compact**, and then click **Next** to display the wizard's final page.

18 Type Alphabetical List of Products as the title, and click **Finish** to preview the report.

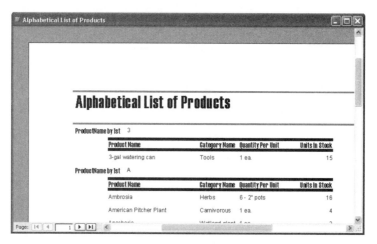

19 Close the report window.

CLOSE the *GardenCo* database.

Modifying a Report

*Microsoft
Office
Specialist*

You can use the *Report Wizard* to get a quick start on a report, but you will usually want to use Design view to refine the report and add special touches. Refining a report is an iterative process: you switch back and forth between Design view and Print Preview to evaluate each change you make and to plan the next change.

In this exercise, you'll work with the Alphabetical List of Products report from the GardenCo database.

USE the *GardenCo* database in the practice file folder for this topic. This practice file is located in the *My Documents\Microsoft Press\Access 2003 SBS\Reports\Modify* folder and can also be accessed by clicking *Start/All Programs/Microsoft Press/Access 2003 Step by Step*.
OPEN the *GardenCo* database and acknowledge the safety warning, if necessary.

1   On the **Objects** bar, click **Reports**.

2   Click **Alphabetical List of Products**, and then click the **Preview** button to open the report in Print Preview.

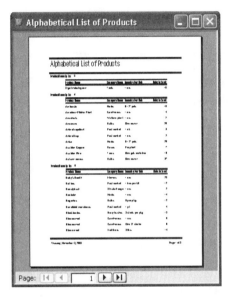

3   Enlarge the window, and then move the pointer over the page. The pointer changes to a magnifying glass with a plus sign in it to indicate that you can zoom in on the page. Click once to zoom in, and notice some of the following problems with the report design:

- There is no date below the title.

- Some horizontal lines need to be removed or added.

- There is some extraneous text.

- Labels and text boxes need to be rearranged.

- The list breaks in mid-group.

- There are a number of general formatting issues.

View

4   Click the **View** button to view the report in Design view.

Report Header selector   Grouping Header selector
Report selector   Page Header selector   Report Header section

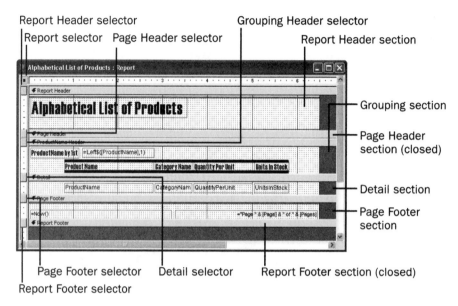

— Grouping section

— Page Header section (closed)

— Detail section

— Page Footer section

Page Footer selector   Detail selector   Report Footer section (closed)
Report Footer selector

5   Point to the top of the **Page Header** selector. When the pointer changes to a two-headed vertical arrow, drag the selector down about a quarter inch.

> **Tip**   There are rulers above and to the left of the form to help you judge the size of the printed report. You can toggle these and the grid dots on and off by right-clicking the report and clicking Ruler or Grid.

You should now be able to see the double lines below the title. (The horizontal lines inserted by the wizard actually consist of sets of two lines.)

6   In the **Report Header** section, click one of the lines above the title, and press ⬚. Then repeat this step to delete the other line above the title and one of the lines below it.

> **Troubleshooting**   Small black handles indicate your selection.

Toolbox

7   Click the **Toolbox** button to open it, if necessary.

8   Click the **Text Box** control in the toolbox, and then click in the blank area at the right end of the **Report Header** section to insert a text box and its label.

ab|
Text Box

9   Click the new label, and delete it.

10   Drag the text box to just below the title, and align it with the left edge. With the text box still selected, press the ⬚ key to display the **Properties** dialog box.

11   On the **Data** tab, click **Control Source**, and type the following:

=Format(Date(), "dd mmm, yyyy")

12 Press Enter.

A custom date format is created. The Date() function returns the current date and time. The Format() function determines the manner in which the date and time are displayed. Each time you preview or print the report, this expression will insert the current date in the text box, and format it in this fashion: *17 Feb, 2003*.

13 Close the **Properties** dialog box.

Tip You can quickly insert a text box that displays the date and/or time in one of several standard formats. In Design view, on the Insert menu, click Date and Time. A dialog box appears in which you can specify the format. When you click OK, Access inserts a text box in the Header section if it exists, or in the Detail section if it doesn't. You can then move the text box to where you want it. For detailed information about date formats, search for *date formats* in Access online Help.

14 In the **ProductName Header** section, delete all the bold lines above and below the labels. (There are two sets of two.)

15 Delete the **Product Name by 1st** label, and drag the text box to the left edge of the section.

16 In the **Page Footer** section, click the text box containing **=Now()**, and click Del.

17 Drag a rectangle around all the labels in the **ProductName Header** section and the text boxes in the **Detail** section to select them.

Selection handles appear around the borders of all the controls, and you can now move them as a group.

18 Move the controls to the left until the left edge of **Product Name** lines up with the half-inch mark on the ruler at the top of the window.

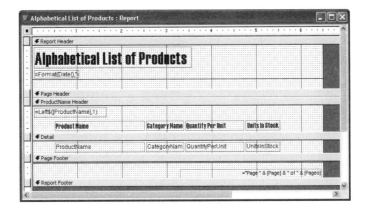

19 Save your changes, and then switch to Print Preview.

The report is displayed in Print Preview. You still need to add a thin line at the bottom of each group, and you need to prevent the groups from breaking across pages.

Sorting and
Grouping

20 Switch back to Design view, and then click the **Sorting and Grouping** button on the toolbar.

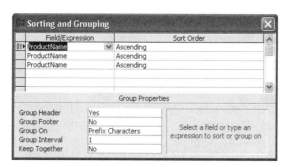

The Sorting and Grouping dialog box appears. The top field, which should already be selected, has an icon in its row selector indicating that it is the field on which records are grouped. Because Group Header is set to *Yes* and Group Footer is set to *No* in the Group Properties area, a ProductName header is displayed in your report, but a ProductName footer isn't.

21 In the **Group Properties** area, double-click **Group Footer** to change it to **Yes**.

A ProductName Footer section selector appears in the Design view window, above the Page Footer section.

22 Change the **Keep Together** setting to **Whole Group**, and close the **Sorting and Grouping** dialog box.

Line

23 Click the **Line** control in the toolbox, and then click near the top of the **ProductName Footer** section to insert a short horizontal line.

24 Press [F4] to display the **Properties** dialog box, if necessary, and then click the **Format** tab.

25 Type 0 as the **Left** property, and 6.5 as the **Width** property.

26 Close the **Properties** dialog box, save your changes, and then switch to Print Preview to see how the report looks.

The report is displayed in Print Preview. You still need to remove the set of lines above the page number and realign the columns.

27 Switch to Design view, and delete the two lines at the top of the **Page Footer** section.

If you can't see the lines, drag a rectangle starting below the lines and move upward to select them. This will select them, even if you can't see them.

28 In the **ProductName Header** and **Detail** sections, select the label and text box for **Units In Stock**, and drag them to the right until their right edges touch the right edge of the background grid.

29 In the same two sections, move the label and text box for **Quantity Per Unit** to the right until the left edge is at about 3.75 inches.

30 Lengthen the label and text box for **CategoryName** and the text box for **QuantityPerUnit**.

Tip To make changes to two or more controls, you can drag a rectangle to group and select them, and then drag a handle on any selected control to change all of them the same way.

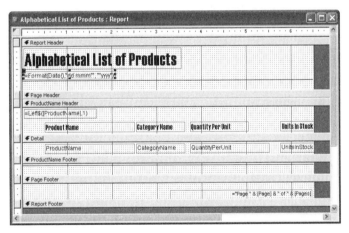

31 Save your changes, and preview the report.

32 Close the report.

CLOSE the *GardenCo* database.

Creating a Report from Scratch

Microsoft Office Specialist

When you want to create a report that displays records from one or more tables, the Report Wizard is the fastest way to create the report and include all the desired field captions and contents. However, sometimes a *main report* simply serves as a shell for one or more subreports, and the main report displays little or no information from the underlying tables. In this case, it is often easier to create the main report by hand in Design view.

In this exercise, you will use a query as the basis for the shell for a report that lists sales by category. A CategoryName section will list the current category, but the Page Header, Detail, and Page Footer sections will contain no information.

USE the *GardenCo* database in the practice file folder for this topic. This practice file is located in the *My Documents\Microsoft Press\Access 2003 SBS\Reports\ByDesign* folder and can also be accessed by clicking *Start/All Programs/Microsoft Press/Access 2003 Step by Step*.
OPEN the *GardenCo* database and acknowledge the safety warning, if necessary.

1   On the **Objects** bar, click **Queries**.

2   Click **Sales by Category** to select it.

3   On the **Insert** menu, click **Report**.

4   Double-click **Design View** to open a blank report.

> **Tip**   The Page Header, Detail, and Page Footer sections you see in Design view are the default sections for a new report, but you don't have to use them all, and you can add others.

A small window also opens, displaying a list of the fields in the Sales by Category query.

5   On the **View** menu, click **Report Header/Footer**.

The sections are now enclosed in the Report Header and Report Footer sections.

> **Troubleshooting**   If the page header and footer disappear from your report, on the View menu, click Page/Header/Footer to restore them, and then click Report Header/Footer.

6   On the **View** menu, click **Sorting and Grouping**.

The Sorting and Grouping dialog box appears, in which you can specify the fields that will be used to group the records in the report.

7   Click the down-arrow to the right of the **Field/Expression** box, and click **CategoryName**.

8   In the **Group Properties** area, set **Group Header** to **Yes**.

An icon appears in the selector button to the left of CategoryName to indicate that it is a group heading, and the CategoryName Header section selector appears in the Design view window.

9   Close the **Sorting and Grouping** dialog box.

10   Click the **Report** selector in the upper-left corner of the report, and then press [F4] to open the **Properties** dialog box.

> **Tip**   If the report is already selected, the Report selector has a small black square in it.

11   In the **Properties** dialog box, click the **Format** tab, and scroll down until you see the **Grid X** and **Grid Y** properties. Set them each to 10.

The grid, which is represented by dots in the report background, becomes easier to use when aligning controls.

12   On the **Format** tab, set the height of each section by clicking the section selector and then setting the **Height** property as follows:

Section	Setting
Report Header	1"
Page Header	0"
Category/Name Header	2.2"
Detail	0"
Page Footer	0.2"
Report Footer	0"

> **Tip**   You can also set the height of a section by dragging the top of the section selector up or down.

13   Move the **Properties** dialog box to view the results. (Resize the window to see all sections, if necessary.)

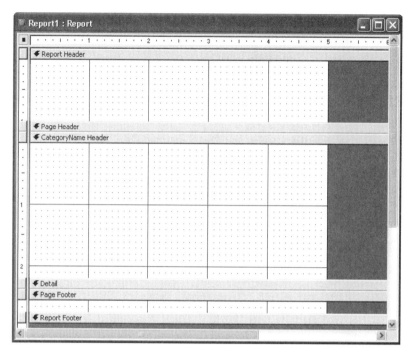

Save

14 Click the **Save** button, type Sales by Category as the name of the report, and then click **OK**.

Toolbox

15 If the toolbox isn't displayed, click the **Toolbox** button on the toolbar.

The toolbox is now displayed.

Label

16 To give the report a title, click the **Label** control in the toolbox, and then click the top of the **Report Header** section, about 2 inches from the left edge.

Access inserts a very narrow label.

17 Type Sales by Category, and press [Enter].

The label expands to hold the text you type, and when you press [Enter], Access selects the label control and displays its properties in the Properties dialog box.

18 Scroll down, and set the label's font properties as follows:

Property	Setting
Font Name	Times New Roman
Font Size	20
Font Weight	Bold
Font Italic	Yes

The text in the label reflects each change. By the time you finish making all the changes, the text has outgrown its frame.

19   On the **Format** menu, point to **Size**, and then click **To Fit**.

Troubleshooting   After the focus leaves this control, Access displays an error warning that the new label is not associated with a control. Click the icon to display a shortcut menu, and then click Ignore Error.

20   On the **Insert** menu, click **Date and Time** to display the **Date and Time** dialog box.

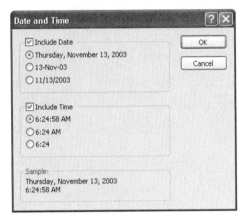

21   Make sure that **Include Date** and the first (long) date format are selected, clear the **Include Time** check box, and click **OK**.

A text box containing =Date() appears in the upper-left corner of the Report Header section. If the report has no Report Header section, the text box appears in the Detail section.

Center

22   Drag the new text box containing =Date() below the title, adjust the width of the box to match the width of the title, and click the **Center** button on the Formatting toolbar to center the date in the box.

23   Drag the **CategoryName** field from the field list window to the top of the **CategoryName Header** section. (You might have to scroll up to see this field.)

24   Delete the **Category Name** label that was inserted with the text box.

25   Select the text box, and set its font properties to the same settings as those used for the report title, in step 18.

26   On the **Format** menu, point to **Size**, and then click **To Fit**.

27 Position the text box with its top against the top of the section and its left edge 0.2 inch (two dots) in from the left, and then drag the right edge of the text box to about the 2.4-inch mark.

28 Click the **Save** button to save the report, and then display it in Print Preview.

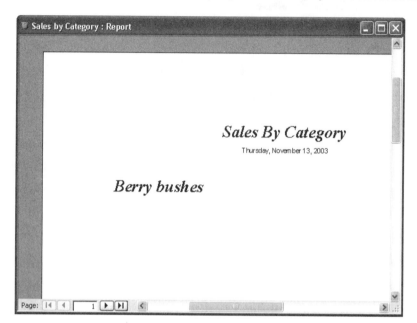

29 Return to Design view, and add a label below **CategoryName**. Click the **Label** button in the toolbox, click directly below the left edge of the text box, type Product:, and then press [Enter].

Because this label is not associated with a control, you will see another error. Click the icon, and then click Ignore Error.

30 Set the font properties that you set for **CategoryName** in step 25, except for **Font Size**, which should be **12**.

31 Right-click the label, point to **Size** on the shortcut menu, and then click **To Fit**.

32 Position the label at the bottom of the **CategoryName** text box, aligning their left edges.

33 Insert a page number in the **Page Footer** section by clicking **Page Numbers** on the **Insert** menu to display the **Page Numbers** dialog box.

34   In the **Format** area, select the **Page N of M** option; and in the **Position** area, select the **Bottom of Page [Footer]** option. Click the down arrow to the right of the **Alignment** box, and click **Center**. Then click **OK**.

Access centers a text box containing the expression =*"Page " & [Page] & " of " & [Pages]* in the Page Footer section.

35   Save the report, and then preview the results.

36   Close the report.

CLOSE the *GardenCo* database.

Adding a Subreport to a Report

Microsoft Office Specialist

You can use a wizard to quickly create a report that is bound to the information in one table or in several related tables. However, reports often include multiple sets of information that are related to the topic of the report but that are not necessarily related to each other. A report might, for example, include charts, spreadsheets, and other forms of information about several divisions or activities of a company. Or it might include information about production, marketing, sales, compensation, and the company's 401(k) plan. All these topics are related to running the business, but they don't all fit nicely into the structure of a single Access report.

One solution to this problem is to create separate reports, print them, and put them in one binder. An easier solution is to use *subreports*. A subreport is simply a report that you insert in another report. You create the subreport as you would any other report, and then use a wizard to insert it. You can also use a wizard to insert a subreport control in the main report, and then let the wizard guide you through the process of creating the subreport in the control. In either case, you end up with both the main report and the subreport listed as objects in the Reports pane of the database window.

Often you will use queries as the basis for reports that require summary calculations or statistics. But you can also enhance the usefulness of both regular reports and subreports by performing calculations in the reports themselves. By inserting *unbound* controls and then using the Expression Builder to create the expressions that tell Access what to calculate and how, you can make information readily available in one place instead of several.

Tip If the correct relationships have been established, you can quickly add an existing report as a subreport by opening the main report in Design view and then dragging the second report from the Reports pane to the section of the main report where you want to insert it.

In this exercise, you will add a subreport to the main report created in the previous exercise. This subreport will display the total sales for each of the products in the category that is selected in the main report, as well as a calculated control for the total sales for the category.

USE the *GardenCo* database in the practice file folder for this topic. This practice file is located in the *My Documents\Microsoft Press\Access 2003 SBS\Reports\Subreport* folder and can also be accessed by clicking *Start/All Programs/Microsoft Press/Access 2003 Step by Step*.
OPEN the *GardenCo* database and acknowledge the safety warning, if necessary.

1 Open the **Sales by Category** report in Design view.

Subform/
Subreport

2 Click **Subform/Subreport** in the toolbox, and then click a point even with the left edge of the **Product** label and about two grid intervals below it.

Access opens a blank, unbound subreport in the main report and displays the first page of the SubReport Wizard.

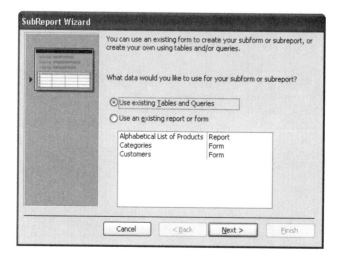

3 Make sure that the **Use existing Tables and Queries** option is selected, and then click **Next**.

4 Click the down arrow to the right of the **Tables/Queries** box, and then click **Query: Sales by Category**.

5 Double-click **CategoryID**, **ProductName**, and **ProductSales** to move them from the **Available Fields** list to the **Selected Fields** list, and then click **Next**.

6 Make sure the **Choose from a list** option is selected, and click **Next**.

7 Accept the suggested name, *Sales by Category subreport*, and click **Finish**.

The Sales by Category subreport takes the place of the unbound subreport in the main report.

8 Click the subreport control, and press F4 to display the **Properties** dialog box, if necessary.

9 On the **Format** tab, change the width of the subreport to 5" and the height to 1.5". Then press Enter.

10 In the subreport, right-click the **Report Header** section selector, and click **Report Header/Footer** on the shortcut menu to delete the header and footer. Click **Yes** in the alert box.

11 In the subreport, right-click the **Page Header** section selector, click **Page Header/Footer** on the shortcut menu, and click **Yes** in the alert box.

The subreport now has only a Detail section.

Tip Step 11 deletes the Page Header and Footer from the report. To redisplay the Page Header/Footer sections, on the View menu, click Page Header/Footer. If there are controls in those sections when you choose this command, Access warns you that the controls will be deleted.

12 In the **Detail** section, click the **CategoryID** text box, and then press the Del key.

13 Click the **ProductName** text box, and change its width to 2.125".

14 Click the **ProductSales** text box, and change its **Left** property to 2.3" and its **Width** property to 1".

The labels overlap.

15 In the main report, click the partially hidden **Sales by Category** subreport label, and delete it.

Tip If you accidentally delete something, press Ctrl+Z or click the Undo button to undo the deletion.

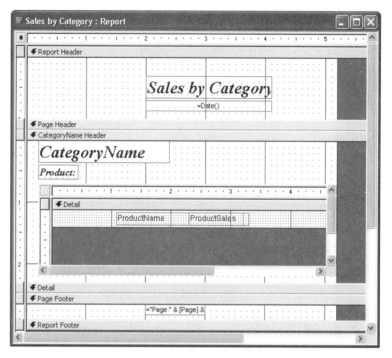

16 Click the selector in the upper-left corner of the subreport twice (the first click selects the subreport, the second puts a black square in the selector), and then on the **View** menu, click **Report Header/Footer** to display those sections.

17 Scroll the subreport to display the **Report Footer** section (you might have to adjust the Report window to see the scrollbar), click the **Text Box** control in the toolbox, and then click in the center of the **Report Footer** section grid.

Access inserts an unbound control and its label. You will use this control to perform the calculation.

18 In the **Properties** dialog box, change the label's caption to Total:, and set the **Font Name** property to **Arial**, the **Font Size** property to **9**, and the **Font Weight** property to **Bold**.

19 Click the unbound text box control, in the **Properties** dialog box click the **Data** tab, click **Control Source**, and click the ... button to open the **Expression Builder**.

20 In the first column, double-click **Functions**, and click **Built-In Functions**. Then scroll down in the third column, and double-click **Sum**.

Access displays *Sum (<<expr>>)* in the expression box.

21 Click **<<expr>>**, click **Sales by Category subreport** in the first column, and double-click **ProductSales** in the second column.

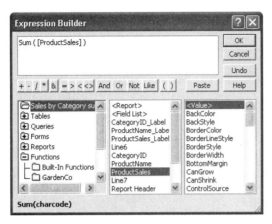

22 Click **OK** to close the **Expression Builder**, and then press [Enter] to enter the calculation in the unbound text box in the **Properties** dialog box.

23 Click the **Format** tab, and set the font properties as you did in step 18.

24 At the top of the **Format** tab of the **Properties** dialog box, click the down-arrow to the right of the **Format** box, click **Currency**, and then press [Enter].

Now the results of the calculation will be displayed as currency.

25 Position and adjust the size of the calculated control and its label to match those in the **Detail** section. Drag the left edge of the label to 1.1" and the right edge of the text box to 3.2 inches.

26 Save your changes, and switch to Print Preview to see the results.

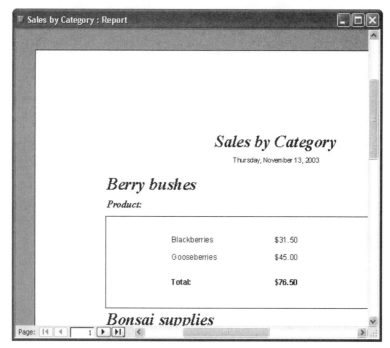

27 Switch to Design view, and click the subreport to select it.

Tip Several factors affect the layout of the subreport in the main report when it is displayed in Print Preview. The width of the subreport sets the width of the space available for the display of text. The height of the subreport sets the minimum height of the area where product information is displayed (because the Can Shrink property for the subreport is set to *No*). The maximum height of the product display area is the length of the list (because the Can Grow property is set to *Yes*) plus the space between the bottom of the subreport and the bottom of the Detail section.

28 On the **Format** tab of the **Properties** dialog box, change the **Border Style** property to **Transparent**.

29 Save your changes, preview the report, and then close it.

CLOSE the *GardenCo* database.

Previewing and Printing a Report

Microsoft Office Specialist

Print Preview in Access is very similar to Print Preview in other Microsoft Office System products. If you check out your reports carefully in Print Preview, you won't be in for any major surprises when you print them. But Access also provides a "quick and dirty" preview option called Layout Preview that displays only enough of the report for you to see all the elements. This view often produces a shorter report that is faster to print and provides just enough information to help you refine the layout.

Most people don't spend a lot of time studying the preview and print options, so in this exercise you will review them, in case there are a few you haven't tried yet. Then you'll print a report.

USE the *GardenCo* database in the practice file folder for this topic. This practice file is located in the *My Documents\Microsoft Press\Access 2003 SBS\Reports\Print* folder and can also be accessed by clicking *Start/All Programs/Microsoft Press/Access 2003 Step by Step*.
OPEN the *GardenCo* database and acknowledge the safety warning, if necessary.

1 Open the **Alphabetical List of Products** report in Design view.

2 Click the down arrow to the right of the **View** button to display the list of views.

View

Each of the three choices—Design view, Print Preview, and Layout Preview—has an associated icon. The Design view icon has a border, and is highlighted with a background color, indicating it is the current view. The Print Preview icon is duplicated on the View button, indicating that it is the default view if you simply click the button rather than display this menu and choose a view. When you are in Design view, both Print Preview and Layout Preview are available.

3 Click **Print Preview**.

In the preview environment, the Formatting and Report Design toolbars are hidden, the toolbox is hidden, and an image of how the report will look when it is printed is displayed, along with the Print Preview toolbar. If you can't see an entire page in the window, you can maximize the window, or click the Zoom button to toggle the page magnification.

Tip When the pointer appears as a plus sign, clicking it zooms in on (magnifies) the report. When it is a minus sign, clicking it decreases magnification.

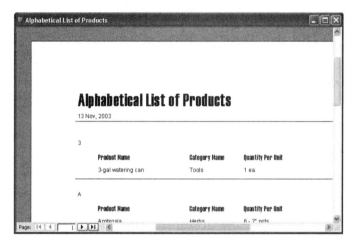

Next Page

4 On the Navigation bar, click the **Next Page** button repeatedly to view each of the 10 pages of this report.

Close

5 On the Print Preview toolbar, click the **Close** button.

New in Office 2003
Automatic error checking

Tip A new feature with Access 2003 is automatic error checking. Error checking identifies common errors in forms and reports and gives you a chance to fix them. For example, Access informs you if a report is wider than the page it will be printed on. To enable error checking, on the Tools menu, click Options, click the Error Checking tab, click the "Enable error checking" checkbox, and under Form/Report Design Rules, click the options you want to enable, and then click OK.

6 Click the down arrow to the right of the **View** button, and click **Layout Preview**.

The Print Preview toolbar is displayed, and the report looks similar to the way it does in Print Preview. However, not all products are listed in each group. (If you can't see the page clearly, zoom in.)

7 Click the **Next Page** button.

In Layout Preview, the report has only one or two pages.

8 Click the **Close** button to return to Design view.

9 On the **File** menu, click **Print** to display the **Print** dialog box.

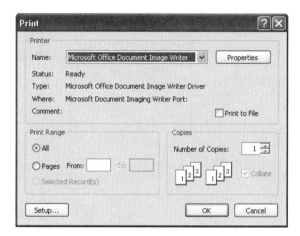

You can click the Setup button to open the Page Setup dialog box, or you can click Properties to open a dialog box in which you can set properties specific to the printer designated in the Name box. You can also specify which pages to print and the number of copies of each.

10 Click **Cancel** to close the **Print** dialog box.

11 Close the report.

CLOSE the *GardenCo* database.

Key Points

- A report created in Access 2003 typically summarizes and organizes information. When designing a report, consider the point you are trying to make, the intended audience, and the level of information they will need.

- You can use a wizard to create a report, or you can create one from scratch. Once the report is created, you can switch back and forth between Design view and Print Preview to refine your report.

- You can create a main report that serves as a shell for one or more subreports.

- To your report and/or subreport, you can add controls and set the properties of the controls. You can display information from one or more records from one or more tables or queries, and you can have multiple sets of headers and footers.

- If your report needs summary calculations or statistics, you can use a query as the basis for the report. You can enhance the usefulness of a report or subreport by performing calculations in the reports themselves. You can use the Expression Builder to create the expressions that tell Access what and how to calculate.

- Print Preview lets you check reports before printing them. The Layout Preview option displays only enough of the report to show all the elements. It's shorter, prints faster, and gives just enough information to help you refine the layout.

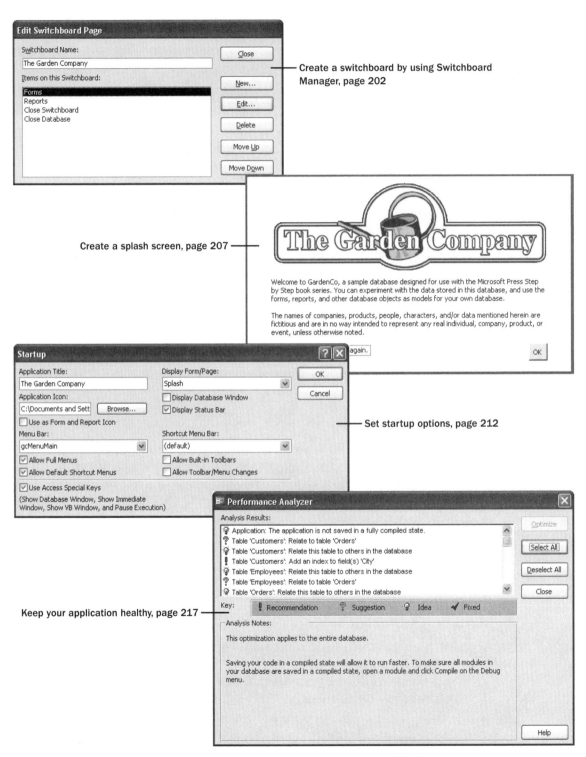

Create a switchboard by using Switchboard Manager, page 202

Create a splash screen, page 207

Set startup options, page 212

Keep your application healthy, page 217

Chapter 8 at a Glance

8 Making It Easy for Others to Use Your Database

In this chapter you will learn to:

✔ Create a switchboard by using Switchboard Manager.

✔ Create a splash screen.

✔ Set startup options.

✔ Keep your application healthy.

A database created with Microsoft Office Access 2003 is a complex combination of objects and information, and the tools required to manage and manipulate them. In the first seven chapters of this book, you have learned how to work with these components to enter, organize, retrieve, and display information. You have become a database developer. You can create databases that you, or others familiar with Access, can use.

However, if information will be entered and retrieved from your database by people who aren't proficient with Access, the information will be safer and the users happier if you take some steps to insulate them from the inner workings of Access. You need to turn your collection of objects and information into an application that organizes related tasks. Then users can focus on the job at hand, not on the program used to develop the application. With a little extra effort on your part, you can add features that make it much easier for others to access and manipulate your data, and much more difficult to unintentionally change or delete it. The most common ways to control access to a database application are through switchboards and startup options.

In this chapter, you will learn how to create and customize your own switchboard, create a splash screen, set various startup options, and use several Access utilities to help maintain the health of a database. You will be working with the GardenCo database files and a few other sample files provided on the book's companion CD.

See Also   Do you need only a quick refresher on the topics in this chapter? See the Quick Reference entries on pages xlii–xlii.

Important Before you can use the practice files in this chapter, you need to install them from the book's companion CD to their default location. See "Using the Book's CD-ROM" on page xiii for more information.

Creating a Switchboard by Using Switchboard Manager

A *switchboard* appears as a hierarchy of pages containing buttons that the user can click to open additional pages, display dialog boxes, present forms for viewing and entering data, preview and print reports, and initiate other activities. For example, sales-people for The Garden Company might use a switchboard to display a form to quickly enter orders or add new customers.

You can create switchboards by hand or with the help of Switchboard Manager. A switchboard created by hand is made up of multiple forms (pages) of your own design that are linked together by macros and Microsoft Visual Basic for Applications (VBA) code. A switchboard created with Switchboard Manager consists of a Switchboard Items table and one generic form containing eight hidden buttons. You can use Design view to change the location of buttons and add other visual elements (such as pictures), but unlike a switchboard created by hand, you can change the number of active buttons and the action that is performed when each button is clicked only by editing information in the Switchboard Items table.

Tip To be able to use a switchboard, you don't really need to know how switchboards created with Switchboard Manager work, but it helps to know what's going on behind the scenes in case you need to make changes. When the switchboard is opened, Access runs VBA code that reads information stored in the Switchboard Items table and uses it to set form properties that determine which buttons are visible in the generic form. The code also assigns labels and actions to the visible buttons. If you click a button to go to a second level in the switchboard hierarchy, the code reads the table again and resets the properties for the generic form to create the page for the new level.

In this exercise, you will use Switchboard Manager to create a simple switchboard for the GardenCo database.

BE SURE TO start Access before beginning this exercise.
USE the *GardenCo* database in the practice file folder for this topic. This practice file is located in the *My Documents\Microsoft Press\Access 2003 SBS\Switchbrd\SBManager* folder and can also be accessed by clicking *Start/All Programs/Microsoft Press/Access 2003 Step by Step*.
OPEN the *GardenCo* database and acknowledge the safety warning, if necessary.

1 On the **Tools** menu, point to **Database Utilities**, and click **Switchboard Manager**. When Access prompts you to create a switchboard, click **Yes**.

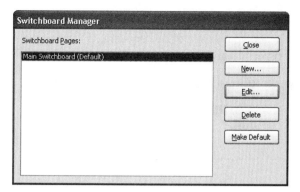

The first page of Switchboard Manager lists any existing switchboard pages. (It lists only pages created by Switchboard Manager; if you created any pages by hand, they are not listed here.) This database doesn't currently have any switchboard pages, but Access lists a default page to get you started.

2   With **Main Switchboard** selected in the **Switchboard Pages** list, click **Edit**.

3   In the **Switchboard Name** box, type The Garden Company to replace *Main Switchboard*, and then click **Close**.

The Garden Company switchboard is now the default for this database.

4   Click **New**.

The Create New dialog box appears, in which you can name new pages you want to add to the switchboard.

5   Type Forms to replace the text that is already selected in the **Switchboard Page Name** box, and then click **OK**.

6   Click **New** again, name the new page Reports, and click **OK**.

The Switchboard Manager displays your new pages.

7   With **The Garden Company (Default)** selected, click **Edit**.

Access displays the Edit Switchboard Page dialog box.

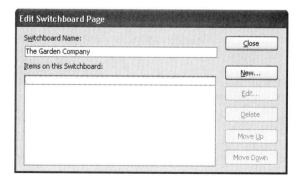

8 Click **New**.

The Edit Switchboard Item dialog box appears, in which you assign properties to one of the buttons on the generic switchboard page.

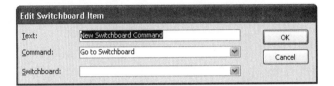

9 In the **Text** box, type Forms as the text that will be the label for a button.

The second box already contains the *Go to Switchboard* command, which is what you want for this example.

10 Click the down arrow to the right of the **Switchboard** box, click **Forms**, and then click **OK**.

The label and list of items in the third box vary depending on the command chosen in the second box.

11 Click **New** again, type Reports in the **Text** box, accept the *Go to Switchboard* command, click the down arrow to the right of the **Switchboard** box, click **Reports**, and click **OK**.

12 Click **New** again, and in the **Text** box, type Close Switchboard.

13 Click the down arrow in the right side of the **Command** box, and click **Run Macro**.

The label for the third box changes to *Macro*.

14 Click the down arrow to display the list of macros, scroll down, click **Switchboard.closeSB**, and then click **OK** to close the dialog box and save the changes.

Tip The Switchboard.closeSB macro does not come with Access; it was written specifically for this exercise. You can review this macro, and several others in the GardenCo database, by clicking Macros on the Objects bar and then opening a macro in Design view.

Access will open the macro group called *Switchboard* and start running the macro at the line named *closeSB*.

15 Click **New** again. Then in the **Text** box, type Close Database, click the down arrow to the right of the **Command** box, and click **Exit Application**. This command does not require a parameter, so the third box is no longer available. Click **OK** to close the dialog box and save the changes.

The Edit Switchboard Page dialog box now lists the items you've just created.

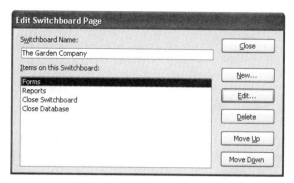

16 Click **Close** to return to **Switchboard Manager**.

17 In the list of Switchboard pages, click **Forms**, and then click **Edit**.

18 In the **Edit Switchboard Page** dialog box, add these five new buttons with the following properties. (Click **New** to open the **Edit Switchboard Item** dialog box for each new entry, and then click **OK** to accept each item added.)

Text	Command	Third box
Edit/Enter Categories	Open Form in Edit Mode	Categories
Edit/Enter Orders	Open Form in Edit Mode	Orders
Edit/Enter Products	Open Form in Edit Mode	Products
Edit/Enter Suppliers	Open Form in Edit Mode	Suppliers
Return	Go to Switchboard	The Garden Company

19 Click **Close** to return to **Switchboard Manager**.

20 Select the **Reports** page, click **Edit**, and add five buttons with these properties:

Text	Command	Third box
Preview/Print Catalog	Open Report	Catalog
Preview/Print Customer Labels	Open Report	Customer Labels
Preview/Print Invoices	Open Report	Invoice
Preview/Print Products	Open Report	Alphabetical List of Products
Return	Go to Switchboard	The Garden Company

21 Click **Close** twice to close the **Edit Switchboard Page** dialog box and **Switchboard Manager**.

22 On the **Objects** bar, click **Forms**, and double-click **Switchboard**. (You might have to scroll to the right to see the form.)

Your new switchboard opens in Form view.

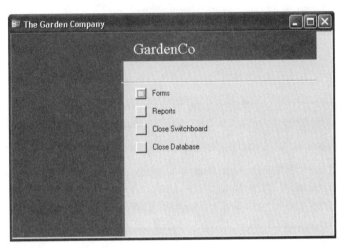

23 Click **Forms** on your new Switchboard, and then click **Edit/Enter Categories** to look at the Categories form. When you are finished, close the form.

24 Click **Return** to return to the first-level switchboard window.

25 Click the **View** button to view the switchboard in Design view.

View

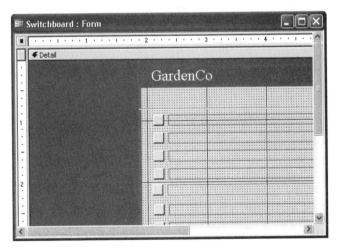

The form has eight buttons and no label text.

26 Click the first button, press F4 to open the **Properties** dialog box, click the **Format** tab, and look at the **Visible** property.

The first button and label are both set to Yes.

27 Click the rest of the buttons in the form, one at a time.

The Visible property of the rest of the buttons is set to No (not visible). When the form is displayed in Form view, it reads the Switchboard Items table and uses the data there to set the Visible property of the buttons and labels.

Tip You can reopen Switchboard Manager to add more pages or commands, and you can open the Switchboard form in Design view to add graphics or other objects. Because everything needed to produce the working switchboard is contained in the Switchboard form and its underlying Switchboard Items table, you can copy or import the form and the table to any other database in which you might want a similar switchboard, modifying them as needed with Switchboard Manager.

28 Click the **Event** tab, and then look at the **On Click** event for the buttons and labels.

Each event is associated with a variable. In the Switchboard Items table, created by the Switchboard Manager to store information about the switchboard's buttons, this variable is in turn associated with the command and parameters (if any) you specified. When you click a button in Form view, Access checks the On Click property, looks up the variable in the Switchboard Items table, and carries out the associated command.

29 Close the **Properties** dialog box, and then close the **Switchboard** form, clicking **Yes** to save the form.

CLOSE the *GardenCo* database.

Creating a Splash Screen

Many applications display a *splash screen* upon starting. This screen is sometimes an animation or piece of artwork, sometimes an advertisement for the company that created the database application, and occasionally a useful dialog box that displays information or instructions. The hidden purpose of a splash screen is often to divert the user's attention while the rest of the application loads into the computer's memory. The Access applications that you create probably won't take a long time to load, but a splash screen can still be useful.

Because the splash screen is the first thing users see each time they open the application, you can use it to remind them of important points, such as how to get help or how to contact you. This is also a good place to display a randomly selected tip—as long as the tip is more useful than irritating. To avoid having users get annoyed at anything that stands between them and the use of your application, you should always provide the option of not having the splash screen appear in the future.

A splash screen that users can interact with in some manner—by clicking buttons or entering text—is a specialized type of dialog box. You create this type of dialog box in Access by adding controls to a form.

In this exercise you will create a simple splash screen for the GardenCo database.

USE the *GardenCo* database, *tgc_logo1* icon, and *Paragraphs* text file in the practice file folder for this topic. These practice files are located in the *My Documents\Microsoft Press\Access 2003 SBS\Switchbrd\Splash* folder and can also be accessed by clicking *Start/All Programs/Microsoft Press/Access 2003 Step by Step*. OPEN the *GardenCo* database and acknowledge the safety warning, if necessary.

1 On the **Objects** bar, click **Forms**, and then double-click **Create form in Design view**. (You might have to scroll left to see this option.)

Save

2 Click the **Save** button, and in the **Form Name** box, type Splash. Then click **OK**.

3 If the **Properties** dialog box is not already displayed, press [F4].

The Form object should already be selected in the list at the top of the dialog box.

4 Click the **Format** tab, and set the following properties:

Property	Setting
Scroll Bars	Neither
Record Selectors	No
Navigation Buttons	No
Dividing Lines	No
Auto Center	Yes
Border Style	None
Control Box	No
Min Max Buttons	None
Close Button	No
Width	5.5"

Toolbox

5 If the Toolbox is not displayed, click the **Toolbox** button.

The Toolbox is now displayed.

Rectangle

6 In the Toolbox, click the **Rectangle** button, and then click anywhere in the **Detail** section.

A small rectangle appears where you clicked.

7 On the **Format** tab of the **Properties** dialog box, set the following properties for the rectangle:

Property	Setting
Left	0
Top	0
Width	5.5"
Height	3.25"
Back Style	Normal
Special Effect	Flat
Border Style	Solid
Border Color	32768
Border Width	6 pt

The form changes in the background as you change each setting.

Image

8 In the Toolbox, click the **Image** button, and then click in the rectangle, near the top.

Access inserts an image frame and displays the Insert Picture dialog box.

9 Navigate to the *My Documents\Microsoft Press\Access 2003 SBS\Switchbrd\Splash* folder, and double-click **tgc_logo1**.

Access inserts The Garden Company's logo in the image control.

10 Drag the image to center the logo along the top of the form, just below the border.

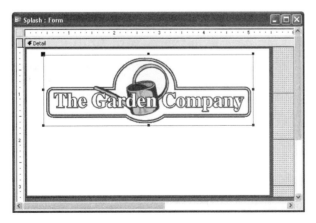

Label

11 In the Toolbox, click the **Label** button, and then click below the left corner of the logo to insert a label. In the label, type Placeholder, and press Enter.

12 Align the left edge of the label with the left edge of the logo, and set the top just below the bottom of the logo.

13 Drag the handle at the lower-right corner of the label down and to the right until the label is as wide as the logo and about an inch high. (You might have to resize your window.)

14 Open any text editor, such as Microsoft Notepad. On the **File** menu, click **Open**, navigate to the *My Documents\Microsoft Press\Access 2003 SBS\Switchbrd\Splash* folder, and then double-click **Paragraphs**. Copy the two paragraphs in that file to the clipboard, and then press [Alt]+[Tab] to return to the Splash form, select the *Placeholder* text, and paste the two paragraphs into the label control.

Check Box

15 In the Toolbox, click the **Check Box** button, and then click about a quarter inch below the label, aligned with its left edge, to insert a check box.

16 In the **Properties** dialog box, click the **Other** tab, and name the control chkHideSplash. Then on the **Data** tab, set the **Default Value** property to 0 (meaning *No*).

17 Click the label associated with the check box, and on the **Format** tab, type Don't show this screen again as its **Caption** property.

18 With the label still selected, on the **Format** menu, click **Size**, and then click **To Fit**.

The entire caption is now displayed.

Control
Wizards

19 If the **Control Wizards** button is not active (orange) in the Toolbox, click it.

Command
Button

20 Click the **Command Button** button, and insert a command button near the right edge of the form, opposite the check box.

Access adds a button to the form and starts the Command Button Wizard.

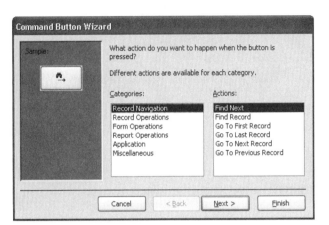

21 In the **Categories** list, click **Form Operations**.

22 In the **Actions** list, click **Close Form**, and click **Next**.

23 Click **Text**, change the caption text from *Close Form* to OK, and then click **Next**.

24 Type OK to name the button, and then click **Finish**.

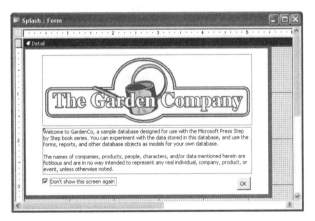

View

25 Save the design, and then click the **View** button to switch to Form view.

The form has a gray border because it doesn't quite fill the design grid.

26 Switch back to Design view.

27 Click the **Form Section Selector**, and then on the **Format** tab in the **Properties** dialog box, set the width to 5.5".

28   Save and close the **Splash** form and reopen it in Form view.

29   Click **OK** in the form to close the splash screen.

CLOSE the *GardenCo* database and the text editor you opened in step **14**.

Setting Startup Options

You can start Access and open a database in a variety of ways. Here are the most common ways:

- Click Start, point to All Programs, and click Microsoft Access.

- Double-click a shortcut to MSACCESS.

- Double-click a shortcut to a database file.

- Double-click a database file name in a folder.

With the first two methods, Access starts, displaying a blank window from which a new database can be created or an existing one opened. With the last two methods, Access starts, and then it opens the specified database.

Tip   When you start a program by clicking a command on the Start button's All Programs submenu, you are in fact clicking a shortcut. The entire Start menu is a hierarchical arrangement of shortcuts.

If your database will be used by people with little or no experience with Access, you might want to control which features are available when a database opens. There are several ways to do this. If you want users to be able to open only one database, you can add one or more options to the shortcut used to start Access. These options can open a specific database, run macros, and perform other tasks. A more common way to control the user's environment is to set startup options in each database. You can use startup options to control the menus and toolbars available to the user, the form displayed (such as a splash screen or switchboard), and other features. The startup form can include macros and VBA procedures that run automatically to set other conditions.

Tip   This exercise uses custom toolbars and menus that were created specially for the sample database. For information about how to create this type of item, search for *toolbar* in Access online Help. Also, the Orders form in this exercise uses several custom macros. You can review these macros by clicking Macros on the Objects bar and then opening orderForm in Design view. The exercise also uses VBA code attached to the splash screen. You can review this code by selecting the Splash form and then clicking the Code button on the Access window's toolbar.

In this exercise, you will set startup options that tie together a splash screen, a switch-board, and some custom menus to create a version of the GardenCo database that is appropriate for inexperienced users.

USE the *GardenCo* database in the practice file folder for this topic. This practice file is located in the *My Documents\Microsoft Press\Access 2003 SBS\Switchbrd\Startup* folder and can also be accessed by clicking *Start/All Programs/Microsoft Press/Access 2003 Step by Step*.
OPEN the *GardenCo* database and acknowledge the safety warning, if necessary.

1   On the **Tools** menu, click **Startup**.

The Startup dialog box appears.

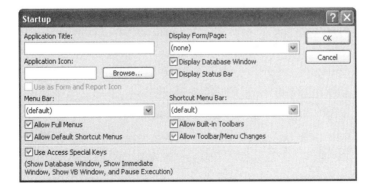

2 With the insertion point in the **Application Title** box, type The Garden Company, and press Tab.

The text you just entered will be displayed in the Access title bar, replacing the usual *Microsoft Access* title.

3 Click the **Browse** button at the end of the **Application Icon** box, and navigate to the *My Documents\Microsoft Press\Access 2003 SBS\Switchbrd\Startup* folder. Click **icon_tgc**, and then click **OK** to enter it as the application icon.

This icon will appear in the left corner of the title bar, followed by *The Garden Company*.

Troubleshooting   The full path to the icon is recorded. As long as you don't move the icon, you can move the database to another folder on the same computer, and Access will still find the icon. If you plan to move the database to a different computer, you should instead use the icon's Universal Naming Convention (UNC) path.

4 Click the down arrow to the right of the **Menu Bar** box, and then click **gcMenuMain**.

This is a menu bar created specifically for this exercise. The alternative, (default), is the standard menu bar.

5 In the **Display Form/Page** box, click the down arrow to display the list of forms, and select **Splash**.

This database's splash screen will be displayed each time the database is opened.

6 Clear the **Display Database Window** check box, but leave **Display Status Bar** checked.

Tip   For experienced users, the database window is like a home page: it is where everything starts. But having this window available could be confusing for someone whose only job is entering orders, and it could be disastrous if inexperienced people make changes to critical data.

7 Leave the **Shortcut Menu Bar** box set to *(default)*.

8 Clear both the **Allow Built-in Toolbars** and the **Allow Toolbar/Menu Changes** check boxes.

None of the built-in toolbars can be displayed, preventing the user from making changes to custom toolbars and menus.

9 For the time being, leave **Use Access Special Keys** selected.

When this option is selected, several special key combinations are available, including Ctrl+F11, which toggles the standard menu on.

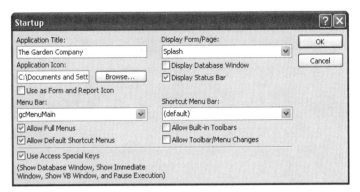

10 Click **OK** to close the **Startup** dialog box.

Most startup options don't go into effect until you close and restart the database. The only changes you should see now are the icon and the name in the Access window's title bar.

11 Close and reopen the **GardenCo** database, enabling macros if necessary.

The startup options go into effect: you see the new title bar, the custom menu bar, and the splash screen.

12 On the splash screen, click **OK**.

Troubleshooting   If you get an error when you click OK on the splash screen, click the Reset button. The Visual Basic Editor will be displayed. On the Tools menu, click References, scroll down, click Microsoft DAO 3.6 Object Library, and click OK. Then repeat your tests.

The VBA code attached to the Splash form in the GardenCo database causes the switchboard to be displayed.

13 On the switchboard, click **Forms**, and then click **Edit/Enter Orders** on the second-level switchboard page.

The Orders form and its associated custom toolbar appear.

Tip   If the toolbar appears in the Orders form, you can drag it and dock it below the menu bar.

Custom menu bar

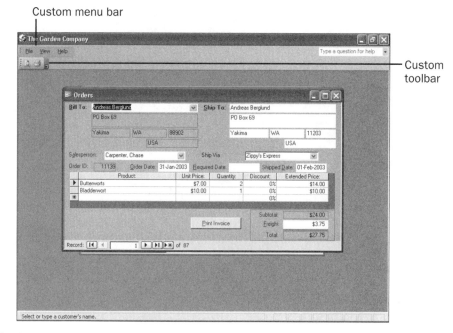

Custom toolbar

14 On the **View** menu, click **Customers**.

The Customers form opens on top of the Orders form, and your custom toolbar disappears because it is associated only with the Orders form.

15 Close the **Customers** form.

The custom toolbar reappears.

16 Right-click the **Orders** form.

The standard shortcut menu appears.

Tip Being able to display the shortcut menu could be a problem if you don't want to give users the means to alter the form's design. You can solve this problem by creating a custom shortcut menu and specifying it in the form's properties.

17 Press Esc to close the shortcut menu, and then close the **Orders** form.

18 Press Ctrl+F11.

The standard menu bar replaces the custom one. (If you missed that change, you can press Ctrl+F11 again to toggle between the standard menu bar and the custom one.)

Tip Toggling between the menu bars is possible because you did not clear the "Use Access Special Keys" check box in the Startup dialog box. It is handy to have this option available while you are developing a database, but you might want to disable it when the database is ready to put into service.

19 Press **F11**.

This Access Special Key displays the database window—another reason why the Access Special Keys probably should not be available to users.

Tip The only way to prevent a user from bypassing your startup options is to write and run a VBA procedure that creates the AllowByPassKey property and sets it to *False*. There is no way to set this property through Access. For information about how to do this, search for *AllowByPassKey* in the Help file available when you are working in the Visual Basic Editor.

20 Close the database window, which closes the **GardenCo** database.

21 While holding down the **Shift** key, open the **GardenCo** database again.

Holding down the **Shift** key while you start the database bypasses all the startup options, so the database starts the same way it did before you set these options. You must continue to hold the **Shift** key down while you acknowledge the safety warning.

CLOSE the *GardenCo* database.

Keeping Your Application Healthy

In the day-to-day use of an Access database—adding and deleting records, modifying forms and reports, and so on—various problems can develop. This is especially true if the database is stored on a local area network and is accessed by multiple users. Access monitors the health of database files as you open and work with them. If it sees a problem developing, it attempts to fix it. If Access can't fix a problem, it usually displays a message suggesting that you take some action. But Access doesn't always spot problems before they affect the database, and sometimes database performance seems to slow down or become erratic. Even if no serious errors creep in, simply using a database causes its internal structure to become fragmented, resulting in a bloated file and inefficient use of disk space.

You don't have to wait for Access to spot a problem. There are various things you can do to help keep your database healthy and running smoothly. Your first line of defense against damage or corruption in any kind of file is the maintenance of backups. Database files rapidly become too large to conveniently back up to floppy disk, but you have many other options: you can copy the file to another computer on the network, send it as an e-mail attachment to another location, use a tape backup, burn a CD-ROM, or copy it to some other removable media.

There are several utilities that you can use to keep your database running smoothly. The following list describes a few of these utilities:

- Compact and Repair Database. The repair portion of this utility attempts to repair corruption in tables, forms, reports, and modules. Compacting the database rearranges how the file is stored on your hard disk, which optimizes performance.

- Performance Analyzer. This utility analyzes the objects in your database and offers feedback divided into three categories: ideas, suggestions, and recommendations. If you would like to follow through on any of the suggestions or recommendations, you can click a button to have Access optimize the file.

- Documenter. This tool, which is part of the Performance Analyzer, produces a detailed report that can be saved and printed. It includes enough information to rebuild the database structure if that were ever necessary.

- Detect and Repair. This command, which appears on the Help menu, is not a command to be clicked casually. Running this utility might make changes to files and registry settings that affect all Office programs.

In this exercise, you will back up the GardenCo database, and then compact and repair it. You will then run the Performance Analyzer and Documenter.

USE the *GardenCo* database in the practice file folder for this topic. This practice file is located in the *My Documents\Microsoft Press\Access 2003 SBS\Switchbrd\Health* folder and can also be accessed by clicking *Start/All Programs/Microsoft Press/Access 2003 Step by Step*.
OPEN the *GardenCo* database and acknowledge the safety warning, if necessary.

New in
Office 2003
Back Up
Database

1 On the **File** menu, click **Back Up Database**.

> **Tip** You can also access this command on the Tools menu by clicking Database Utilities, and then clicking Back Up Database.

2 In the **Save Backup As** dialog box, navigate to the *My Documents\Microsoft Press\Access 2003 SBS\Switchbrd\Health* folder, accept the file name Access provides, and click **Save**.

> **Tip** When you create a back up file, Access appends the current date to the file name in the following format: *GardenCo_2003-04-22.mdb*. You can change the file name to suit your needs.

A copy of the database is created and stored in the specified folder.

3 Acknowledge the safety warning to reopen the GardenCo database.

4 On the **File** menu, click **Database Properties** to open the dialog box.

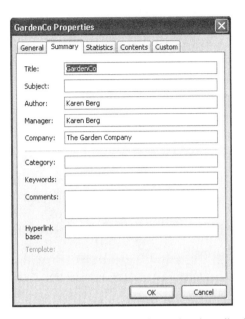

This dialog box contains five tabs that display information about your database.

5   Click the **General** tab, and note the size of the database.

6   Click **OK** to close the dialog box.

7   On the **Tools** menu, point to **Database Utilities**, and then click **Compact and Repair Database**, acknowledging the safety warning when prompted.

The utility takes only a few seconds to run, and you will see no difference in the appearance of the database.

Troubleshooting   If you don't have enough space on your hard disk to store a temporary copy of the database, if you don't have appropriate permissions, or if someone else on your network also has the database open, Compact and Repair Database will not run properly.

8   Display the database's **Properties** dialog box again, and compare the current size to its previous size.

You can expect a 10 to 25 percent reduction in the size of the database if you have been using it for a while.

Tip   It is a good idea to compact and repair the database often. You can have Access do this automatically each time the database is closed, by clicking Options on the Tools menu, selecting the Compact on Close option on the General tab of the Options dialog box, and clicking OK.

9 Click **OK** to close the **Database Properties** dialog box.

10 On the **Tools** menu, point to **Analyze**, and then click **Performance**.

This Performance Analyzer dialog box is displayed:

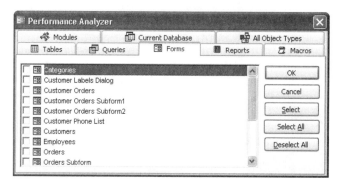

This dialog box contains a tab for each type of object that can be analyzed, and a tab that displays objects of all types.

11 Click the **All Object Types** tab.

12 Click **Select All**, and then click **OK** to start the analyzer.

You will see quite a bit of action on your screen as the analyzer opens and closes windows. (If the splash screen is open, the analyzer skips it.) When it finishes, the analyzer displays its results in the dialog box. (The results you see might be different from those shown here.)

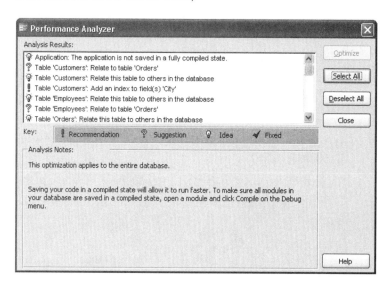

The icons in the left column of the Analysis Results list indicate the category of each entry: *Recommendation*, *Suggestion*, *Idea*, and *Fixed*. (When you first run the Performance Analyzer, there will be no Fixed entries in the list.) Clicking an entry displays information about it in the Analysis Notes section.

13 Scroll through the list, click each entry in turn, and read through all the analysis notes.

Most of the suggestions are valid, though some, such as the one to change the data type of the PostalCode field to Long Integer, are not appropriate for this database.

14 Close the **Performance Analyzer** dialog box.

15 On the **Tools** menu, point to **Analyze**, and then click **Documenter**.

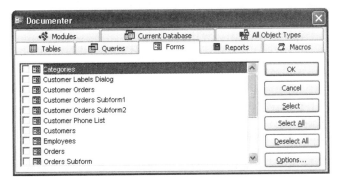

The Documenter dialog box appears. It is similar to the Performance Analyzer dialog box, in that it contains a tab for each object type that it can document. You can select individual objects on one or more tabs, or click All Object Types and make your selections.

16 Click the **Tables** tab, and then click the **Options** button.

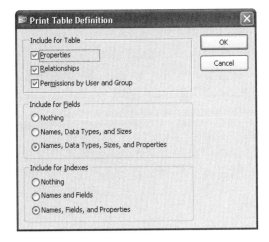

The Options dialog box offers print options associated with the current tab. The options differ for each tab, but all are similar to these, in that you can use them to specify what to include in the documentation for each type of object.

17 Click **Cancel** to close the dialog box.

18 Click the **All Object Types** tab.

19 Click **Select All**, and then click **OK** to start the documentation process.

As the documenter runs, objects are opened and closed, and the status bar displays the progress through the objects. When the process is finished, a report is displayed in Print Preview.

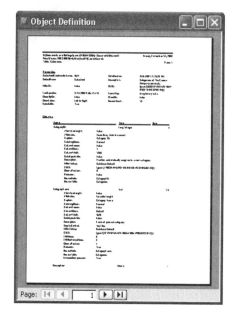

This report can run to hundreds of pages, so you probably don't want to click the Print button right now. However, it is a good idea to save a report such as this for your own databases, in case you ever need to reconstruct them.

You can't save the report generated by the documenter, but you can export it. On the File menu, click Export, and then select a format. The best format is probably RTF, which can be opened in Microsoft Word.

20 Close the report.

CLOSE the *GardenCo* database.

Key Points

- You can create a switchboard and set startup options to make it easier for others to access and manipulate your data, and more difficult to unintentionally change or delete data.

- You can create a splash screen that appears when your database is opened. The splash screen might contain advertising, a graphic logo, or an animation, and can also provide helpful instructions to users.

- There are several utilities that you can use to keep your database running smoothly—Compact and Repair Database, Performance Analyzer, Documenter, and Detect and Repair. You can keep your application healthy by taking advantage of these utilities before Access indicates there is a problem with your database.

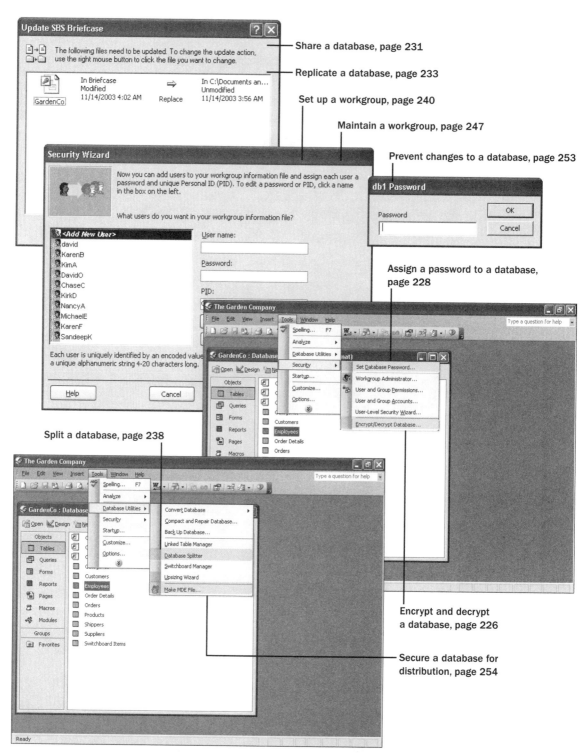

Share a database, page 231

Replicate a database, page 233

Set up a workgroup, page 240

Maintain a workgroup, page 247

Prevent changes to a database, page 253

Assign a password to a database, page 228

Split a database, page 238

Encrypt and decrypt a database, page 226

Secure a database for distribution, page 254

9 Keeping Your Information Secure

The need for *database security* is an unfortunate fact of life. As with your house, car, office, or briefcase, the level of security required for your database depends on the value of what you have and whether you are trying to protect it from curious eyes, accidental damage, malicious destruction, or theft.

The security of a company's business information can be critical to its survival. For example, The Garden Company's owners might not be too concerned if a person gained unauthorized access to their products list, but they would be very concerned if a competitor managed to see—or worse, steal—their customer list. And it would be a disaster if someone destroyed their critical order information.

Your goal as a database developer is to provide adequate protection without imposing unnecessary restrictions on the people who should have access to your database. The type of security required to protect a database depends to a large extent on how many people are using it and where it is stored. If your database is never opened by more than one person at a time, you don't have to worry about the potential for corruption caused by several people trying to update the same information at the same time. If many people access the database to work with different types of information, you will want to consider setting up workgroups and assigning permissions to restrict the information each group can see and the actions they can perform. If your database is sold as part of an application, you will want to take steps to prevent it from being misused in any way.

In this chapter, you will explore various ways to protect data from accidental or intentional corruption and to make it difficult for curious eyes to see private information.

See Also Do you need only a quick refresher on the topics in this chapter? See the Quick Reference entries on pages xliii–xlv.

Important Before you can use the practice files in this chapter, you need to install them from the book's companion CD to their default location. See "Using the Book's CD-ROM" on page xiii for more information.

Encrypting and Decrypting a Database

A database created with Microsoft Office Access 2003 is a *binary file*, meaning that it is composed of mostly unreadable characters. If you open it in a word processor or a text editor, at first glance it looks like gibberish. However, if you poke around in the file long enough, you will discover quite a bit of information. Most likely, not enough information is exposed to allow someone to steal anything valuable. But if you are concerned that someone might scan your database file with a utility that looks for key words, you can *encrypt* the file to make it really unreadable.

Encrypting a file doesn't prevent it from being opened and viewed in Access. It does not add password protection or any other kind of security. But it does keep people who don't have a copy of Access from being able to read and perhaps make sense of the data in your file. The only difference you might notice when opening an encrypted database in Access is that some tasks might take slightly longer. If this is an issue, you will want to *decrypt* it before you work with it.

In this exercise, you will encrypt and decrypt the GardenCo database.

BE SURE TO start Access before beginning this exercise.
USE the *GardenCo* database in the practice file folder for this topic. This practice file is located in the *My Documents\Microsoft Press\Access 2003 SBS\Secure\Encrypt* folder and can also be accessed by clicking *Start/All Programs/Microsoft Press/Access 2003 Step by Step*.
OPEN the *GardenCo* database and acknowledge the safety warning, if necessary.

1 On the **Tools** menu, point to **Security**, and then click **Encode/Decode Database**.

The Encode Database As dialog box appears.

2 Navigate to the *My Documents\Microsoft Press\Access 2003 SBS\Secure\Encrypt* folder, type GardenCo_Encode as the name of the encrypted file you want to create, click **Save**, and acknowledge the safety warning.

An encrypted version of the database is created, but you continue to work in the original GardenCo database. You could have saved the encrypted database with the same name (you would be warned that you were overwriting an existing file), but this way you can compare the two versions.

3 Close the database, and start a text editor, such as Microsoft Notepad. On the **File** menu, click **Open**. In the **Files of type** box, click **All Files**, navigate to the *My Documents\Microsoft Press\Access 2003 SBS\Secure\Encrypt* folder, and then click **GardenCo**.

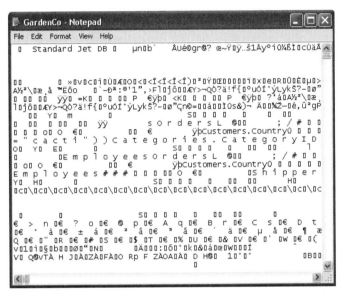

4 Close the **GardenCo** database, and open **GardenCo_Encode** in the same text editor.

It would be difficult to make much sense of the original file, and the same section of the encrypted version is even less meaningful.

5 Close the text editor.

6 Start Access, and navigate to the *My Documents\Microsoft Press\Access 2003 SBS \Secure\Encrypt* folder. Double-click **GardenCo_Encode**, and acknowledge the safety warning, if necessary.

The encrypted file looks identical to the original.

Tip Encrypting a database compresses it, but the amount of *compression* is minimal. Using the Compact and Repair utility provides more compression. Using a third-party compression program such as WinZip provides far more compression than either of the other methods and has the added benefit of effectively encrypting the database.

7 Close the **GardenCo_Encrypt** database.

8 To decrypt the encrypted database, on the **Tools** menu, point to **Security**, and click **Encode/Decode Database**.

9 In the **Encode/Decode Database** dialog box, navigate to the *My Documents \Microsoft Press\Access 2003 SBS\Secure\Encrypt* folder, click **GardenCo_Encode**, and then click **OK**.

The Decode Database As dialog box appears.

10 In the **File name** box, type GardenCo_Decode, and click **Save**.

11 Quit Access.

12 Click the Windows **Start** button, navigate to the *My Documents\Microsoft Press \Access 2003 SBS\Secure\Encrypt* folder, and then compare the size of the three databases.

Decrypting a database doesn't uncompress it, so usually the difference in size between the encrypted file and the decrypted file, if any, is minimal.

Assigning a Password to a Database

You can prevent unauthorized users from opening a database by assigning it a *password*. Anyone attempting to open the database will be asked for the password. If they enter it correctly, they will have full access to the database; if they don't, the database won't open.

Tip You can use anything as a password as long as you remember these rules. Passwords are case-sensitive and can range from 1 to 20 characters. You can include letters, accented characters, numbers, spaces, and most symbols. A password can't start with a space, and it can't include any of the following: \ [ ] : | < > + = ; , . ? *. A good password should not be a word found in a dictionary, and it should include upper and lower case letters, and symbols or numbers.

A database password is easy to set, and it is better than no protection at all in that it keeps most honest people out of the database. However, many inexpensive password recovery utilities are available, theoretically to help people recover a lost password. Anyone can buy one of these utilities and "recover" the password to your database. Also, the same password works for all users, and nothing prevents one person from giving the password to many other people. As a result, simple password protection is most appropriate for a single-user database. If your database is on a *network server* and can be opened by more than one person at a time (multi-user), you should consider setting up a workgroup and assigning a security account password.

When setting or removing a password, you must open a database for *exclusive use*, meaning that nobody else can have the database open. This will not be a problem for the database used in the exercise, but if you want to set or remove a password for a real database that is on a network, you will need to make sure nobody else is using it.

In this exercise, you will assign a password to the GardenCo database.

BE SURE TO start Access before beginning this exercise, but don't open the *GardenCo* database yet.
USE the *GardenCo* database in the practice file folder for this topic. This practice file is located in the *My Documents\Microsoft Press\Access 2003 SBS\Secure\Password* folder and can also be accessed by clicking *Start/All Programs/Microsoft Press/Access 2003 Step by Step*.

Open

1 On the Access toolbar, click the **Open** button to display the **Open** dialog box.

2 Navigate to the *My Documents\Microsoft Press\Access 2003 SBS\Secure\Password* folder, click **GardenCo**, and then click the down arrow to the right of the **Open** button to display the menu.

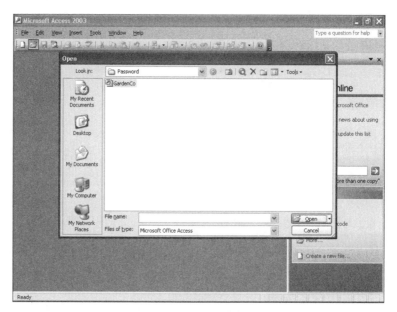

3 Click **Open Exclusive**, and enable macros, if necessary.

4 On the **Tools** menu, point to **Security**, and click **Set Database Password**.

The Set Database Password dialog box appears.

5 In the **Password** box, type Nos!Len, and press [Tab].

6 In the **Verify** box, type Nos!Len, and then click **OK**.

Tip To remove the password, repeat steps 2 through 4 to open the database exclusively (you will have to enter the password), and on the Tools menu point to Security, and click Unset Database Password. Type the password in the dialog box, and press [Enter]. Access removes the password, and anyone can then open the database.

7 Close and reopen the database.

The Password Required dialog box appears.

8   Type something other than the correct password, and click **OK**.

Access warns you that the password is not valid.

9   Click **OK** to close the message, type the correct password (Nos!Len), and then click **OK** again.

10   Acknowledge the safety warning, if necessary.

The database opens.

CLOSE the *GardenCo* database.

Sharing a Database

When a limited number of people are working on a local area network (LAN), *sharing a database* is easy. You simply place the database file in a folder that everyone can access, and then limit who can do what to the database by using the same *network security* you use to protect other information on the network. The number of people who can share a database in this manner depends on how many access it at the same time and what they want to do.

Access manages multiple users fairly well, but you will want to take precautions to prevent multiple users from attempting to update the same record at the same time. For example, if more than one employee at The Garden Company tried to change the same record in the Products table at exactly the same time, the results would be unpredictable if no precautions were in place. For small groups of people, you might want to implement *pessimistic locking*, which locks a record for the entire time it is being edited. For larger groups, you might want to implement *optimistic locking*, which locks a record only for the brief time that Access is saving the changes.

Important   When sharing a database on a LAN, each workstation on which the database will be opened must have a copy of Access installed.

In this exercise, you will explore several options that are designed to ensure that a database can be shared without any problem.

USE the *GardenCo* database in the practice file folder for this topic. This practice file is located in the *My Documents\Microsoft Press\Access 2003 SBS\Secure\Share* folder and can also be accessed by clicking *Start/All Programs/Microsoft Press/Access 2003 Step by Step.*
OPEN the *GardenCo* database and acknowledge the safety warning, if necessary.

1 On the **Tools** menu, click **Options** to display the **Options** dialog box.

2 Click the **Advanced** tab.

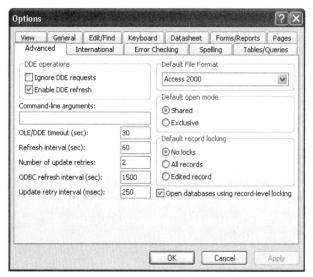

3 In the **Default open mode** area, make sure that the **Shared** option is selected.

If the Exclusive option is selected, only one person at a time can open the database. If Shared is selected, more than one person can have the database open. (The Shared option can be overridden by selecting Open Exclusive in the Open dialog box.)

4 In the **Default record locking** area, select the **Edited record** option.

Only the record that is being edited will be locked.

5 Make sure the **Open database using record-level locking** check box is selected.

6 Confirm that the following *properties* are still set to their default values, which should be appropriate for most situations:

Property	Setting
Refresh interval (sec)	60
Number of update retries	2
ODBC refresh interval (sec)	1500
Update retry interval (msec)	250

Tip These properties work together to determine what happens when two users attempt to update a record at the same time. For more information about these properties, click the Help button (?) in the upper-right corner of the dialog box, and then click the box containing a setting.

7 Click **OK** to close the dialog box.

Now when someone is editing a record in this shared database, no one else will be able to make a change to a record that is currently in use.

8 Close the database.

CLOSE the *GardenCo* database.

Replicating a Database

Database *replication* is the process of converting your database to a new version, called a *Design Master*, and then creating *replicas* of that master database that can be distributed to different people, who can then edit the data. Each person working on the database must have his or her own replica.

When you create a replica with the Create Replica command, Access closes the database and creates a master and a replica (named *Replica of <database>*). You repeat this for every replica you want to create. The name of each replica is made unique by the addition of a number. After users have made changes to their replicas, the modified replicas are returned to you, and you use the other commands on the Replication submenu to synchronize the versions and resolve conflicts. For more information on this process, search on *replication* in Access online Help.

Database *synchronization* is the process of comparing the information between two members of the replica set (two versions of the master database) and merging any changes. If changes to the same field in the same record cause any conflicts, a winner and a loser are determined by priorities assigned to the members of the set.

(For example, the replica that was edited by The Garden Company's sales manager would probably have a higher priority than the one edited by a sales clerk.) The winning change is applied to the master database, and the losing change is recorded as a conflict. After the master database has been compared to each replica, all changes have been recorded, and all conflicts have been resolved (you can use the *Conflict Resolution Wizard* to help with this process), all the replicas are updated with the current information from the Design Master and are sent back to the remote locations.

Tip This process sounds complex, and it is. If you think you need replication, you should look into acquiring Microsoft Office XP Developer (MOD). Several of the more difficult tasks are made easier with the help of the Replication Manager, which is included with MOD.

The primary use of replication is in *data warehouses* where, for example, daily database updates might be sent from branch stores to be synchronized with a master database at night. Updated information about stock levels and specials would then be returned to the branch stores in the morning.

A full-scale exercise demonstrating database replication is too complex for the simple format of this book, but one fairly simple form of database replication can be useful to the average user. Microsoft Windows comes with *Briefcase*, which uses replication to keep files in sync when you work on different computers in different locations. For example, the owner of The Garden Company might want to take the GardenCo database home at night to work with on her laptop.

In this exercise, you will replicate a database to the Briefcase folder on the desktop of your computer. (It is assumed that you don't currently have a Briefcase folder on your computer.)

USE the *GardenCo* database in the practice file folder for this topic. This practice file is located in the *My Documents\Microsoft Press\Access 2003 SBS\Secure\Replicate* folder and can also be accessed by clicking *Start/All Programs/Microsoft Press/Access 2003 Step by Step*.

1 Right-click the desktop, point to **New,** and then click **Briefcase** on the shortcut menu.

A New Briefcase icon appears on your desktop.

Tip If the Briefcase program isn't installed on your computer, you will need to install it by using the Add/Remove Programs icon in Control Panel.

2 Rename *New Briefcase* **SBS Briefcase** by clicking the icon, clicking its name, replacing *New* with **SBS,** and pressing [Enter].

3 Click the Windows **Start** button, and navigate to the *My Documents\Microsoft Press \Access 2003 SBS\Secure\Replicate* folder.

4 Reduce the size of the window, and position it so that you can see both the **GardenCo** database file and **SBS Briefcase** on your desktop.

Tip The Briefcase folder doesn't have to be on the desktop. You can follow these steps from within any folder to create a folder named *New Briefcase* in that folder.

5 Drag **GardenCo** to **SBS Briefcase**.

The Updating Briefcase alert box displays the message *Copying from 'Replicate' to 'SBS Briefcase'*, and after a moment, a message appears.

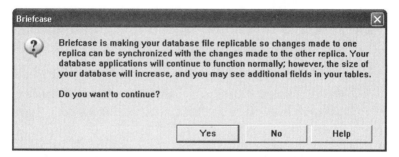

6 Click **Yes** to continue.

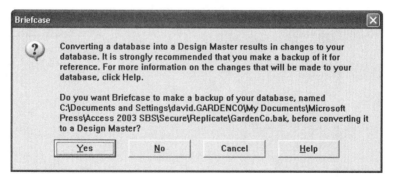

7 Click **Yes** to have Briefcase make a backup copy of your database.

A dialog box appears, informing you that Briefcase has converted your database to a Design Master and placed a replica in the SBS Briefcase folder.

8 Click **OK** to accept the option to allow design changes only in the original copy of the database and to finish the replication process.

9 Navigate to the practice file folder (which should still be open), and notice the difference in size between the Design Master (*GardenCo*) and the backup (*GardenCo.bak*). Replication substantially increases the size of the original database.

The Design Master and a backup copy of the database are in the practice file folder, and a replica of the database is in the SBS Briefcase folder. If you want to work on the database on a different computer that is not connected to this one through a LAN, you can copy the replica (or the entire SBS Briefcase folder) to removable media, such as a Zip disk or CD-ROM. (It's almost certainly too big for a floppy disk.)

Tip   If you want to work on a laptop connected through a LAN to the computer containing the GardenCo database, you can drag the database to the Briefcase on your laptop.

10 To simulate the editing and synchronizing process, start by double-clicking the **SBS Briefcase** folder to open it.

11 In the **Welcome to the Windows Briefcase** dialog box, click **Finish**.

The Briefcase is similar to a normal Windows folder. Notice that the Sync Copy In column has a path to the Design Master, and the setting in the Status column is *Up-to-date*.

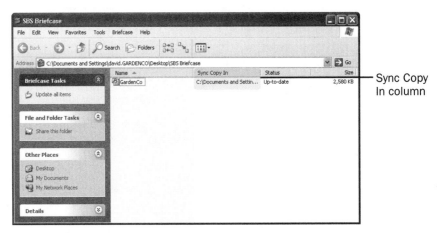

Sync Copy In column

12 Double-click **GardenCo** to start Access, and to open the database.

A replication symbol appears to the left of each table, form, and other object name. Note that design changes can be made only in the original file.

13 On the **Objects** bar, click **Forms**, and then double-click **Products** to open the Products form.

14 Change the name of the first product from *Magic Lily* to Mystic Lily.

15 Close the form and the database.

16 Quit Access, and then close the SBS Briefcase window.

If you were working on a different computer, at this point you would be ready to synchronize the replica with the master database stored on the office computer.

17 On your desktop, double-click the **SBS Briefcase** folder.

The setting in the Status column has changed to *Needs updating*.

Tip   You changed the replica stored on the same computer as the master database, so rather than closing and opening the SBS Briefcase folder, you could have pressed F5 to refresh the status.

18 On the **Briefcase** menu, click **Update All**.

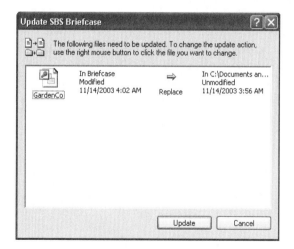

The Update SBS Briefcase dialog box appears, showing the condition of both databases. Because only the replica has changed, an arrow pointing toward the master database suggests that the changes in the replica replace the information in the master. If only the master had changed, or if both databases had changed, the arrows would be different. You can accept the suggestion, or you can right-click an entry and select another option to override the suggestion.

19 Click **Update** to update the master database.

A status message appears, indicating the update is being performed. When it is finished, press F5 to update the folder to reflect the *Up-to-date* status.

20 Close the SBS Briefcase window.

21 Start Access, navigate to the *My Documents\Microsoft Press\Access 2003 SBS \Secure\Replicate* folder, double-click **GardenCo**, and acknowledge the safety warning, if necessary.

22 Open the **Products** form, and confirm that the change you just made appears there.

23 Close the **Products** form.

CLOSE the *GardenCo* database.

Splitting a Database

Microsoft Office Specialist

In a large organization, different people will have different uses for the information in a database. They might want to develop their own variations of your queries, forms, and reports, or even create their own. Allowing dozens of people to edit the objects in a database leads at best to confusion and at worst to disaster.

One easy solution to this problem is to split the database into a *back-end database*, containing the tables, and a *front-end database*, containing the other database objects. You can store the back-end database on a server and distribute the front-end database to all the people who work with the data. They can use the queries, forms, reports, pages, macros, and Microsoft Visual Basic for Applications (VBA) code that you developed, or they can write their own. Although everyone still has access to the data in the tables, and there is still some potential for corrupting the data, the rest of your database objects are secure.

Tip Before splitting a database, you should make a backup copy of it. To back up an open database, on the File menu, click Back Up Database. Access appends the date to the database name and offers to store it in the same folder.

In this exercise, you will split the GardenCo database into back-end and front-end *components*.

USE the *GardenCo* database in the practice file folder for this topic. This practice file is located in the *My Documents\Microsoft Press\Access 2003 SBS\Secure\Split* folder and can also be accessed by clicking *Start/All Programs/Microsoft Press/Access 2003 Step by Step*.
OPEN the *GardenCo* database and acknowledge the safety warning, if necessary.

1 On the **Tools** menu, point to **Database Utilities**, and click **Database Splitter**.

The Database Splitter Wizard appears.

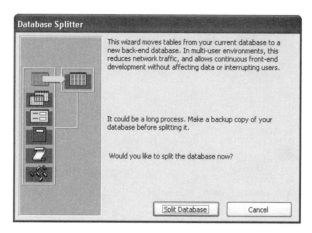

2   Click **Split Database**.

The Create Back-end Database dialog box appears so that you can specify where the back-end database should be stored and provide a name.

3   In the **Create Back-end Database** dialog box, navigate to the *My Documents \Microsoft Press\Access 2003 SBS\Secure\Split* folder, and click **Split** to accept the default name of GardenCo_be.mdb.

4   After the database is successfully split, click **OK** to return to the database window.

Notice that now, in the list of tables, each table name is preceded by an arrow, indicating that it is linked to a table in a different database.

5   Attempt to open the **Categories** table in Design view.

A message box appears informing you that this is a linked table with some properties that can't be modified.

6   Click **Yes** to open the table, and then click each field name in the top section of the Design view window.

A message displayed in red in the Field Properties section informs you that the properties for the selected field cannot be modified. If you click the properties in the lower part of the window, you will find that some can be changed and some can't.

7   Close the table.

8   On the **Objects** bar, click the other object types.

Each type appears to be intact, and you can modify the object if necessary.

9   Close **GardenCo**, and open **GardenCo_be**.

This database contains only tables. Other types of objects are listed on the Objects bar but do not exist in this database.

10 Open the **Categories** table in Design view.

The properties of the fields in the table in this database can be modified.

11 Close the table.

CLOSE the *GardenCo_be* database.

Setting Up a Workgroup

As you develop a database and it grows in size, it can contain an enormous amount of interrelated information about your company. Different departments might need to view different parts of this information. For example, The Garden Company's management group might need to see financial information, the marketing and sales groups might need to see order information, and the human resources group might need to see employee and timekeeping information. Although representatives of each group might need access to some of the information in the database, it is not appropriate for everyone to be able to see everything. In fact, it might not be appropriate for some employees to open the database at all.

You can control the access of individuals or groups to the entire database or to specific objects in it by implementing user-level security. The Access user-level security model is based on the following four elements:

■ *Objects*: The tables, queries, forms, reports, and so on that make up the structure of a database.

■ *Permissions*: A set of attributes that specify the kind of access a user has to data or objects in a database.

■ *Users*: The individual people authorized to access a database. You can assign each user a unique user name and password and grant explicit permission to view or change specific objects in the database.

■ *Groups*: Sets of users authorized to access a database. If multiple users require the same permissions, you can create a group, assign permissions to it, and add the users to the group. After users are added, they "inherit" the permissions of the group.

Information about these four elements is stored in a *workgroup information file (WIF)*. When you install Access, the setup program creates a default *workgroup* and sets up two groups, Admins and Users, within that workgroup. Until you take over management of database security, Access assigns everyone to both groups, with a default user name of *Admin* and a blank password. Because of the blank password, nobody has to log in, and everyone has permission to open, view, and modify all data and objects in any new database created while the default workgroup is active. All information about the security setup of the default workgroup is stored in the default WIF.

If you want to set up some kind of security for a database, you could modify the default WIF to change the default setup, but it is wiser to create a new workgroup by creating a new WIF. If you need many groups and permission levels, setting up a user-level security system by hand can be quite a chore. But if your needs are relatively simple, the Security Wizard will guide you through the process and set up a system that you can later modify.

Tip Access user-level security is conceptually similar to the security systems that can be set up for Microsoft Windows servers. If you have any experience with those systems, implementing security for a database will be relatively easy.

In this exercise, you will use the Security Wizard to secure the GardenCo database by creating a new workgroup and adding groups, users, passwords, and permissions.

USE the *GardenCo* database in the practice file folder for this topic and the next one. This practice file is located in the *My Documents\Microsoft Press\Access 2003 SBS\Secure\Multi* folder and can also be accessed by clicking *Start/All Programs/Microsoft Press/Access 2003 Step by Step*.
OPEN the *GardenCo* database and acknowledge the safety warning, if necessary.

1   On the **Tools** menu, point to **Security**, and then click **User-Level Security Wizard** to display the first page of the wizard.

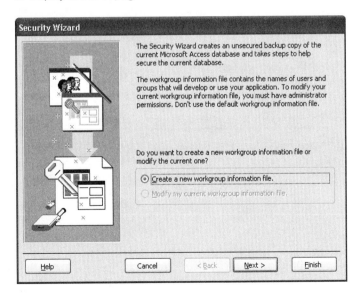

2 Click **Next** to create a new workgroup information file (WIF).

A new workgroup is created, to which you can assign the users or groups you want to be able to use this database.

3 Replace the text in the **WID** box by selecting it and typing sbsTGC1234.

Tip It is a good idea to create a new workgroup ID, but if you do, it is important that you record this ID in a safe place.

4 In the **Your name (optional)** box, replace *Microsoft Access* with Karen Berg (the owner of The Garden Company).

5 In the **Company (optional)** box, type The Garden Company.

6 Accept the default selection to create a shortcut to open the security-enhanced database, and click **Next**.

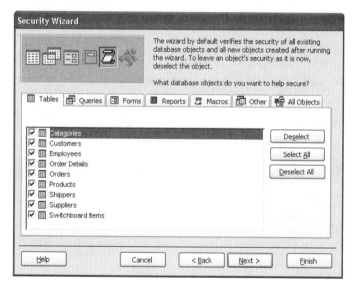

7 Click **Next** to accept the default selections and secure all objects.

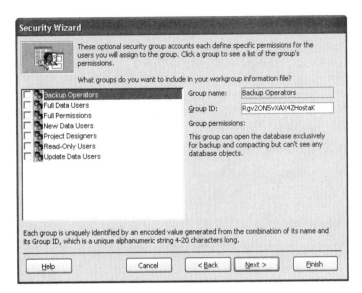

Tip The Group ID number you see will be different from what is shown above. You can click a group's name (not its check box) and see what permissions it has in the Group Permissions box.

8 Select the check boxes for **Full Data Users** and **New Data Users**, and then click **Next**.

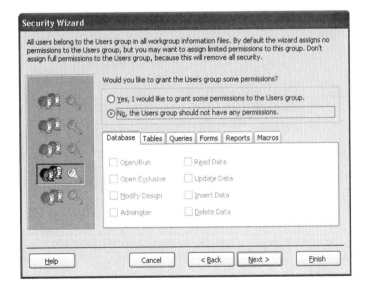

9   Click **Next**.

Tip   Depending on your operating system and security plan, your own logon name might be in this list already. This is fine…just treat yourself as another employee of The Garden Company.

10   In the **User name** box, type KarenB, in the **Password** box, type pw0, and then click **Add This User to the List**.

KarenB is added to the list of users.

Tip   When securing a real database, you should use more complex passwords, or you can leave them blank and have each user set his or her own password later.

11   Repeat step 10 to add the following users:

Name	Password
KimA	pw1
DavidO	pw2
ChaseC	pw3
KirkD	pw4
NancyA	pw5
MichaelE	pw6
KarenF	pw7
SandeepK	pw8

The new users appear in the list.

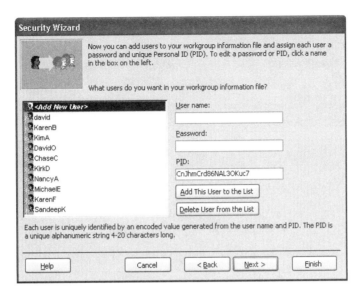

12 Click **Next**.

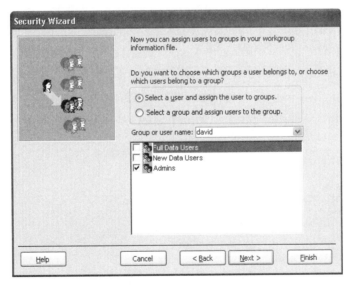

13 Select the **Select a group and assign users to the group** option, click the down arrow to the right of the **Group or User name** box, and click **Admins**.

Existing groups can be selected from the "Group or user name" list, and all users are listed in the large area below it.

14 Select the **KarenB** check box, if necessary.

15 Click the down arrow to the right of the **Group or user name box**, click **New Data Users**, and then select the check box for **NancyA**.

16 Click the down arrow to the right of the **Group or user name box**, click **Full Data Users**, add **KimA**, **DavidO**, **MichaelE**, **KarenF**, and **SandeepK** to this group, and then click **Next**.

> **Tip** On the last page of the wizard is a box you can check to display Access Help topics about managing user and group accounts. If you would like more information about this subject, this is a good place to start.

17 Click **Finish** in the wizard's final page to accept the default name for the backup copy of your unsecured database.

Access displays a report listing all the settings you have made. You can print the report, or export it to a text file and store it in a secure location.

18 Close the report, declining the offer to save it.

The Security Wizard encrypts and closes the database.

19 In a message informing you that you must close and reopen Access to use the new workgroup, click **OK**.

20 Quit Access.

21 On the desktop, double-click the new **GardenCo.mdb** shortcut icon.

The properties of the shortcut icon include information that starts Access with the database's workgroup active.

The Logon dialog box appears.

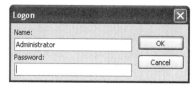

Your user name might appear in the Name box.

22 In the **Name** box, type KarenB, and in the **Password** box, type pw0. Then click **OK**.

The database opens as usual. As long as you use the shortcut icon, you will be able to open this database.

Tip   If you move a secured database and want to continue using the desktop shortcut to open it, you can edit the shortcut's properties. Right-click the shortcut icon, and click Properties. Press the ⎡Home⎤ key to move the insertion point to the left end of the Target box, and then hold down the ⎡→⎤ key to scroll through the target setting, which consists of three sections. The first starts Access, the second specifies the path of the database Access should open, and the third specifies the path of the WIF. To update this target, change the second and third paths to point to the current locations of the database file and the WIF. (The latter has an extension of *.mdw*.) Then change the path in the "Start in" box, and click OK.

CLOSE the *GardenCo* database.

Maintaining a Workgroup

When you want to secure a multi-user database, the Security Wizard guides you through the process of creating a workgroup, adding groups and users, and assigning passwords and permissions. After the workgroup has been created, you can either use workgroup commands to maintain it or run the wizard again to modify the WIF.

The following workgroup commands are grouped together on the Security submenu of the Tools menu:

Command	Purpose
Workgroup Administrator	Change the current workgroup.
User and Group Permissions	Change the permissions that groups or users have for all database objects.
User and Group Accounts	Add and delete users and groups. Assign users to groups. Clear any password or change the logon password for the user currently logged on.
User-Level Security Wizard	Create and modify workgroups.

What users can do with these commands is determined by their permissions.

In this exercise, you will explore these commands and change a user password. To complete this exercise, you must have first worked through the previous exercise.

BE SURE TO complete the previous exercise before beginning this one. Start Access before beginning this exercise, but don't open the *GardenCo* database yet.

USE the *GardenCo* database and the *Security* workgroup information file from the previous exercise for this topic. These practice files are located in the *My Documents\Microsoft Press\Access 2003 SBS \Secure\Multi* folder and can also be accessed by clicking *Start/All Programs/Microsoft Press /Access 2003 Step by Step*.

Open

1 Try to open the GardenCo database by clicking the **Open** button on the Access toolbar, navigating to the *My Documents\Microsoft Press\Access 2003 SBS\Secure \Multi* folder, and double-clicking **GardenCo**.

A message appears, telling you that you don't have the permissions necessary to open this database.

2 Click **OK**.

Access remains on your screen, but no database is open.

3 On the **Tools** menu, point to **Security**, and then click **Workgroup Administrator** to open the dialog box.

Tip Your dialog box will not display the same user, company, and path information that you see in this graphic.

4 Write down the name and path of the current workgroup. You will need this information later.

Important It is very important that you accurately record the path to the current WIF. However, if you somehow lose this, you can probably find it in C:\Documents and Settings*xxx*\Application Data\Microsoft\Access, where *xxx* is your user account.

5 Click **Join**.

The Workgroup Information File dialog box appears.

6 Click **Browse**, navigate to the *My Documents\Microsoft Press\Access 2003 SBS \Secure\Multi* folder, select **Security** (this WIF file was already created and named by the wizard), and click **Open**.

7 Click **OK** to accept the path and name for the selected WIF.

An alert box informs you that you have joined the selected workgroup.

8 Click **OK** to close the alert box, and click **OK** again to close the **Workgroup Administrator** dialog box.

9 Try again to open **GardenCo** by double-clicking its file name in the practice file folder.

This time, Access displays the Logon dialog box.

10 In the **Name** box, type KarenB, and then in the **Password** box, type pw0. Click **OK**.

The database opens.

Important Access to different secured databases can be controlled by different WIFs, and you can have multiple WIFs on one computer. However, only one workgroup can be active on a computer at any time. After you join a workgroup, you remain in that workgroup until you join a different one. The current workgroup is stored in the computer's registry as an attribute of Access. Because this workgroup requires users to log on, any user trying to open any Access database from this computer will be asked for a user name and password. (A user on a different computer could connect through the LAN and open any non-secured database stored on this computer without logging on, but that user could not open a secured database.)

11 On the **Tools** menu, point to **Security**, and click **User and Group Permissions**.

Any member of the Admins group can use this dialog box to set permissions for an individual user or a group. Permissions are set separately for each user and each object type. You select the user in the User/Group Name box, select the object in the Object Type drop-down list, and then select one or more of the objects of that type in the Object Name list. Finally, click each permission you want to assign.

12 In the **List** section, click **Groups**.

When this workgroup was created, permissions for groups were set and users were assigned to the groups. Users inherit the permissions of the groups they belong to, so this is a quick way to set permissions for several people at one time.

13 Click each group name, and watch the permissions change.

Note that New Data Users cannot modify table design.

14 Click **Cancel** to close this dialog box, and then quit Access.

15 Start Access again, and open the **GardenCo** database located in the practice file folder, this time logging on as **NancyA** with a password of **pw5**. (Nancy is a member of the New Data Users group.)

16 Attempt to open any table in Design view.

Access warns that you don't have permission to modify the table and asks if you want to open it as read-only. You would see a similar message if you tried to delete a record, but not if you tried to add a record.

17 Click **No** to close the alert box, and then quit Access.

18 Start Access, and reopen the same database as **KarenB**, with the password **pw0**.

19 On the **Tools** menu, point to **Security**, and then click **User and Group Accounts** to display the dialog box.

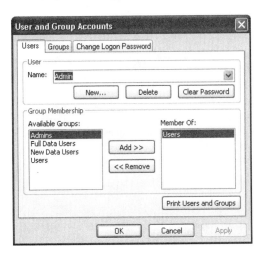

As a member of the Admins group, Karen can add and remove users and groups. She can also clear the password of any user so that the user can log on and set a new password.

Tip Any user can change his or her own password. Members of the Admins group can clear the password of any user, but they can't change any password except their own.

20 Click the **Change Logon Password** tab to display the options.

21 In the **Old Password** box, type pw0 (the current password), press ⟨Tab⟩, type Nos27Len (the new password), press ⟨Tab⟩ again, and verify the new password by typing it again. Then click **OK**.

The next time Karen logs on, she will have to use the new password.

22 On the **Tools** menu, point to **Security**, and then click **User-Level Security Wizard**.

You can use the wizard to modify the current workgroup. You can change anything you set when you used this wizard to create the workgroup, except the user names and passwords of existing users.

23 Click **Cancel**, and then quit Access.

24 Click **Start**, navigate to the *My Documents\Microsoft Press\Access 2003 SBS* folder, and try to open any non-secured database by double-clicking its file name in one of the subfolders.

Access prompts you to log on because the active workgroup requires it.

25 Click **Cancel**.

26 Navigate to the *My Documents\Microsoft Press\Access 2003 SBS\Secure\Multi* folder, and open the **GardenCo** database, logging on as KarenB with the new password Nos27Len.

27 On the **Tools** menu, point to **Security**, and then click **Workgroup Administrator**.

Troubleshooting If you are using Microsoft Windows 2000 or Microsoft Windows XP, one of the folders in the path to your original workgroup might be hidden. To browse to it, you will have to set Windows Explorer to show hidden files and folders. To do this, start Windows Explorer, click Folder Options on the Tools menu, click the View tab, click "Show hidden files and folders", and click OK.

28 Click **Join**, click **Browse**, browse to the WIF whose name and path you wrote down in step 4, and click **Open**.

29 Click **OK** to close the **Workgroup Information File** dialog box, and click **OK** twice more to close the message box and the dialog box.

A message appears, informing you that you don't have permission to open this database. (It is a secured database and you are no longer a part of its workgroup.)

30 Click **OK**, navigate to any of the *My Documents\Microsoft Press\Access 2003 SBS* practice file folders, and try to open one of the non-secured GardenCo databases.

The database opens without prompting you to log on because the default workgroup doesn't require it.

CLOSE the *GardenCo* database.

Preventing Changes to a Database

If you have added VBA procedures to a database, you certainly don't want users who aren't qualified or authorized to make changes to your code. You can prevent unauthorized access in two ways: you can protect your VBA code with a password, or you can save the database as a Microsoft Database Executable (MDE) file. If you set a password for the code, it remains available for editing by anyone who knows the password. If you save the database as an MDE file, people using the file can run your code, but they can't view or edit it.

In this exercise, you will secure the VBA code in a database by assigning a password to it.

USE the *GardenCo* database in the practice file folder for this topic. This practice file is located in the *My Documents\Microsoft Press\Access 2003 SBS\Secure\VBA* folder and can also be accessed by clicking *Start/All Programs/Microsoft Press/Access 2003 Step by Step*.
OPEN the *GardenCo* database and acknowledge the safety warning, if necessary.

1   Press [Alt]+[F11] to open the Visual Basic Editor.

2   On the Visual Basic Editor's **Tools** menu, click **db1 Properties**.

3   In the **Project Properties** dialog box, click the **Protection** tab.

4   Select the **Lock project for viewing** check box.

5   In the **Password** box, type 2003!VBA, and press [Tab].

6   In the **Confirm Password box**, type the password again, and then click **OK**.

The password is set, but it won't be active until the next time you open the database.

7 Close the Visual Basic Editor, and then close the database.

8 Open the database again, acknowledge the safety warning, if necessary, and then press ⎇+Fⁿ to open the Visual Basic Editor.

The editor opens, but all that is displayed in the Project Explorer is the name of the project. The Code window is closed.

9 Click the plus sign to the left of the GardenCo project name to expand the project.

Access displays a Password dialog box.

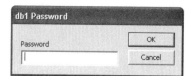

10 Type 2003!VBA, and click **OK**.

The project expands to display its components.

Tip You have to enter the password only once per database session. In other words, you won't have to enter it again unless you close and reopen the database.

11 To remove the password, on the **Tools** menu, click **db1 Properties**.

12 Click the **Protection** tab, clear the **Lock project for viewing** check box, delete the asterisks in the two password boxes, and click **OK**.

Tip The lock and password settings operate independently. Clicking the "Lock project for viewing" check box requires the user to enter the password to view the project. If a password has been set and the "Lock project for viewing" check box is cleared, the user can view the project code but has to enter the password to open the Project Properties dialog box.

13 Close the Visual Basic Editor.

CLOSE the *GardenCo* database.

Securing a Database for Distribution

When a database is used only in one office or on a local area network (LAN) or wide area network (WAN), you have considerable control over who has access to it. But if you send the database out into the world—on its own or as part of a larger application—you lose that control. There is no way you can know who is using it or what tools they might have available to hack into it. If thinking about this keeps you awake at night, you should distribute your database as a *Microsoft Database Executable (MDE)* file.

Suppose the owners of The Garden Company want to make a database available for use by gardening clubs in the area, but they don't want people to be able to change its objects and perhaps "break" things. Saving a database as an MDE file compiles all modules, removes all editable source code, and compacts the destination database. Users of the MDE file can view forms and reports and update information, as well as run queries, macros, and VBA code. They *cannot* do the following:

■   View, edit, or create forms, reports, or modules in Design view.

■   Add, delete, or change references to other objects or databases.

■   Change VBA code.

■   Import or export forms, reports, or modules.

Access can save a database as an MDE file only if it is in Access 2002 format. Although Access 2000 is the default format for databases created with Access 2002 and Access 2003, Access can't save an Access 2000 database as MDE: you first have to convert it to 2002 format.

In this exercise, you will convert the GardenCo database to Access 2002 format, and then secure it by saving it as a distributable MDE file. Although The Garden Company probably wouldn't distribute their main database to garden clubs even as an MDE file, we will use that database for this exercise. You start this exercise with the GardenCo database closed.

USE the *GardenCo* database in the practice file folder for this topic. This practice file is located in the *My Documents\Microsoft Press\Access 2003 SBS\Secure\MDE* folder and can also be accessed by clicking *Start/All Programs/Microsoft Press/Access 2003 Step by Step*.

1   Start Access.

> **Important**   If you are working in a multi-user environment, first make sure that all other users close the database for which you want to create an MDE file.

2   On the **Tools** menu, point to **Database Utilities**, point to **Convert Database**, and click **To Access 2002 – 2003 File Format**.

3   In the **Database to Convert From** dialog box, navigate to the *My Documents \Microsoft Press\Access 2003 SBS\Secure\MDE* folder, and double-click **GardenCo**.

4   In the **File name** box, type GardenCo_New, and click **Save**.

5   Click **OK**.

A database you can secure as an MDE file is created.

> **Important** You cannot convert a database back from the MDE format, so before you save a database as an MDE file, create a backup copy. If you need to make changes to forms, reports, or VBA code, you will have to make them in the original database and then save it as MDE again.

6 On the **Tools** menu, point to **Database Utilities**, and click **Make MDE File**.

7 In the **Database To Save As MDE** dialog box, navigate to the *My Documents \Microsoft Press\Access 2003 SBS\Secure\MDE* folder, click **GardenCo_New**, click **Make MDE**, and then acknowledge the safety warning, if necessary.

8 In the **File name** box, type TGC, and click **Save**.

The process only takes a moment; no message alerts you when it is completed.

Open

9 Click the **Open** button, navigate to the practice file folder, double-click **TGC**, and acknowledge the safety warning, if necessary.

10 Click each of the object types on the **Objects** bar while watching the **Design** button at the top of the database window.

The Design button is available for tables, queries, and macros, but unavailable for all other object types.

> **Tip** If you intend to distribute your database for installation on systems where the setup is unknown, you should look into the Package and Deployment Wizard in Microsoft Office XP Developer.

CLOSE the *GardenCo* database.

Key Points

■ Your goal as a database developer is to provide adequate protection without imposing unnecessary restrictions on the people who should have access to your database. The type of security required to protect a database depends on how many people are using it and where it is stored.

■ You can encrypt a database, which does not prevent it from being opened and viewed in Access, but does keep people who don't have a copy of Access from reading or making sense of the data.

■ You can assign a password to your database, preventing unauthorized users from opening it.

- You can share a database on a local area network (LAN) and limit what users can do with the database by using the same network security you use to protect other information on the network. To prevent multiple users from attempting to update the same record at the same time, you can implement pessimistic locking, which locks a record for the entire time it is being edited, or optimistic locking, which locks a record only for the brief time that Access is saving the changes.

- You can convert your database to a new version, called a Design Master, and then create replicas of that master database to distribute to remote locations. The replicas can then be synchronized and changes merged with the master database. After all changes have been recorded, all of the replicas are updated with the current information from the Design Master and sent back to the remote locations.

- You can split your database into a back-end database, containing the tables, and a front-end database, containing the other database objects. You can store the back-end database on a server and distribute the front-end database to all the people who work with the data. They can use all the objects that you created (other than the tables, which are not available for editing), or create their own.

- You can control the access of individuals or groups to your entire database or to specific objects in it by implementing user-level security. You can create new workgroups and add groups, users, passwords and permissions to each workgroup. All this information is stored in a Workgroup Information File (WIF) that you can easily generate by using the Security Wizard. After the workgroup has been created, you can either use workgroup commands to maintain it or run the Security Wizard again to modify the WIF.

- If you have added VBA procedures to a database, you can protect your VBA code with a password, or by saving the database as a Microsoft Database Executable (MDE) file. If you set a password for the code, it remains available for editing by anyone who knows the password. If you save the database as an MDE file, people using the file can run your code, but they can't view or edit it.

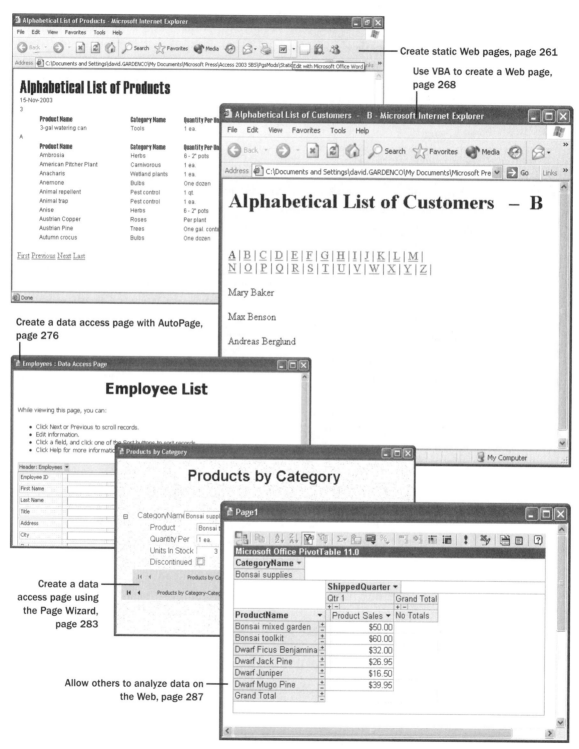

Create static Web pages, page 261

Use VBA to create a Web page, page 268

Create a data access page with AutoPage, page 276

Create a data access page using the Page Wizard, page 283

Allow others to analyze data on the Web, page 287

10 Working with Pages and Modules

In this chapter you will learn to:

✔ Create static Web pages.

✔ Explore Visual Basic for Applications (VBA).

✔ Use VBA to create a Web page.

✔ Create a data access page with AutoPage.

✔ Create a data access page using the Page Wizard.

✔ Allow others to analyze data on the Web.

The World Wide Web is the largest public clearinghouse of information in the world. It has become the place to publish and distribute books, software, and data of all types. If your organization has an Internet presence, you will want to take advantage of features in Microsoft Office Access 2003 that can be used to publish your database information so that it is accessible through an intranet or the Internet.

Important This discussion assumes that you are already familiar with the Internet, Internet service providers, and methods of placing HTML pages on a Web site for publication. If this is not the case, you should still be able to follow along and work through the exercises, but you might need help moving your files to the Web. A good source of information about creating and publishing a Web site is *Microsoft Office FrontPage 2003 Step by Step* (Microsoft Press, 2003).

Information on the Web is viewed with a *Web browser*. The two most popular Web browsers are Microsoft Internet Explorer and Netscape Navigator; however, both of these browsers are available in many versions, and other browsers are also available. All browsers are capable of viewing files based on a simple set of *Hypertext Markup Language (HTML)* tags. Newer versions of the popular browsers also recognize non-standard HTML tags and other file formats, such as *Dynamic Hypertext Markup Language (DHTML)* and *Extensible Markup Language (XML)*.

Important If you intend to place database information on the Web, give careful thought to what operating system and browser will be used by people viewing your site. If you would like your site to be available to the general public, then you will have to forgo cutting-edge technology, such as data access pages, in favor of static Web pages or *Active Server Pages (ASP)*.

You can use Access to create two types of Web pages:

- *Static HTML pages,* which provide a snapshot of some portion of the database contents at one point in time. These pages can be viewed by any modern browser and can be stored on a server running any server software.

- *Dynamic Web pages,* which are created in response to some action on the part of each user.

There are two main types of dynamic Web pages:

- *Data access pages,* with which users can directly manipulate data in your database. Users can add, edit, and delete records, and change their view of the data, in much the same way as they would in a form. To take full advantage of data access pages, users must be running Internet Explorer version 5.0 or later.

- *Active Server Pages,* which are stored on a *network server* and generate different views of the data in response to choices users make on a Web page. The pages can be viewed with any modern browser, but the server where the pages are stored must be running Microsoft Windows NT 4, Microsoft Windows 2000, or Microsoft Windows XP. Although Access can export a form or report as an Active Server Page, you will not do that in this chapter. Search for *ASP* in Access online Help for more information.

In this chapter, you will create static and dynamic Web pages. You will get an overview of Microsoft Visual Basic for Applications (VBA) and see how VBA procedures stored in Access modules can be used to create Web pages. You will also add controls to data access pages to allow other people to view your data, add and edit records, make projections, and analyze your data. You will be working with the GardenCo database files and several other sample files provided on the book's companion CD.

See Also   Do you need only a quick refresher on the topics in this chapter? See the Quick Reference entries on pages xlv–xlvii.

Important   Before you can use the practice files in this chapter, you need to install them from the book's companion CD to their default location. See "Using the Book's CD-ROM" on page xiii for more information.

Creating Static Web Pages

The most basic form of an HTML page is a static page. If you want any Web browser that supports HTML 3.2 or later to be able to view your data, you should display the data in static HTML pages. Static pages are downloaded and displayed in their entirety; the user can't edit them, and there are no tricky bits that pop up or change format as the user moves through the page.

Access can export tables, queries, forms, and reports as static HTML pages. Exported tables, queries, and forms are displayed in datasheet format. (If you have a lot of data, the Web page might be very long.) Exported reports are displayed on a series of short pages, similar to reports in Access.

In this exercise, you will export the Alphabetical List of Products report from the GardenCo database to a set of static HTML pages. You must have a printer installed to complete this exercise.

BE SURE TO start Access before beginning this exercise.
USE the *GardenCo* database in the practice file folder for this topic. This practice file is located in the *My Documents\Microsoft Press\Access 2003 SBS\PgsMods\Static* folder and can also be accessed by clicking *Start/All Programs/Microsoft Press/Access 2003 Step by Step*.
OPEN the *GardenCo* database and acknowledge the safety warning, if necessary.

1 On the **Objects** bar, click **Reports**.

2 Open the **Alphabetical List of Products** report in Print Preview, to see what it looks like.

3 Close the report.

4 On the **File** menu, click **Export** to display the **Export** dialog box.

5 Navigate to the *My Documents\Microsoft Press\Access 2003 SBS\PgsMods\Static* folder, in the **File name** box, type AlphaProd, in the **Save as type** box, click **HTML Documents**, select the **Autostart** check box, and then click **Export**.

6 In the **HTML Output Options** dialog box, make sure the **Select a HTML Template** check box is cleared, and then click **OK**.

Access displays its progress as it exports the report to HTML pages. Because you clicked Autostart, when the export process is complete, the first HTML page opens in your Web browser. (It might appear as a blinking button on the taskbar.)

Tip If you are prompted to install a printer, click OK, and follow the directions.

7 If you don't see the HTML page, on the taskbar, click **Alphabetical List of Products** to display it.

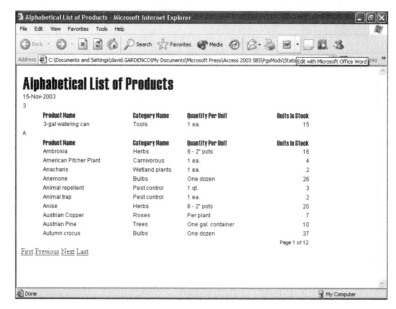

A title appears in the title bar, the data is in the body of the page, and navigation links and a page number have been added at the bottom.

8 Click **Start**, and then navigate to the *My Documents\Microsoft Press\Access 2003 SBS \PgsMods\Static* folder.

A file named *AlphaProd*, which is the first page of the report, and nine more files named *AlphaProd2* through *AlphaProd12*, which are the remaining pages, are listed.

9 Return to the HTML page, and click the **Next** hyperlink repeatedly to scroll through the 12 pages of the report.

Tip If you are interested in seeing the HTML code that makes this page look the way it does, you can view it in Internet Explorer by right-clicking the body of the page and clicking View Source. If you are running Netscape Navigator, click View Document Source or View Page Source on the View menu, depending on the version of Netscape you are using.

10 Close the HTML report.

CLOSE the *GardenCo* database.

Exploring Visual Basic for Applications (VBA)

Microsoft Visual Basic for Applications (VBA) is a high-level programming language developed for the purpose of creating Windows applications. A common set of VBA instructions can be used with all Microsoft Office products, and each product also has its own set. VBA includes hundreds of commands and can be extended indefinitely with third-party controls and routines you write yourself.

You can use VBA to integrate features of Microsoft Word, Microsoft Excel, Microsoft Outlook, and other applications, as well as Access. If you work with Office applications and have any interest in programming, VBA is well worth learning. This topic provides an overview of VBA. For more information about this subject, see the VBA online Help file and other books from Microsoft Press.

Tip The VBA online Help file is not installed in the default Office setup. However, if you attempt to use it by clicking Microsoft Visual Basic Help on the Help menu displayed from within the Visual Basic Editor, you will be prompted to insert the installation CD, and the files will be installed.

VBA programs are called *procedures* or simply *code*. Access refers to VBA procedures as *modules* and represents them with the Modules object on the Objects bar. In VBA itself, there are two types of modules: *class modules*, which are associated with a specific form or report, and *standard modules*, which contain general procedures that are not associated with any object. When you use the Switchboard Manager or the Command Button tool in the Toolbox, VBA code is automatically attached to your forms, so you might have already used VBA without realizing it.

When you write or edit VBA code, you do so in the *Visual Basic Editor*, sometimes referred to as the *Visual Basic Integrated Development Environment (IDE)*. If you are working in Access and you have selected a form, report, or module in the database window, a Code button becomes available on the Access window's toolbar. Clicking this button opens the Visual Basic Editor and places the insertion point in the code for the highlighted object. If you are working in Access without having selected an object and want to switch to the Visual Basic Editor, press [Alt]+[F11]. (This method works for all Microsoft Office applications.)

Here is the Visual Basic Editor as it would look if you selected the Switchboard form in the GardenCo database and clicked the Code button:

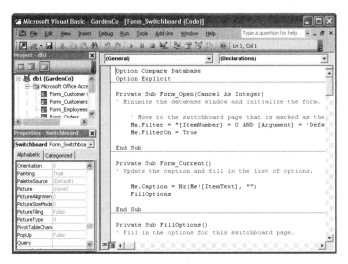

You can display or hide most of the VBE components by clicking the appropriate button or a command on the View menu in the editor. You can also use the following buttons to change how information is displayed:

- When you click the Project Explorer button, the pane for the Project Explorer is displayed. You use the Project Explorer to find and display the VBA objects in the active database.

- When you click the Toggle Folders button at the top of the Project Explorer to toggle it on, the VBA objects are categorized in the Class Objects and Modules folders. When the Toggle Folders button is toggled off, the objects are listed without being categorized.

- When you click the Full Module View button at the bottom of the Code window, all the procedures from the module selected in the Project Explorer pane are displayed.

- When you click the Procedures View button, only the active procedure—the one containing the insertion point—is displayed.

The Object box, on the upper-left side of the Code window, lists all the objects, such as command buttons, labels, and text boxes that appear in the form. Even the form itself is an object. When you select an object in this list, a placeholder for the most common event associated with that object is created in the Code window below.

The Procedure box, on the upper-right side of the Code window, lists all the procedures associated with the currently selected object. These procedures are associated with events, such as a mouse click on a command button. When you select a procedure in this list, the name of the event is added to the first line of the object's placeholder in the Code window below.

In the Code window itself, everything above the first horizontal line is the Declarations section of the module. This section sets the module's requirements and defaults. Two declarations, Option Compare Database and Option Explicit, are usually included by default. You can add others.

Important   When you use the Option Explicit declaration, you must explicitly declare all variables before using them. If you attempt to use an undeclared variable, an error occurs when the code is compiled. Variables are discussed later in this chapter.

The Code window below the Declarations section displays the procedures included in the module. Procedures can be categorized as follows:

- *Sub procedures*, which are a series of VBA statements enclosed by Sub and End Sub statements that perform actions but don't return a value.

- *Function procedures*, which are enclosed in Function and End Function statements and return a value.

Each procedure is a block of code that accomplishes a specific task. In the previous graphic, each procedure was created by the Switchboard Manager to respond to requests to create a switchboard, and respond to the click of a button on the switchboard page.

The VBA statements in a procedure are often interspersed with *comments*. These are notes that help someone reading the code understand the code's purpose. Comments are declared by an apostrophe; anything after an apostrophe in a line of code is a comment. The Visual Basic Editor makes comments obvious by formatting them as green text.

Within each line of code, you will see that some words are blue and others are black. The blue words are *keywords*, reserved as part of the VBA programming language. The black words are variables or values supplied by the programmer.

One of the first things done in many procedures is to use Dim (dimension) statements to define (declare) the *variables* that will be used in the procedure. Declaring a variable sets its type. (VBA supports the data types used for Access fields and other types.) Declaring a variable also sets the exact appearance of the word representing the variable—the combination of uppercase and lowercase characters.

Tip   If you always include at least one uppercase character in variable declarations and always type the variable name in lowercase, you can take advantage of the fact that when VBA recognizes a variable or keyword, it changes it to the capitalization style of its definition. So if you misspell a word, you won't see it changed, which is a hint to check your spelling.

Every programming language has certain formatting conventions. Most of them have no impact on whether the code runs, but many make it easier to visually follow what is going on in the code and locate problems. Indenting is one such convention. When typing VBA code, use a tab to indent lines that are part of a larger element. In the switchboard code shown earlier, everything between the beginning and end of the procedures is indented by one tab, and the code for some statements, such as For...Next loops and If...Then...Else statements, is indented another tab.

As you type words that are part of the VBA programming language (keywords), the Visual Basic Editor often offers hints and autocomplete options. If, for example, you are using the DoCmd statement, when you type the period after DoCmd, a list of all possible methods appears.

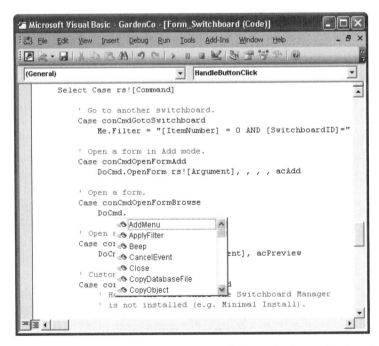

You can either continue to type, or scroll down the list and select the method you want. When you complete the command and press the [Space⎯⎯⎯], a box displays the syntax for the rest of the command.

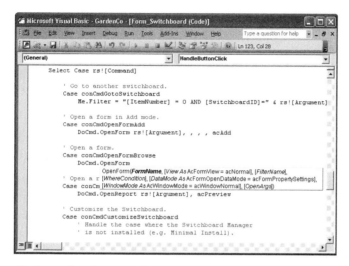

If a line of code extends beyond the edge of the screen, it will still run, but it is hard to read. You can break a long line of code by typing a space and an underscore, and then pressing [Enter]. (You can press [Tab] to set the second line of code off from the first, but that's not a requirement.) Although the code will continue on the next line, it will be treated as one line of code.

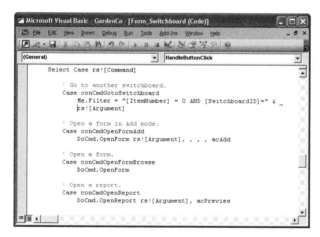

You can get more information about any VBA command by highlighting it in the Visual Basic Editor and pressing [F1] to open Visual Basic Help.

Using VBA to Create a Web Page

Exporting an Access object to static Web pages is quick and easy, but if you want to manipulate the data as you create the static pages, the export process won't be of much use. A better way is to create a module containing VBA code that manipulates the data.

As an example, suppose The Garden Company wants to use data in the Customers table to create a set of 26 Web pages, one for each letter of the alphabet. Each page will list the customers whose last names start with the correlating letter and will contain links to all the other pages in the set. All the legwork for setting up the pages can be done with VBA code.

The sample GardenCo database for this exercise includes HTML_final, a finished and fully commented version of the HTML module you will be creating. If you don't want to type the code as instructed, you can copy it from each Step# module provided in the sample database, paste it into your new HTML module, and then delete the comment from the copied code.

Tip The more complex a program is, the more ways there are to write it. This exercise doesn't pretend to illustrate the best programming methods and doesn't take the time to explain every code detail. You can learn more about each VBA command by clicking it and then pressing [F1] to read about it in Access online Help.

In this exercise, you will follow the typical programming process of writing a module in stages, testing each stage before moving on to the next. In the first stage, you will write code to open the database and look at each record in the Customers table. In the second stage, you will figure out how to spot the change in the first letter of each person's last name. In the third stage, you will open a new text file for each letter and add some HTML code to it. In the fourth and final stage, you'll do some house-keeping and close all the files.

USE the *GardenCo* database in the practice file folder for this topic. This practice file is located in the *My Documents\Microsoft Press\Access 2003 SBS\PgsMods\VBA* folder and can also be accessed by clicking *Start/All Programs/Microsoft Press/Access 2003 Step by Step*.
OPEN the *GardenCo* database and acknowledge the safety warning, if necessary.

1 On the **Objects** bar, click **Modules**.

2 On the database window's toolbar, click the **New** button.

The Visual Basic Editor opens, with a new module highlighted in the Project Explorer.

Tip If the Project Explorer window is closed, on the View menu, click Project Explorer, or press [Ctrl]+[R] to display it.

Save

3 On the Visual Basic Editor toolbar, click the **Save GardenCo** button, name the module HTML, and click **OK**.

4   Click in the Code window to place the insertion point there.

5   On the **Insert** menu, click **Procedure** to display the **Add Procedure** dialog box.

6   In the **Name** box, type createHTML, and then click **OK** to accept the default settings.

A new sub procedure is inserted in the Code window.

7   If Option Explicit isn't in the **Declarations** section at the top of the Code window, position the insertion point at the end of Option Compare Database, press Enter, type Option Explicit, and press Enter again.

Any variables now must be declared before running the program. If they aren't, the program won't run, and you will have to stop and declare the variables.

Tip   To have the editor add Option Explicit to every new module, on the Tools menu, click Options. On the Editor tab of the Options dialog box, click Require Variable Declaration. It is a good idea to select all the options on this tab. Press the F1 key with the tab visible to read information about the options.

8   Click the empty line below Public Sub, press the Tab key, and then either copy and paste the following lines from Step08, or type them, pressing Enter at the end of each line:

```
Dim con As Object
Dim rs As Object
Dim stSql As String
Dim firstRec As Boolean
Dim activeDir As String
Dim curWord As String
Dim curLtr As String
Dim oldLtr As String
Dim skipLtr As String
Dim qt As String
Dim i As Integer
```

Important If you want to copy and paste a code block from the Step# modules, double-click the module name in the Project Explorer, select the code in the Code window, press ⌃+Ⓒ, click the Code window to activate it, position the insertion point where you want the copied code to appear, and press ⌃+Ⓥ. Close the Step# Code window. You will then need to remove the comments so that the code will be run with the rest of the procedure. To do this, right-click a blank area on the Visual Basic Editor's toolbar, click Edit to display the Edit toolbar, select the commented code block, and click the Uncomment Block button. Then make any necessary adjustments to the indents to make the lines match what you see in the instructions.

The Dim (dimension) statement declares all the variables you will use in this procedure. You would normally do this as you found a need for each variable.

9   Press Ⓔⓝⓣⓔⓡ twice to leave a couple of blank lines. (You will add code here later.) Then either copy and paste the following lines from Step09, or type them, pressing Ⓔⓝⓣⓔⓡ at the end of each line:

```
qt = Chr(34)
Set con = Application.CurrentProject.Connection
stSql = "SELECT * FROM [Customers] ORDER BY LastName"
Set rs = CreateObject("ADODB.Recordset")
rs.Open stSql, con, 1   ' 1 = adOpenKeyset
```

The first line sets the value of the variable *qt* to represent a quotation mark. You use this trick to print a quotation mark, because simply typing the quotation mark in the code would be interpreted as part of the code. The rest of the lines connect to the current database and run a query that selects all records from the Customers table, sorted by LastName.

Tip When you press Ⓔⓝⓣⓔⓡ after typing a line of code, the line is analyzed, its *syntax* is checked, and all variable names and keywords are set to the appropriate capitalization style. If you get in the habit of declaring variables with mixed case and typing all code in lowercase, you will be able to spot typos more easily.

10   Add a few more blank lines, and then copy and paste the following lines from Step10, or type them. (Press Ⓣⓐⓑ to indent the second line, and press the Ⓑⓐⓒⓚⓢⓟⓐⓒⓔ key to remove the indent before typing the last line.)

```
Do Until rs.EOF
    curWord = rs!LastName
    Debug.Print curWord
    rs.MoveNext
Loop
```

This segment (called a *Do...Loop statement*) opens the first record in the Customers table, sets the variable *curWord* to the value of the LastName field, prints the value of *curWord*, and then moves to the next record. This set of steps is repeated until the last record is printed.

11 Add a few more blank lines, and copy and paste the following lines from Step11, or type them:

```
rs.Close
Set rs = Nothing
Set con = Nothing
```

These lines close the database and free up the object variables by disassociating them from the actual objects, which in turn frees up memory and system resources.

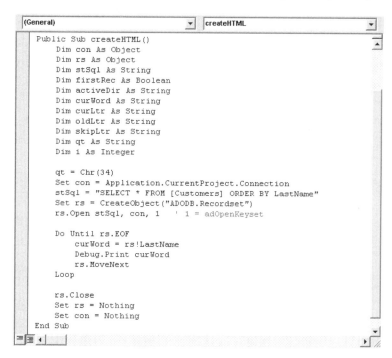

```
(General)                                    createHTML

    Public Sub createHTML()
        Dim con As Object
        Dim rs As Object
        Dim stSql As String
        Dim firstRec As Boolean
        Dim activeDir As String
        Dim curWord As String
        Dim curLtr As String
        Dim oldLtr As String
        Dim skipLtr As String
        Dim qt As String
        Dim i As Integer

        qt = Chr(34)
        Set con = Application.CurrentProject.Connection
        stSql = "SELECT * FROM [Customers] ORDER BY LastName"
        Set rs = CreateObject("ADODB.Recordset")
        rs.Open stSql, con, 1   ' 1 = adOpenKeyset

        Do Until rs.EOF
            curWord = rs!LastName
            Debug.Print curWord
            rs.MoveNext
        Loop

        rs.Close
        Set rs = Nothing
        Set con = Nothing
    End Sub
```

Tip   You should save your work often by clicking the Save button on the toolbar.

12 On the **View** menu, click **Immediate Window**.

The Immediate window is displayed below the Code window. You can use the Immediate window to test a line of code or to change the value of a variable. In this case, you will use it as an output window to view the results of the Debug.Print command.

Run
Sub/UserForm

13 Click anywhere within your sub procedure, and then click the **Run Sub/UserForm** button on the toolbar.

The procedure runs, and the last name of each customer from the Customers table is printed in the Immediate window.

14 Click in the Immediate window, press ⌃+Ⓐ to select all its content, and press the Ⅾⅇⅼ key to delete the selection.

15 Click your code to shift the focus to the procedure, and press ⌷F8⌷ to begin stepping through the code.

The first line of the sub procedure is highlighted in yellow, indicating that it will be the next line of code processed.

16 Press ⌷F8⌷ again.

The highlight skips the Dim statements and moves to the *qt = Chr(34)* line.

17 Continue pressing ⌷F8⌷ and watching the highlight until it has passed *Loop* and returned to *Do Until rs.EOF.*

This loop is the core of the program. It will execute one time for each record in the table. The first time through, it sets *curWord* to the value of the last name in the first record of the table, prints that value in the Immediate window, and then moves to the next record.

18 Press ⌷F8⌷ to move the highlight to *curWord = rs!LastName.*

19 Hold the pointer over *curWord* for a few seconds, and then do the same over *rs!LastName.*

The current value of the variable is displayed in a ScreenTip.

20 Press ⌷F8⌷ again, and check the values displayed on both sides of the expression on the line above.

The values are the same.

21 Press ⌷F5⌷ to finish running the procedure.

Your procedure now opens the database and gets the last name from each record in the Customers table.

22 Replace the *Debug.Print* line in your code with the following code, by either copying and pasting it from Step22 or typing it:

```
curLtr = UCase(Left(curWord, 1))
If curLtr <> oldLtr Then 'we have a new letter
    Debug.Print curLtr
    oldLtr = curLtr
End If
```

The first line changes the leftmost character of *curWord* to uppercase if it isn't already, and sets it as the value of *curLtr.* The If statement compares the value of *curLtr* to *oldLtr.* (At this point *oldLtr* will be blank, because its value hasn't been set.) If the value is different, it is printed, and then *oldLtr* is set to the current value of *curLtr;* otherwise, the flow of code passes to the next line after the If statement, which moves to the next record.

23 Press ⌷F5⌷ to run the program.

The letters of the alphabet are printed in the Immediate window, below the list of customer names. If you scroll through the window's contents, you will see that several letters are missing, not because something is wrong with your code, but because no customers have last names beginning with those letters.

24 In the blank lines you left below the last Dim statement, copy and paste these lines of code from Step24, or type them:

```
activeDir = Application.CurrentProject.path
If Dir(activeDir & "\html_pages", vbDirectory) = "" Then
    MkDir activeDir & "\html_pages"
End If
```

The first line sets the value of activeDir to the path of the folder (or directory) containing the database. The If statement checks to see if that directory has a subdirectory named html_pages in which to store the HTML pages you create. If it doesn't, the MkDir command creates the subdirectory.

25 Insert a line above the Do...Loop statement, and then copy and paste this line from Step25, or type it:

```
firstRec = True
```

You need to differentiate between the first record of a letter and all remaining records. Variables such as *firstRec* are often referred to as *flags* that can be set to true or false.

26 Delete the *Debug.Print* line above the line that compares *oldLtr* to *curLtr*.

27 Click at the end of the line that compares *oldLtr* to *curLtr*, press ⏎ to insert a new line, press ⇥ to indent, and copy and paste the following code from Step27, or type it:

```
If Not firstRec Then 'end the previous page
    Print #1, "</body>"
    Print #1, "</html>"
    Close #1
Else
    firstRec = False
End If

Open activeDir & "\html_pages\" & "cust" & curLtr & ".htm" _
    For Output As #1
Print #1, "<html>"
Print #1, "<head><title>Alphabetical List of Customers  " _
    & "&ndash;   " & curLtr & "</title></head>"
Print #1, "<body bgcolor=yellow link=red>"
Print #1, "<h1>Alphabetical List of Customers   &ndash;" _
    & "  " & curLtr & "</h1>"
Print #1, "<br>"
Print #1, "<br>"
```

Important In the previous step, and in some of the following steps, lines of code have been broken to fit the width of this book. When you break a line of code in the Visual Basic Editor, use a space followed by an underscore.

This code checks to see if the record being processed is the first one: if not, it writes the tags to close out the previous HTML file. It then opens a new HTML file and writes tags to it.

28 Insert a line above *rs.MoveNext*, and copy and paste from Step28, or type:

```
Print #1, "<p>" & rs!FirstName & " " & rs!LastName
```

This creates a paragraph in the HTML file containing the first and last names of the customer, separated by a space.

29 Insert a line after *Loop*, and then insert this code from Step29, or type it:

```
Print #1, "<body>"
Print #1, "</html>"
Close #1
```

This adds the closing HTML tags to the last file, and closes it.

30 Click the **Save** button, and then click the **Run Sub/UserForm** button to run the program, which will create a series of HTML files in a new folder called *html_pages* in the working folder for this exercise. It should take only a few seconds.

Troubleshooting A typo or a misplaced instruction can cause a program to go into an endless loop. If your program seems to be running far too long, you can press ⌨Ctrl+ the Pause/Break key to switch to debug mode, where you can run the program one step at a time to try to locate the problem.

31 In Windows Explorer, browse to the *html_pages* folder in the working folder.

The folder contains a series of HTML files, one for almost every letter of the alphabet.

32 Double-click **custA** to open it in your browser.

33 View the HTML source code for the page. (If you are using Internet Explorer, right-click the body of the page, and click **View Source**.)

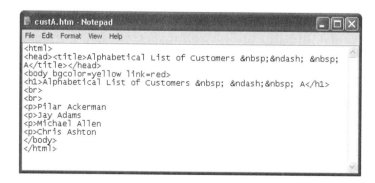

```
<html>
<head><title>Alphabetical List of Customers  &ndash;  
A</title></head>
<body bgcolor=yellow link=red>
<h1>Alphabetical List of Customers   &ndash;  A</h1>
<br>
<br>
<p>Pilar Ackerman
<p>Jay Adams
<p>Michael Allen
<p>Chris Ashton
</body>
</html>
```

Your VBA code wrote the HTML tags and database information to the file.

34 Close the source window and your browser, and then return to the Visual Basic Editor.

35 Insert a line between *Print #1, "<br>"* and *End If*, if necessary, and copy and paste the following code from Step35, or type it:

```
For i = 65 To 77
  Print #1, "<font color=" & qt & "purple" & qt & "size=+1><a href=" _
    & qt & "cust" & Chr(i) & ".htm" & qt & ">" & Chr(i) & _
    "</a> | </font>"
Next i
Print #1, "<br>"
For i = 78 To 90
  Print #1, "<font color=" & qt & "purple" & qt & "size=+1><a href=" _
    & qt & "cust" & Chr(i) & ".htm" & qt & ">" & Chr(i) & _
    "</a> | </font>"
Next i
Print #1, "<p>"
```

This code prints the letters *A* through *M* on one row at the top of each page, and *N* through *Z* on the next row. Each letter is a link to the HTML page for that letter.

36 Save your changes, and run the program again. Then return to the *html_files* folder, and open **custB** to display the Web page.

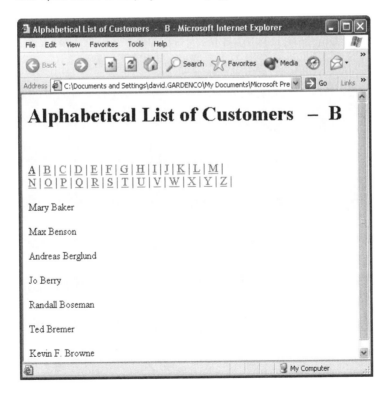

37 Click **F** to jump to the page containing last names starting with *F*.

The appropriate page is displayed.

38 Click **X**.

An error tells you that the page you requested cannot be displayed. No customers have a last name starting with *X*, so your VBA code didn't create a page for it. If you were going to release these pages to the public, you would want to modify the code so it either created blank pages for the missing letters, or didn't include a letter in the header if there were no names starting with that letter.

39 Close your browser, and close the Visual Basic Editor.

CLOSE the *GardenCo* database.

Creating a Data Access Page with AutoPage

If you are confident that everyone who will need to access your data on the Internet or an intranet will be using Internet Explorer version 5.0 or later, and that they will have Microsoft Office 2003 Web Components installed, you can take advantage of the special capabilities of *data access pages*. (Office 2003 Web Components is a set of ready-made controls that you use to work interactively with information in a data access page.)

A data access page is similar to a form, in that it can be used to view, enter, edit, or delete data from a Microsoft Access or a Microsoft SQL Server database. Like a form, a data access page is an Access object. Unlike a form, a page is not stored as part of your database: it is an external HTML file that is linked to your database in such a way that it makes the information in the database available over an intranet or the Internet. The window displayed when you click Pages on the Objects bar contains shortcuts to any pages you have created, and each page contains code that connects it to the appropriate database when the page is opened in Internet Explorer.

In Design view, a data access page looks somewhat like a form or report in Design view, but there are several differences.

■ In a form or report, the entire object is contained within the sections. In a data access page, the sections contain and control data that is *bound* to the database. The space above and below the sections is also part of the page, and you can place text and other controls in it.

■ The Field List for a form or report displays only the fields in the specific table or query to which the object is bound. The Field List for a data access page displays fields from all available tables and queries.

You can view a data access page in Access or in Internet Explorer. For example, suppose The Garden Company's head buyer is visiting suppliers and she wants to check the store's stock of particular kinds of gardening tools. She can connect to the Internet, start Internet Explorer, open an Inventory data access page, check current stock levels, and change the On Order field to show the number of items she is about to order from the supplier.

Important To interact with and use the full functionality of a data access page, users must have Office 2003 installed on their computers. If they don't, they can view the data but they can't add, delete, or edit data.

There are four ways to create a data access page: in Design view, from an existing Web page, with the Page Wizard, or with AutoPage. AutoPage is the simplest method. Like AutoForm and AutoReport, AutoPage uses all the available fields and creates a simple page with minimal formatting.

In this exercise, you will create a data access page with which people can update entries in the Employees table in the GardenCo database through the Internet.

USE the *GardenCo* database in the practice file folder for this topic. This practice file is located in the *My Documents\Microsoft Press\Access 2003 SBS\PgsMods\AutoPage* folder and can also be accessed by clicking *Start/All Programs/Microsoft Press/Access 2003 Step by Step*.
OPEN the *GardenCo* database and acknowledge the safety warning, if necessary.

1 On the **Objects** bar, click **Pages**.

2 On the database window's toolbar, click the **New** button to display the **New Data Access Page** dialog box.

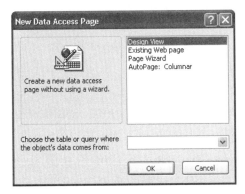

3 Click **AutoPage: Columnar**, click **Employees** in the list of tables and queries, and then click **OK**.

A simple data access page is created and displayed in Page view.

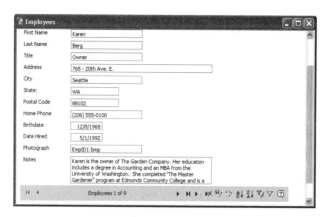

Every field in the underlying Employees table, along with its caption, is listed in one column. (AutoPage creates only columnar pages.) Below the *fields* is a navigation bar, which is included by default in all data access pages. (You might have to increase the size of the window to see this bar.)

Save

4 On the toolbar, click the **Save** button to save your new page.

5 In the **Save As Data Access Page** dialog box, click **Save** to save the file in the practice file folder with the suggested name of *Employees*.

6 If Access displays a warning message that the connection string for this page uses an absolute path, click **OK** to dismiss the message.

Tip Because you are using a file on your own computer and not a network computer, a *UNC path* is not appropriate.

7 Hold the pointer over each navigation button until a ScreenTip displays the name of the button.

Next

8 On the navigation bar, click the **Next** button to move to the next record.

Help

9 Click the **Help** button.

Access online Help displays the topic *About data access pages*.

10 Close Help.

11 Click the Windows **Start** button, navigate to the *My Documents\Microsoft Press \Access 2003 SBS\PgsMods\AutoPage* folder, and double-click **Employees** to open it in Internet Explorer. Close the folder.

The page should look and function the same as it did in Access.

Tip   You can view data access pages only in Internet Explorer 5.0 or later. (You must also have Internet Explorer 5.0 or later installed on your computer to create data access pages.) These exercises were developed using Internet Explorer 6.0. If you are using Internet Explorer 5.0, you might notice slight differences in the screens and in the options available.

Sort Ascending

12   Click the **Last Name** field, and then on the navigation bar, click the **Sort Ascending** button.

The records are sorted in ascending order, based on the last name.

View

13   Press Alt + Tab to return to Access, and on the toolbar, click the **View** button to view the Employees page in Design view.

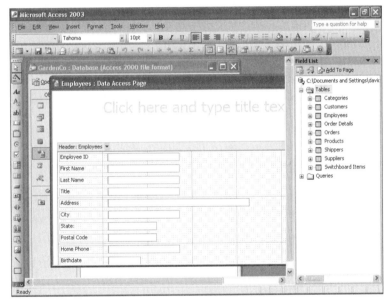

14   Click the **Close** button in the upper-right corner of the **Field List** so that you can see the entire page window. You might have to scroll up.

15   Click the placeholder text *Click here and type title text*, and type **Employee List**.

The words are styled as *Heading 1*, indicated in the Style box on the Formatting toolbar.

16   Press the ↓ key to move to the line below the heading.

The Style box shows that this paragraph is styled as Normal.

17 Type the following:

While viewing this page, you can:

Bullets

18 Press ⌜Enter⌝, on the Formatting toolbar, click the **Bullets** button, and type the following lines, pressing ⌜Enter⌝ after each:

Click Next or Previous to scroll records.

Edit information.

Click a field, and click one of the Sort buttons to sort records.

Click Help for more information about using this page.

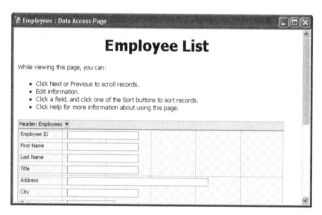

Bold

19 Double-click the word *Next* in the first bulleted item, and on the Formatting toolbar, click the **Bold** button.

20 Repeat step 20 for the words *Previous*, *Sort*, and *Help* in the bulleted list.

21 Scroll down the page, click below the navigation bar, and type:

Copyright 2003, The Garden Company.

Tip You can add a © symbol by clicking where you want the symbol to appear, and then with ⌜Num Lock⌝ turned on, holding down the ⌜Alt⌝ key and typing **0169** on the numeric keypad. When you release the ⌜Alt⌝ key, the copyright symbol is inserted.

22 Select the line you just typed, on the Formatting toolbar, click the down arrow to the right of the **Font Size** box, and click **8**.

The size of the text changes to 8 points.

View

23 Save the page, and then click the **View** button to switch to Page view.

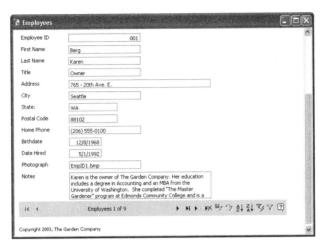

24 Return to Design view.

25 Delete the **Last Name** label, drag the **LastName** text box to the right, and then drag both the **FirstName** text box and its label down until the text box is in line with the **LastName** text box.

26 Click any blank spot to deselect the label and text box, then double-click the **First Name** label to open the **Properties** dialog box, click the **Other** tab, and change the **InnerText** property to **Name**.

> **Tip** You can also view the properties for an element of a data access page by clicking it and then, on the View menu, clicking Properties, or by right-clicking the element and, on the shortcut menu, clicking Properties. Pressing [F4] doesn't toggle the display of properties for data access pages as it does with other objects.

27 Click the **View** button to switch to Page view.

28 Select the **Employee ID** number, and press [Tab] three times.

> **Tip** The order in which the insertion point moves through the fields is determined by the TabIndex property.

29 Switch back to Design view.

30 Click the navigation bar at the bottom of the data access page. (You might have to move or resize the window to see the navigation bar.)

The entire bar is selected, and its properties appear in the Properties dialog box.

Delete

31 On the navigation bar, click the **Delete** button.

Only that button is selected, and its properties are displayed.

32 In the **Properties** dialog box, click the **Format** tab to display the properties.

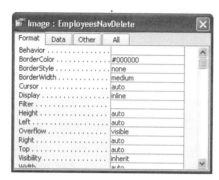

33 Scroll down, click the **Visibility** property, and then select **hidden**.

This will prevent viewers from deleting records.

34 On the toolbar, click the **View** button to change to Page view.

The page is displayed, and the Delete button no longer appears on the navigation bar.

35 On the toolbar, click the **Save** button.

36 Press [Alt]+[Tab] to switch to Internet Explorer, and click the **Refresh** button.

When the browser reloads the Web page, the Delete button is no longer available.

37 Close Internet Explorer, and close the **Employees** page.

Refresh

CLOSE the *GardenCo* database.

Lost Database or Data Access Page?

A data access page is an HTML file that is connected to a *data source*—in this case, an Access database. The data source can be located on the same computer as the data access page or on some other computer on an intranet or the Internet. Where it's located is not important as long as the data access page can locate and open the database.

The page's ConnectionString property, which is stored in the HTML file, includes a path to the data source and other information that allows it to connect to the source. If you create a data access page while you have the data source open on your own computer, the ConnectionString property includes a path to your hard drive, in the usual C:\ path format. When the page is opened on another computer, the page is downloaded to that computer. The ConnectionString information is read, the computer attempts to follow the path to the data source, and the attempt fails. Using a UNC path ensures that the data source can be found because it specifies the computer on which the data source is stored, as well as the drive and folders.

Just as you can "lose" a data source, you can also "lose" data access pages. If you create a data access page and later move it or rename the folder where it is stored, you will get an error when you attempt to open it in either Access or Internet Explorer. To fix this problem, try to open the page in Page view. When you see the message that the file can't be found, click the Update Link button, and locate the HTML file. You will then be able to open the page, but you will get another error stating that the page can't find the database. Switch to Design view, click the title bar to select the page, and then click Properties on the View menu to open the Properties dialog box for the page. On the Data tab, click ConnectionString, and click its ... button. In the Data Link Properties dialog box, click the Connection tab, edit or browse to the correct path in the first box, and click OK.

Creating a Data Access Page Using the Page Wizard

Using AutoPage is a quick way to create a simple data access page in columnar format. But if you want more control over the content and layout, you can use the Page Wizard. With this wizard, you can select the initial fields to include on the data access page, create groups, and pick a theme from the dozens of those available. The theme you select is applied to the page when viewed in Access or Internet Explorer.

In this exercise, you will use the Page Wizard to create a data access page based on the Products by Category query in the GardenCo database.

USE the *GardenCo* database in the practice file folder for this topic. This practice file is located in the *My Documents\Microsoft Press\Access 2003 SBS\PgsMods\Wizard* folder and can also be accessed by clicking *Start/All Programs/Microsoft Press/Access 2003 Step by Step.*
OPEN the *GardenCo* database and acknowledge the safety warning, if necessary.

1   On the **Objects** bar, click **Pages**.

2   At the top of the database window, click the **New** button.

3   In the **New Data Access Page** dialog box, click **Page Wizard**. In the list of tables and queries, click **Products by Category**, and then click **OK**.

The same wizard is displayed when you create a form or report.

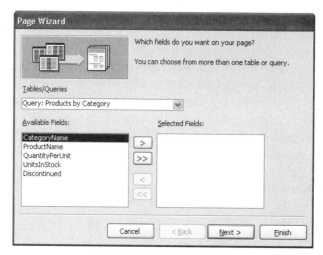

4 Click the **>>** button to move all the fields from the **Available Fields** list to the **Selected Fields** list, and then click **Next**.

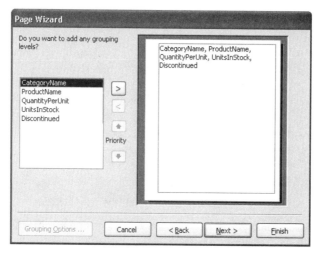

5 Double-click **CategoryName**, and then click **Next**.

6 In the first sort box, click **ProductName**, and click **Next**.

7 Select the **Do you want to apply a theme to your page** check box, and then click **Finish**.

The page is created and displayed in Design view, and the Theme dialog box appears.

You can click the name of any theme to see a sample. You can also use the check boxes at the bottom of the dialog box to modify the theme, and you can set the selected theme as the default for all new pages.

8 Scroll to the bottom of the list, click **Watermark**, and then click **OK**.

The new page appears in Design view.

9 If necessary, close the **Properties** dialog box, and then scroll to the top of the page.

10 Click the placeholder title text at the top of the page, and type Products by Category.

View

11 Click the **View** button to change to Page view.

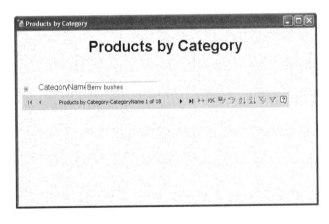

Next

12 On the navigation bar, click the **Next** button to move to the next category.

13 Click the **+** button to the left of **CategoryName**.

The display expands to show a product record under the category name, and a second navigation bar is displayed under the first.

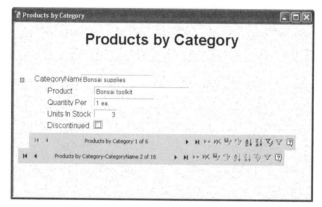

14 On the upper navigation bar, click **Next** to view the next product record in that category.

15 On the lower navigation bar, click **Next** to move to the next category.

The next category name is displayed, and the Products section disappears. You don't want to have to click the + button to display the section every time you move to a new category, so you need to make a change.

16 Switch to Design view, right-click the top header (**Products by Category-CategoryName**), and on the shortcut menu, click **Group Level Properties**.

The GroupLevel Properties dialog box appears.

17 Double-click the **ExpandedByDefault** setting to change it to **True**.

18 Return to Page view, and on the lower navigation bar, click the **Next** button several times.

The Product section remains expanded as you move from category to category.

19 Close the page, saving it if you feel that you would like to explore it some more.

If you save the page, it will be stored in the practice file folder.

CLOSE the *GardenCo* database.

Allowing Others to Analyze Data On the Web

Microsoft Office Specialist
A *PivotTable* is an interactive table that is linked to a database. Similarly, a *PivotChart* is an intereactive chart that is linked to a database. If you add a PivotTable or a PivotChart to a data access page and publish it on the Web, people with the appropriate software can connect to it and analyze your data in various ways.

New in Office 2003

PivotTables and Pivot-Charts

You use PivotTables to summarize the data in a database table or query in tabular format. You can rotate the columns and rows to summarize the data from different points of view. For example, you might want to use a PivotTable view of an order details table to see the total sales for a particular product or the total sales for all products in a particular month. Similarly, you use PivotCharts to summarize data visually so that it is easy to make data comparisons at a glance.

Important   Users must have Internet Explorer version 5.0 or later, Microsoft Office 2003 Web Components, and a valid Microsoft Office 2003 license to work interactively with a PivotTable or PivotChart on a data access page. Consider who your users will be before deciding to present information in this format.

In this exercise, you will create a data access page by hand and add a PivotTable to analyze product sales.

USE the *GardenCo* database in the practice file folder for this topic. This practice file is located in the *My Documents\Microsoft Press\Access 2003 SBS\PgsMods\Analyze* folder and can also be accessed by clicking *Start/All Programs/Microsoft Press/Access 2003 Step by Step*.
OPEN the *GardenCo* database and acknowledge the safety warning, if necessary.

1   On the **Objects** bar, click **Pages**.

2   Double-click **Create data access page in Design view** to open a blank data access page. If Access displays a warning that earlier versions of Access cannot open the page in Design view, click **OK**.

Field List

3   If the **Field List** is not displayed, on the toolbar, click the **Field List** button.

The Field List is now displayed.

Toolbox

4   If the Toolbox is not displayed, on the toolbar, click the **Toolbox** button.

5   Size and arrange the page window, Toolbox, and **Field List** so that you can see them all. (If the **Properties** dialog box is open, you can either close, or move it to the side for now.)

Office
PivotTable

6 In the Toolbox, click the **Office PivotTable** button, and then click in the upper-left corner of the blank section at the top of the page.

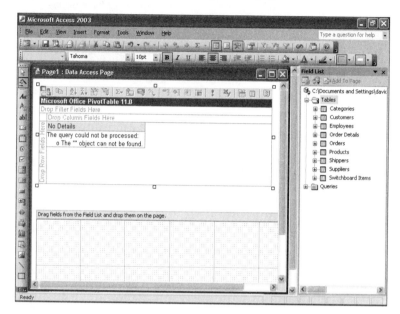

The PivotTable frame contains horizontal and vertical boxes labeled with the type of data they can hold: Filter Fields, Column Fields, Row Fields, and Details.

7 Click inside the PivotTable, and then double-click its frame to open the **Properties** dialog box.

Tip Pressing [F4] in a data access page does not open the Properties dialog box, as it does in other objects.

The title of the Properties dialog box is *Object : PivotTable0*.

8 Click the **Other** tab, click the **DataMember** property, click **Product Sales for 2003** from the list, and close the **Properties** dialog box.

The PivotTable will now be based on the Product Sales for 2003 query in the GardenCo database.

9 In the **Field List**, click the plus sign to the left of **Queries**, and then click the plus sign to the left of **Product Sales for 2003**.

You can now see all the fields in this query.

10 Drag the **CategoryName** field from the **Field List** to the horizontal box labeled **Drop Filter Fields Here**.

11 Click the down arrow to the right of **CategoryName** to see a list of all the product categories in the database. Then clear the **All** check box, select the **Bonsai Supplies** check box, and click **OK**.

12 Drag the **ProductName** field to the vertical box that's labeled **Drop Row Fields Here**.

You see all the products in the Bonsai Supplies category.

13 Drag the **ShippedQuarter** field to the horizontal box labeled **Drop Column Fields Here**.

14 Drag the **ProductSales** field to the box labeled **Drop Totals or Detail Fields Here**.

15 Click the **View** button to switch to Page view.

View

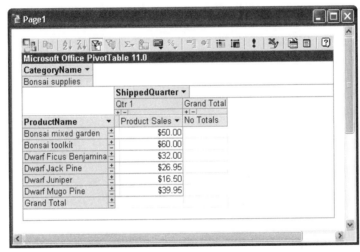

16 Experiment with the PivotTable by selecting different categories, products, and quarters from their drop-down lists.

17 Save the page as Product Sales for 2003 DAP. If Access displays a warning message that the connection string for this page uses an absolute path, click **OK**.

Office Chart

18 Switch to Design view, in the Toolbox, click the **Office Chart** button, and drag a rectangle below the PivotTable and about the same width and height as the table (the grid will move down when you release the mouse button).

When you release the mouse button, you see a placeholder for the Office Chart Web component.

19 Click in the component to display the dialog box.

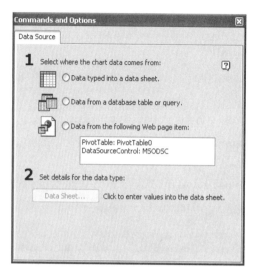

20 Select the **Data from the following Web page item** option, and then click **DataSourceControl:MSODSC**.

21 Click the **Data Details** tab, click the down arrow to the right of the **Data member, table, view,** or **cube name** box, and click **Product Sales for 2003**.

22 Click the **Type** tab, click **Column** in the left pane and the upper-left column chart option in the right pane, and then click the **Close** button to close the dialog box and see the results.

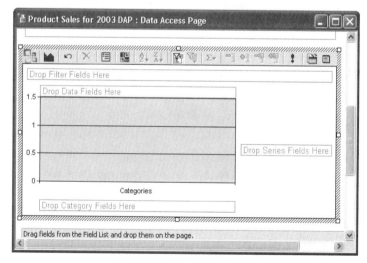

23 Drag **CategoryName** from the **Field List** to the **Drop Filter Fields Here** box. Then click the down arrow, clear the **All** check box, select the **Bonsai Supplies** check box, and click **OK**.

24 Drag **ProductName** to the **Drop Category Fields Here** box, drag **ShippedQuarter** to the **Drop Series Fields Here** box, and drag **ProductSales** to the **Drop Data Fields Here** box.

25 Click the **View** button to see the results.

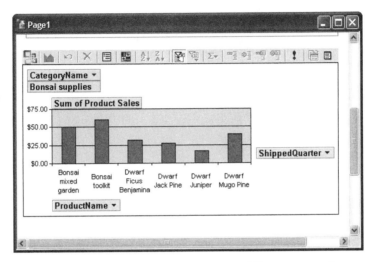

26 Experiment with the PivotChart by selecting different categories, products, and quarters from their drop-down lists.

27 Save the Product Sales for 2003 DAP page.

28 Close the page.

CLOSE the *GardenCo* database, and quit Access.

Key Points

- You can use Access 2003 to publish your database information so that it is accessible through an intranet or the Internet.

- With Access, you can export tables, queries, forms, and reports as static HTML pages, which provide a snapshot of some portion of the database at one point in time. You can also write VBA code that manipulates Access data as it creates HTML pages.

- You can also create Dynamic Web pages, of which there are two types: Data access pages, with which users can directly manipulate data in your database; and Active Server pages, which are stored on a network server and generate different views of the data in response to choices users make on a Web page.

- You can add a PivotTable or PivotChart (an interactive table or chart that is linked to a database) to a data access page and publish it on the Web, making your data available for people with the appropriate software to analyze in various ways.

Glossary

action query   A type of query that updates or makes changes to multiple records in one operation.

Active Server Pages (ASP)   Pages stored on a server that generate different views of the data in response to choices users make on a Web page. A function that groups and performs calculations on multiple fields.

aggregate function   A function that groups and performs calculations on multiple fields.

append query   A query that adds a group of records from one or more tables to the end of one or more tables.

arithmetic operator   An operator that performs an arithmetic operation: + (addition), - (subtraction), * (multiplication), or / (division).

ASCII   Acronym for *American Standard Code for Information Interchange*, a coding scheme for text characters developed in 1968. ASCII files have the extension *.asc*.

ASP   See *Active Server Pages*.

AutoForm   A feature that efficiently creates forms using all the available fields and minimal formatting.

back-end database   The part of a split database that is stored on a server for security reasons, and which usually consists of the tables and other objects that you don't want people to be able to modify. See also *front-end database*.

binary file   A file coded so that its data can be read by a computer.

Boolean   A data type that can hold either of two mutually exclusive values, often expressed as *yes/no, 1/10, on/off*, or *true/false*.

bound   Linked, as when a form used to view information in a table is linked to that table.

Briefcase   A replication folder that you use to keep files in sync when you work on different computers in different locations.

class module   One of two types of modules in Microsoft Visual Basic for Applications (VBA). A class module is associated with a specific form or report. See also *standard module*.

code   VBA programs; also called *procedures*, referred to in Access as modules. See also *class module; standard module*.

combo box   A control in which you can either select from a drop-down list or type an option.

comma-delimited text file   A data file consisting of fields and records, stored as text, in which the fields are separated from each other by commas.

command button   A control shaped like a button to which you can attach code that runs when the button is clicked.

comment   A note embedded in code that helps people reading the code understand its purpose.

comparison operator   An operator that compares values, such as < (less than), > (greater than), and = (equal to).

component   A part of a database that is used to store and organize information. Also known as a database object.

compression   A means of compacting information for more efficient means of transportation.

constant   A named item that retains a constant value throughout the execution of a program, as opposed to a variable, whose value can change during execution.

control   An object such as a label, text box, option button, or check box in a form or report that allows you to view or manipulate information stored in tables or queries.

control property   A setting that determines the appearance of a control, what data it displays, and how that data looks. A control's properties can be viewed and changed in its Properties dialog box.

control source   The source of a control's data—the field, table, or query whose data will be displayed in the control.

criteria   The specifications you give to Access so that it can find matching fields and records. Criteria can be simple, such as all the records with a postal code of 98052, or complex, such as the phone numbers of all customers who have placed orders for over $500 worth of live plants within the last two weeks and who live in postal codes 98052, 98053, and 98054.

crosstab query   A query that calculates and restructures data for easier analysis. See also *select query*, *parameter query*, and *action query*.

data access page   A dynamic Web page that allows users to directly manipulate data in a database via the Internet.

data source   A database or file to which a data access page is connected.

data type   The type of data that can be entered in a field: text, memo, number, date/time, currency, AutoNumber, Boolean (Yes/No), OLE object, and hyperlink. You set the data type by displaying the table in Design view.

data warehouse   A company that serves as a data repository for a variety of data and that may make use of replication to keep each database synchronized when more than one version of the database is updated in more than one remote location.

database application   A database that is refined and made simpler for the user by the sophisticated use of queries, forms, reports, a switchboard, and various other tools.

database program   A program that stores data. Programs range from those that can store one table per file (referred to as a flat database) to those that can store many related tables per file (referred to as a relational database).

database security   The protection of database information from accidental damage, destruction, or theft through the use of encryption, passwords, access permissions, replication, and other security measures.

database window   The window from which all database objects can be manipulated or accessed.

Datasheet view   The view in which the information in a table or query can be viewed and manipulated. See also *views*.

decrypting   "Unscrambling" a database that has been encrypted for security reasons.

delete query   A query that deletes a group of records from one or more tables.

delimited text file   A type of text file format in which each record and each field is separated from the next by a known character called a *delimiter*.

delimiter   A character such as a comma (,), semicolon (;), or backslash (\), or pairs of characters such as quotation marks (" ") or braces ({}), that are used to separate records and fields in a delimited text file.

design grid   The name given to the structure used in Design view to manually construct and modify advanced filters and queries.

Design Master   In replication, the term for the version of the database from which replicas are made and where changes made to replicas are copied and synchronized.

Design view   The view in which the structure of a table or query can be viewed and manipulated. See also *views*.

DHTML   See *Dynamic Hypertext Markup Language*.

duplicate query   A form of select query that locates records that have the same information in one or more fields that you specify.

Dynamic Hypertext Markup Language (DHTML)   A new version of the standard authoring language, HTML, that includes codes for dynamic Web page elements.

dynamic Web page   A page whose content is created in response to some action on the part of a user who is viewing the page over the Internet. See also *static HTML page*.

encrypting   "Scrambling" data for security reasons.

event   An action performed by a user or by Access, to which a programmed response can be attached. Common user events include Click, Double Click, Mouse Down, Mouse Move, and Mouse Up. You can use macros or VBA modules to determine how Access responds when one of these events occurs.

exclusive use   A setting used when you want to be the only person who currently has a database open. You must open a database for exclusive use when setting or removing a password that limits database access.

exporting   The process of creating a file containing the information in a database table in a format that can be used by other programs.

expression   A combination of functions, field values, constants, and operators that yield a result. Expressions can be simple, such as *>100*, or complex, such as *((ProductPrice*Quantity)*.90)+(Shipping+Handling)*.

Expression Builder   A feature used to create formulas (expressions) used in query criteria, form and report properties, and table validation rules.

Extensible Markup Language (XML)   A refined language developed for Web documents that describes document structure rather than appearance.

field   An individual item of the information that is the same type across all records. Represented in Access as a column in a database table. See also *record*.

fixed-width text file   A common text file format that is often used to transfer data from older applications. Each record is always the same number of characters long, and the same field within the records is always the same number of characters. In other words, the same field always starts the same number of characters from the beginning of each record, and any characters not occupied by real data are filled with zeros.

flag   A marker that can be set to true or false to indicate the state of an object.

flat database   A simple database consisting of one table. See also *relational database*.

form   A database object used to enter, edit, and manipulate information in a database table. A form gives you a simple view of some or all of the fields of one record at a time.

Form view   The view in which you can enter and modify the information in a record. See also *views*.

front-end database   The part of a split database that is distributed to the people who analyze and enter data. The actual data tables are stored on a server for security reasons. See also *back-end database*.

function   A named procedure or routine in a program, often used for mathematical or financial calculations.

function procedure   In VBA, a procedure that is enclosed in Function and End Function statements and returns a value. See also *sub procedure*.

group   One of four elements—the other three being object, permission, and user—on which the Access user-level security model is based.

grouping level   The level by which records are grouped in a report. For example, records might be grouped by state (first level), then by city (second level), and then by postal code (third level).

HTML   See *Hypertext Markup Language*.

HTML tag   An HTML command that determines how the tagged information looks and acts.

Hypertext Markup Language (HTML)   The authoring language used to create Web documents.

importing   The method whereby data is brought into an Access database from a different database or program. See also *exporting*.

input mask   A field property that determines what data can be entered in the field, how the data looks, and the format in which it is stored.

intranet   A secure, proprietary Web-based network used within a company or group and accessible only to its members.

keyword   A word that is part of the VBA programming language.

label control   An area on a form that contains text that appears on the form in Form view.

LAN   See *local area network*.

Layout Preview   A view of a report that shows you how each element will look but without all the detail of Print Preview.

linking   The process of connecting to data in other applications.

local area network (LAN)   A computer network that connects computers, printers, and other hardware to a server or group of servers.

logical operator   One of the Boolean operators: AND, OR and NOT.

Lookup Wizard   The wizard in Access that simplifies the creation of a Lookup list.

macro   A set of automated instructions that perform a sequence of simple tasks.

main form   One form that is linked to one or more tables. See also *subform*.

main report   One report that displays records from one or more tables.
See also *subreport*.

make-table query   A query that creates a new table from all or part of the data in one or more tables. Make-table queries are helpful for creating a table to export to other Microsoft Access databases.

many-to-many relationship   A relationship formed between two tables that each have a one-to-many relationship with a third table. See also *one-to-many relationship*; *one-to-one relationship*.

mapped network drive   A drive to which you have assigned a drive letter. Used for quickly accessing files stored in locations that are not likely to change.
See also *UNC path*.

mask   A field property that determines what data can be entered in a field, how the data looks, and the format in which it is stored.

Microsoft Database Executable (MDE)   A compiled version of a database. Saving a database as an MDE file compiles all modules, removes all editable source code, and compacts the destination database.

Microsoft Visual Basic for Applications (VBA)   A high- level programming language developed for the purpose of creating Windows applications.

MDE   See *Microsoft Database Executable*.

module   A VBA program.

named range   A group of cells in an Excel spreadsheet.

native format   The file format an application uses to produce its own files.

navigation button   One of the buttons found on a form or navigation bar that helps users display specific records.

network security   Technologies to protect your network connections to the Internet or other public networks.

network server   A central computer that stores files and programs and manages system functions for a network.

object   One of the components of an Access database, such as a table, form, or report.

one-to-many relationship   A relationship formed between two tables in which each record in one table has more than one related record in the other table. See also *many-to-many relationship*; *one-to-one relationship*.

one-to-one relationship   A relationship formed between two tables in which each record in one table has only one related record in the other table. See also *many-to-many relationship*; *one-to-many relationship*.

operator   See *arithmetic operator*, *comparison operator*, *logical operator*.

optimistic locking   Locking a record only for the brief time that Access is saving changes to it.

option button   A control on a form that allows users to select preferred settings.

page   See *data access page*.

parameter query   A query that prompts for the information to be used in the query, such as a range of dates.

parsing   In Access, the process of analyzing a document and identifying anything that looks like structured data.

password   A secret sequence of letters and other symbols needed to log on to a database as an authorized user.

permission   An attribute that specifies how a user can access data or objects in a database.

pessimistic locking   Locking a record for the entire time it is being edited.

PivotChart   An interactive chart that is linked to a database.

PivotTable   An interactive table that is linked to a database.

populate   To fill a table or other object with data.

primary key   One or more fields that determine the uniqueness of each record in a database.

Print Preview   A view of a report that allows users to see exactly how the report will look when printed.

procedure   VBA code that performs a specific task or set of tasks.

property   A setting that determines the content and appearance of the object to which it applies.

query   A database object that locates information so that the information can be viewed, changed, or analyzed in various ways. The results of a query can be used as the basis for forms, reports, and data access pages.

record   All the items of information (fields) that pertain to one particular entity, such as a customer, employee, or project. See also *field*.

record selector   The gray bar along the left edge of a table or form.

record source   The place from which information derives between two bound objects, such as a field that pulls information from a table. See also *control source*.

referential integrity   The system of rules Access uses to ensure that relationships between tables are valid and that data cannot be changed in one table without also being changed in all related tables.

relational database   A sophisticated type of database in which data is organized in multiple related tables. Data can be pulled from the tables just as if they were stored in a single table.

relationship   An association between common fields in two tables.

replica   A copy of the Design Master of a database.

replicating   The process of creating a Design Master so that multiple copies of a database can be sent to multiple locations for editing. The copies can then be synchronized with the Design Master so that it reflects all the changes.

report   A database object used to display a table or tables in a formatted, easily accessible manner, either on the screen or on paper.

row selector   The gray box at the left end of a row in a table that, when clicked, selects all the cells in the row.

running a query   The process of telling Access to search the specified table or tables for records that match the criteria you have specified in the query and to display the designated fields from those records in a datasheet (table). See also *criteria*; *query*.

saving   The process of storing the current state of a database or database object for later retrieval. In Access, new records and changes to existing records are saved when you move to a different record; you don't have to do anything to save them. You do have to save new objects and changes to existing objects.

schema   A description of the structure of XML data, as opposed to the content of the data. Applications that export to XML might combine the content and schema in one .xml file or might create an .xml file to hold the content and an .xsd file to hold the schema.

select query   A query that retrieves data matching specified criteria from one or more tables and displays the results in a datasheet.

selector   A small box attached to an object that you click to select the object.

sharing a database   Providing access to a database so more that one person can access it to add or alter its information.

splash screen   An introductory screen containing useful or entertaining information. Often used to divert the user's attention while data is loading.

SQL   See *Structured Query Language*.

SQL database   A database that supports SQL and that can be accessed simultaneously by several users on a LAN.

standard module   A VBA program that contains general procedures that are not associated with any object.

static HTML page   A Web page that provides a snapshot of some portion of the database contents at one point in time.

string   A series of characters enclosed in quotation marks.

Structured Query Language (SQL)   A database sublanguage used in querying, updating, and managing relational databases—the de facto standard for database products.

sub procedure   A series of VBA statements enclosed by Sub and End Sub statements.

subdatasheet   A datasheet that is embedded in another datasheet.

subform   A form inserted in a control that is embedded in another form.

subreport   A report inserted in a control that is embedded in another report.

switchboard   A form used to navigate among the objects of a database application so that users don't have to be familiar with the actual database.

synchronizing   The process of comparing the information in a database replica with the database's Design Master and merging any changes.

syntax   The format that expressions must conform to in order for Access to be able to process them.

table   Information organized in columns (records) and rows (fields).

Table Wizard   The Access tool that helps users construct tables.

tags   Codes in HTML that give instructions for formatting or other actions.

task pane   A pane that provides a quick and easy way of initiating common tasks.

template   A ready-made database application that users can tailor to fit their needs.

text box control   A control on a form or report where data from a table can be entered or edited.

transaction record   The written record of transactions.

unbound   Not linked, as when a control is used to calculate values from two or more fields and is therefore not bound to any particular field. *See also* bound.

UNC   See *universal naming convention*.

universal naming convention (UNC) path   A path format that includes the computer name, drive letter, and nested folder names. See also *mapped network drive*.

unmatched query   A form of select query that locates records in one table that don't have related records in another table.

update query   A select query that changes the query's results in some way, such as by changing a field.

user   A person authorized to access a database but who generally is not involved in establishing its structure.

validation rule   A field property that tests entries to ensure that only the correct types of information become part of a table.

variable   A name or symbol that stands for a value that can change.

VBA   See *Microsoft Visual Basic for Applications.*

VBA procedure   A VBA program.

view   The display of information from a specific perspective.

Visual Basic Editor   The environment in which VBA code is written.

Visual Basic Integrated Development Environment (IDE)   See *Visual Basic Editor.*

Web browser   An application used to view Web pages on the World Wide Web.

WIF   See *workgroup information file.*

wildcard character   A placeholder for an unknown character or characters in search criteria.

wizard   A helpful tool that guides users through the steps for completing a specific task.

workgroup   A group of users in a multiuser environment who share data and the same workgroup information file. When you install Access, the setup program creates a default workgroup and sets up two groups, Admins and Users, within that workgroup.

workgroup information file (WIF)   The file where information about the objects, permissions, users, and groups that comprise a specific workgroup is stored.

worksheet   A page in a Microsoft Excel spreadsheet.

XML   See *Extensible Markup Language.*

Index

A

Access. *See Microsoft Access*
action queries, 130, 146, 293
   See also queries
   append queries, 130
   converting from select
      queries, 168
   creating, 168
   delete queries *(see delete
      queries)*
   make-table queries, 130
   update queries *(see update
      queries)*
actions. *See events*
Active Server Pages
     (ASP) 260, 293
Add Procedure dialog box, 269
advanced filtering xxxiv, 127
   See also filtering
aggregate functions, 140, 293
   See also functions
aligning labels, 90, 210
analyzing performance,
     218, 220
apostrophes in VBA code, 103
append queries, 130, 293
   See also queries
application title, 214
Apply Filter
     button, xxxiv, 124–25
applying
   filters, xxxiv, 125
   smart tags, to fields, 54
   startup options, 215
   styles, 35
   themes, to data access
      pages, 284
area codes
   requiring, 155
   restricting to specific, 158
arithmetic operators, 129, 293
   See also expressions
ASCII, 293
assigning passwords, 230
   See also passwords
authorizing database access, 240

autocomplete, in Visual Basic
     Editor, 266
AutoDialer dialog box, 38
AutoFormat dialog box, 94
AutoFormats, creating, 95
AutoForms, 104–106, 293
automatically
   numbering, 46
   saving, 37
automating actions, 22
AutoNumber data type, 46
AutoPage, creating data access
     pages with, 276

B

back-end databases, 239, 293
   See also databases
backgrounds, form, 91
   resizing, xxxii, 93
   styles for, 105
backgrounds, label, 89
backing up
   databases, 238
   databases, with
      Briefcase, xlii, 235
   tables, 169
binary files, 226, 293
blank databases,
     creating, 41, 146
Bold button (Formatting
     toolbar), 280
Boolean data type, 147, 150, 293
borders, transparent, 196
bound, 293
Briefcase
   backing up databases with, xlii,
     235
   copying files to, 235
   creating new, xlii, 234
   defined, 293
   installing, 234
   opening, 236
   renaming, xlii, 234
   replicating databases to, 234
   updating, 237

browsers, 259
building expressions, 137
   See also expressions
bulleted lists, creating, 280
Bullets button (Formatting
     toolbar), 280
business tables, 42
buttons on data access pages,
     hiding, 282
buttons, command. *See
     command buttons*
buttons, switchboard
   adding, 205
   assigning properties to, 204
   displaying, 207
   labeling, 204
   making visible, 207
   On Click event, 207

C

Calls form, 39
Caption property, 47
captions
   adding to form headers, xxxii
   combo box, 99
   field, 47
   form header, 97
   label, 90
centering text
   in labels, 98
   in text boxes, 189
characters, input mask, 153
Check Box button
     (Toolbox), 210
check boxes, 210 *See also
     controls*
checking spelling, 266
Choose Builder dialog box, 102
class modules, 263, 293
clearing design grids, xxiv, 127
   See also design grids
Close button, 9
Close button (Print Preview
     toolbar), 198

O

P

T

U

X

Y

Z

Learning solutions for every software user

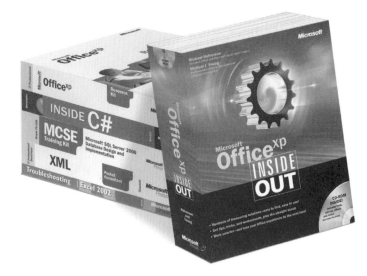

Microsoft Press learning solutions are ideal for every software user—from business users to developers to IT professionals

Microsoft Press® creates comprehensive learning solutions that empower everyone from business professionals and decision makers to software developers and IT professionals to work more productively with Microsoft® software. We design books for every business computer user, from beginners up to tech-savvy power users. We produce in-depth learning and reference titles to help developers work more productively with Microsoft programming tools and technologies. And we give IT professionals the training and technical resources they need to deploy, install, and support Microsoft products during all phases of the software adoption cycle. Whatever technology you're working with and no matter what your skill level, we have a learning tool to help you.

The tools you need to put technology to work.

Microsoft®

microsoft.com/mspress

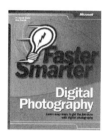

Get a **Free**
e-mail newsletter, updates,
special offers, links to related books,
and more when you
register online!

Register your Microsoft Press® title on our Web site and you'll get a FREE subscription to our e-mail newsletter, *Microsoft Press Book Connections.* You'll find out about newly released and upcoming books and learning tools, online events, software downloads, special offers and coupons for Microsoft Press customers, and information about major Microsoft® product releases. You can also read useful additional information about all the titles we publish, such as detailed book descriptions, tables of contents and indexes, sample chapters, links to related books and book series, author biographies, and reviews by other customers.

Registration is easy. Just visit this Web page and fill in your information:

http://www.microsoft.com/mspress/register

Microsoft®

Proof of Purchase

Use this page as proof of purchase if participating in a promotion or rebate offer on this title. Proof of purchase must be used in conjunction with other proof(s) of payment such as your dated sales receipt—see offer details.

Microsoft® Office Access 2003 Step by Step
0-7356-1517-9

CUSTOMER NAME

Microsoft Press, PO Box 97017, Redmond, WA 98073-9830